Palgrave Macmillan Series in Global Public Diplomacy

Series Editors
Philip Seib
Annenberg School for Communication and Journalism
University of Southern California
Pasadena, CA, USA

Kathy Fitzpatrick
Washington, USA

At no time in history has public diplomacy played a more significant role in world affairs and international relations. As a result, global interest in public diplomacy has escalated, creating a substantial academic and professional audience for new works in the field.

The *Global Public Diplomacy* series examines theory and practice in public diplomacy from a global perspective, looking closely at public diplomacy concepts, policies, and practices in various regions of the world. The purpose is to enhance understanding of the importance of public diplomacy, to advance public diplomacy thinking, and to contribute to improved public diplomacy practices.

More information about this series at
http://www.palgrave.com/gp/series/14680

Stephen Brooks
Editor

Promoting Canadian Studies Abroad

Soft Power and Cultural Diplomacy

Editor
Stephen Brooks
University of Windsor
Windsor, ON, Canada

Palgrave Macmillan Series in Global Public Diplomacy
ISBN 978-3-319-74026-3   ISBN 978-3-319-74027-0   (eBook)
https://doi.org/10.1007/978-3-319-74027-0

Library of Congress Control Number: 2018941869

Cover image: © Pawel Gaul/Getty Images
Cover design by Akihiro Nakayama

Printed on acid-free paper

This Palgrave Macmillan imprint is published by the registered company Springer
International Publishing AG part of Springer Nature
The registered company address is: Gewerbestrasse 11, 6330 Cham, Switzerland

PREFACE

Every Canadianist has a story. It explains how he or she came to study Canada and why, through their research and writing, their teaching, the guidance they provide to the graduate students, and the many administrative tasks they may perform, they have made the study of Canada an important part of their professional life. I have heard many of these stories over the years. One of the things that has long struck me about them, indeed the thread that runs through almost all of them regardless of the particularities of each case, is the enthusiasm for the subject and the conviction that the study of what Bruce Hutchison famously called "The Unknown Country" has relevance beyond the borders of Canada.

I first became aware of this while teaching an American politics course in Leuven, Belgium. That country was in the process of adopting a federal constitution. During my year there, I was asked to give talks on the relations between the French- and English-speaking communities in Canada, on Canada's federal model, and on the independence movement in Quebec. Several years later, and like many thousands before me, I was fortunate enough to be a Fulbright Scholar in the United States. It was during that year that I was introduced to what was then a thriving community of American scholars who had created an impressive national and many regional and state networks for sharing their research and teaching experiences and interacting with colleagues from Canada and other countries. My first direct encounter with this vibrant community of Canadianists was at Columbus, Ohio, where I learned about the hundreds of students who registered each year in Bowling Green State

University's Canadian Studies course each year. The energy and the organization of those who attended this two-day conference was remarkable. It was and continues to be found, if on a diminished scale, across the United States.

Thanks mainly to Jean-Michel Lacroix, the dean of Canadianists in France, I was privileged to hold the Chair in Canadian Studies at the Université de Paris 3 in 2007–2008. Used as they are to imagining that peoples throughout the world admire them and know about their country and its accomplishments, Canadians are usually surprised to learn that only the first of these two beliefs is true. I was struck during that year in France at how little real knowledge of Canada would have existed without the dedication and tireless efforts of French Canadianists. As I quickly found in the courses that I taught in Paris, the fact that goodwill to Canada already exists opens the door and creates a receptiveness among students to learn more about a place, a society and its history that are often hidden in the long shadow of Canada's southern neighbor.

This interest in hearing more about Canada's story exists in countries across much of the world. I recall speaking to a group of professors, graduate students, and state officials in Warsaw on the subject of Canada's immigration policy, labor markets, and multiculturalism. It was a moment in time when the Polish government was considering admitting thousands of workers from China to help improve its transportation infrastructure. In Belgrade I had the chance to speak to a group of international studies students and professors on Canada–US relations and to give a talk on Canada at the opening of a Canadian resource center at another university. Hundreds of Canadianists can tell similar stories. More recently I have been fortunate to assist Sciences Po Lille in placing French students with Canadian parliamentarians as part of that university's excellent internship program. Some of these students will go on to become opinion leaders and decision-makers and will have knowledge, memories, and personal contacts in Canada that may influence their professional activities and, to some degree, the image of Canada that they project to fellow leaders and to citizens in their home country.

Today, the university courses, the invited talks, the seminars and conferences, the Canada Day activities, the internships, the student and faculty exchanges, the visits to Canada, the research and all the other activities that make up the tapestry of Canadian studies across the world continue with very little in the way of financial support from the

Canadian state. Interest in Canada predated the active promotion of academic cultural diplomacy (or, for that matter, any form of public diplomacy) by the Canadian state. This interest continues, if more modestly, since Ottawa's retreat from this support in 2012. The irony is that we live in an age in which the idea that national branding and national standing are important is accepted by most politicians, as is the widespread belief that because of globalization it has never been more important to be able to compete with other national brands clamoring for attention on the world stage. For a country that aspires to have influence on that stage, to turn its back on a key tool of public diplomacy seems rather odd, to say the least.

This book tells the stories of Canadian studies in various parts of the world. In deciding which countries and, in the case of German, language communities to include, I was mindful that I risked offending the many other national and regional associations of Canadianists whose stories are not told in this volume. Cases such as those of the American, British, and French Canadian studies communities had to be included because of the size of their respective memberships, the fact that their pre-institutionalized histories of studying Canada go back many decades, and that all three of these countries have, in their different ways, rather special and intimate relationships to Canada. In selecting the other cases, the size of membership in Canadian studies associations and the scale of their activities were factors also taken into account. But so too were the unique characteristics of each case and also the importance of including non-Western stories in this examination of Canadian studies and cultural diplomacy. We have endeavored to explain the origins, development, and significance of Canadian studies in each national case. At the same time, however, we have attempted to examine the ways in which the academic form of cultural diplomacy can and does contribute to a country's image by encouraging and supporting the individuals and institutions that generate and project this image abroad.

In *Le Temps retrouvé*, Marcel Proust writes, "Un livre est un grand cimetière où sur la plupart des tombes on ne peut plus lire les noms effacés." (A book is a big cemetery where the names have been erased from most of the headstones.) The same may also be said when it comes to the influences that have contributed to the decision to write a particular book. One may think that this or that person, event, or other influence was decisive, but overlook the importance of others. I will only say that I feel especially indebted to David Biette, Mark Kasoff, and Jean-Michel Lacroix, the three of whom are exemplars of Canadian studies abroad. Canadians have been fortunate to have had such unofficial ambassadors.

Windsor, Canada   Stephen Brooks
Lille, France

Contents

NOTES ON CONTRIBUTORS

Yuriy G. Akimov is a professor in the Department of American Studies at St. Petersburg State University and also the chair of the St. Petersburg chapter of the Russian Association for Canadian Studies. He has authored several books and more than 100 articles on Canadian history and politics. In 2011, he received the Pierre Savard award for his book, *North America and Siberia in Late XVI to Mid-XVIII Centuries: An Essay on the Comparative History of Colonization.*

Stephen Brooks is a professor at the University of Windsor and an occasional lecturer at Sciences Po Lille. He held the chair in Canadian Studies at the Université de Paris 3 Sorbonne in 2007–2008. His books deal principally with aspects of Canadian and American politics.

Alan Hallsworth is Professor Emeritus and currently a visiting researcher at the University of Portsmouth. He has held the positions of president, secretary, and treasurer of the British Association for Canadian Studies and served a nine-year term on the Board of the Foundation for Canadian Studies. He is a past and present holder of the Prix du Québec and a member of the International Council for Canadian Studies.

Susan Hodgett is a professor of Area Studies at the University of East Anglia, United Kingdom. She is currently chair of the Area Studies Sub Panel of the UK Research Excellence Framework 2021 and a member of Council of Research England. She was president of the British Association for Canadian Studies 2008–2011, and President of the

International Council for Canadian Studies to 2017. She is currently writing on the future of Area Studies with Patrick James (University of Southern California) for Lexington Press (forthcoming 2018).

Masako Iino is Professor Emeritus and former President of Tsuda College, Tokyo, as well as former president of the Japanese Association for Canadian Studies, and is currently president of the Japan–US Educational Exchange Promotion Foundation (Fulbright Foundation). She was awarded the Governor General's International Award for Canadian Studies in 2001.

She has published many books and papers in the fields of American Studies and Canadian Studies, as well as immigration studies, including *A History of Japanese Canadians* (1997), which received the Prime Minister's Award for Publication, *Another History of US–Japan Relations: Japanese Americans Swayed by the Cooperation and the Disputes between the Two Nations* (2000), *Searching Ethnic America: Multiple Approaches to "E Pluribus Unum"* (2015, editor), and *Ethnic America,* 4th edition (2017, co-author).

Wolfgang Klooss is Professor Emeritus of English and Canadian Studies at Trier University where he served as director of the university's interdisciplinary Centre for Canadian Studies from 1991 until 2017. He was president of the Association for Canadian Studies in German-Speaking Countries (1997–1999). Since 2009 he has been chairman of the German Foundation for Canadian Studies. In 2015, he received the Governor General's International Award for Canadian Studies.

Janne Korkka is a senior lecturer in English at the University of Turku, Finland. His main research interests are in posthumanism, the ethics of encounter, and Canadian literature in English. Currently he works particularly on literary encounters with space and animals as routes to new ways of knowing and on developing ethically informed readings of that which is regarded as ordinary and formulaic in literature. He is the current president of the Nordic Association for Canadian Studies.

Jean-Michel Lacroix is Professor Emeritus of North American Studies at the University of Paris 3 Sorbonne and a member of the Royal Society of Canada. He has been president of the French Association for Canadian studies (1994–2010) and also president of the International Council for Canadian Studies (1987–1991). He has published extensively on Canada and the United States. The 6th edition of his *Histoire des États-Unis* was published in 2018. He is also the author of *Histoire du Canada* (2016).

Kristina Minkova is a senior lecturer in the Department of American Studies at St. Petersburg State University. She has authored several monographs and about 80 articles on Canadian history, foreign policy, and federalism, as well as world trade and the Cold War.

Jeremy Paltiel is a professor of political science at Carleton University in Ottawa. He was a visiting professor in the Department of International Relations at Tsinghua University in Beijing in 2009. He has authored numerous articles on Chinese politics, East Asian foreign relations and Sino-Canadian relations. In 2016, he co-edited *Facing China as a New Superpower* with Huhua Cao. He also co-edited a special issue of *Canadian Foreign Policy* with Laura Macdonald on Canada and emerging markets and contributed "Resolute ambivalence: Canada and the Asia-Pacific." He is the author of *The Empire's New Clothes: Cultural Particularism and Universality in China's Rise to Global Status* (2007).

Robert C. Thomsen is an associate professor of Nationalism and Globalization, and head of the School of Culture and Global Studies at Aalborg University in Denmark. He is the former director of the Canadian Studies Centre at University of Aarhus, and of the Centre for Innovation and Research in Culture and Living in the Arctic at Aalborg University. He has been a member of the executive board of the Nordic Association for Canadian Studies since 2002 and the treasurer of the association since 2005.

He has edited and co-edited a number of volumes in the field of Canadian Studies, including *Canadian Environments: Essays in Culture, Politics and History* (2005) with Nanette L. Hale, and *Heritage and Change in the Arctic: Resources for the Present and the Future* (2017) with Lill R. Bjørst. He is the author of *Nationalism in Stateless Nations: Images of Self and Other in Scotland and Newfoundland* (2010).

LIST OF FIGURES

LIST OF TABLES

Uncertain Embrace: The Rise and Fall of Canadian Studies Abroad as a Tool of Foreign Policy

Stephen Brooks

Michael Goldberg is an American-born academic who moved to Canada in 1968 after competing his doctorate in economics at the University of California at Berkeley. He became a Canadian and, eventually, dean of the University of British Columbia's Sauder School of Business. It was during his time as dean that Goldberg was interviewed for a Canadian Broadcasting Corporation documentary entitled, "What Border? The Americanization of Canada." Here is some of what he said:

> I think Canada is seen as an honest broker worldwide. We're not seen as people who play games with geopolitics. We're seen as a fair, small and honorable people. So it gives us a base for dealing with other people which is a very solid base. In Asia people do business on trust. Canada is seen as trustworthy. That's a huge advantage. The U.S. is seen as less trustworthy, more bullying, and as a result people prefer to diversity their trade relationships outside the U.S. and Canada is a very logical choice. (CBC 1996)

S. Brooks (✉)
Department of Political Science, University of Windsor, Windsor, ON, Canada

© The Author(s) 2019
S. Brooks (ed.), *Promoting Canadian Studies Abroad*,
Palgrave Macmillan Series in Global Public Diplomacy,
https://doi.org/10.1007/978-3-319-74027-0_1

This is, of course, precisely what the advocates of soft power claim. Admiration, trust, standing, respect, and affection are held to be valuable assets in the world of geopolitics. The representatives of a country whose values and institutions are admired, whose achievements are recognized by others, and whose motives are seen to be fair and honest will find it easier to persuade their foreign interlocutors to act in ways that accord with their country's interests, values, and preferences. Goldberg refers specifically to the economic advantages that he believed Canadian businesses enjoyed as a result of their country's positive reputation in Asia. He contrasts this to the United States which, Goldberg claims, compares poorly to Canada in the eyes of Asians—or at least Asian business persons and public officials—when it comes to soft power attributes.

Goldberg may or may not have been correct in claiming that Canada's image in Asia translated into economic advantages over the United States.[1] Nevertheless, the idea that soft power attributes may have consequences for a country's dealings with other countries is widely accepted. Although the term "soft power" is of relatively recent vintage, dating from Joseph Nye's 1990 book, *Bound to Lead: The Changing Nature of American Power* (Nye 1990), the practice is in fact much older. Governments have long acted in ways premised on their belief that *public diplomacy*, involving the communication and dissemination of information and images that present their country in a positive light, may help them to achieve their foreign policy goals. Edmund Gullion, one-time dean of the Fletcher School of Law and Diplomacy and one of the early champions of this tool of foreign policy, offered this classic definition of the term,

> Public diplomacy...deals with the influence of public attitudes on the formation and execution of foreign policies. It encompasses dimensions of international relations beyond traditional diplomacy; the cultivation by governments of public opinion in other countries; the interaction of private groups and interests in one country with those of another; the reporting of foreign affairs and its impact on policy; communication between those whose job is communication, as between diplomats and foreign correspondents; and the processes of inter-cultural communications. (quoted in Cull 2006)

Public diplomacy, as conceptualized in Gullian's definition, may involve a number of state activities. Joseph Nye identifies what he argues are the three main dimensions of public diplomacy: "The first and most immediate dimension is daily communications. The second dimension is strategic communication, which develops a set of simple themes much as a political or advertising campaign does. The third dimension of public diplomacy is the development of lasting relationships with key individuals over many years through scholarships, exchanges, training, seminars, conferences, and access to media channels" (Nye 2010). This third dimension of public diplomacy involves what is generally referred to as *cultural diplomacy.*

There is a good deal of disagreement over the definition of cultural diplomacy and, therefore, what activities, undertaken by whom, and for what purposes fall under this term (see the discussion in Goff 2017). We accept Richard Arndt's distinction between, "[c]ultural relations...the relations between national cultures, those aspects of intellect and education lodged in any society that tend to cross borders and connect with foreign institutions. Cultural relations grow naturally and organically, without government intervention," and cultural diplomacy. The latter, Arndt, argues, "can only be said to take place when formal diplomats, serving national governments, try to shape and channel this natural flow to advance national interests" (Arndt 2005). In his review of the literature on the conceptualization of cultural diplomacy, Tim Rivera quotes a 2014 British Government definition of cultural diplomacy that is similar to Arndt's and quite succinct: "[Cultural diplomacy involves] the promotion of culture and values to further national interests" (quoted in Tim Rivera 2015: 10).

One might argue that the modern roots of cultural diplomacy began in an important way with the creation of Alliance Française in 1883. However, that organization was the creation of very prominent private individuals and Alliance Française has always operated at arm's length from the French state, including maintaining its financial independence. Even today, only about 5% of its revenues are received from the state. The British Council, created in 1934 by the British Foreign Office and financed mainly by the state, perhaps deserves to be thought of as the first major endeavor in the field of cultural diplomacy, as we have defined it. The German Goethe-Institut, created in 1951 principally for language training purposes, acquired an important cultural diplomacy role in the early 1970s under the leadership of Ralf Dahrendorf. The German foreign office had declared culture to be a "third pillar" of the country's foreign policy, expanding the role of the Goethe-Institut in representing German culture abroad. And of course no discussion of twentieth century cultural diplomacy can overlook the extensive activities of the United States government, mainly but not exclusively through the State Department, through such programs as the Voice of America, the Fulbright Program, and the financing of exhibitions and of American artists performing abroad. Much of this effort was driven by the Cold War struggle for the hearts and minds of foreign populations and opinion-leaders.

One of the forms of cultural diplomacy that emerged at the beginning of the Cold War involved government efforts to encourage teaching and research abroad about its country. The prototype and most ambitious of such programs remains the Fulbright Program, created by an act of Congress in 1946. In his book, *The Price of Empire*, Senator J. William Fulbright explained the importance of these efforts:

> Of all the joint ventures in which we might engage, the most productive, in my view, is educational exchange. I have always had great difficulty – since the initiation of the Fulbright scholarships in 1946 – in trying to find the words that would persuasively explain that educational exchange is not merely one of those nice but marginal activities in which we engage in international affairs, but rather, from the standpoint of future world peace and order, probably the most important and potentially rewarding of our foreign-policy activities. (Fulbright 1989)

The Fulbright Program has always been based on the exchange of scholars, teachers, researchers, and students between the United States and most of the countries of the world. It is a two-way street that provides foreigners, many of whom already are or are expected to become opinion-leaders in their home countries, with the opportunity to come to America and—this has always been the expectation—return with a better understanding of American culture and institutions and a sympathetic appreciation of the United States. It also provides Americans with the opportunity to go abroad to study other countries and, in many cases, give talks, participate in conferences, and give interviews that will provide foreign audiences with information and interpretations of America and also American perspectives on issues. The State Department more recently created another much smaller program, Study of the US Institutes for Scholars (SUSIs), which provides foreign scholars with the opportunity to visit the United States for a period of six weeks. The aims of SUSIs are broadly similar to those of the much larger Fulbright

Program. Its stated goal is to, "strengthen curricula and to improve the teaching about the United States in academic institutions abroad" (United States 2017).

Research and teaching about America was already taking place at universities, in research institutes and even in secondary schools in many countries across the world before the Fulbright program was launched. Moreover, intercultural relations at the level of civil society were already quite extensive between the US and many of its allies and major trading partners. But using the definition that we have adopted, this was not, strictly speaking, cultural diplomacy. These activities certainly had implications for how populations and their leaders throughout the world viewed America, but they were not directly promoted by the US government. The Fulbright Program added this element of state sponsorship.

Other countries have followed suit over the years. For example, the Japan Foundation was created in October 1972, associated with the country's Ministry of Foreign Affairs. It has a semi-independent status today, but is still mainly dependent on state money to pay for its extensive activities. These include financing visits to Japan by foreign researchers and teachers, providing grants to Japanese studies associations and centers abroad, and even providing support to such non-Japanese think tanks as the Brookings Institution and the Carnegie Endowment for International Peace to study Japan and issues related to Japan (Japan Foundation 2016). In 2015, the Japan Foundation made grants of US$5 million to each of Georgetown University, the Massachusetts Institute of Technology, and Columbia University to fund endowed professorships in Japanese politics (Redden 2015). The Korean Foundation, established in 1991, provides support for Korean studies associations and centers abroad, including a grant of $2.5 million in 1997 to fund a chair of Korean studies at the University of Pennsylvania, US$2 million for Stanford in 2005 for an endowed chair, and a grant of more than US$1 million in 2016 to Indiana University at Bloomington to finance their Institute for Korean Studies. Korea has given other grants on this scale to finance Korean studies in the UK and elsewhere. A rather different model has been pioneered by China in recent years. Large donations to universities in the United States, the UK, Canada, and elsewhere, sometimes reaching into the hundreds of millions of dollars, have been made by wealthy Chinese businesspersons or by foundations that appear to be fronts for individual donors. The very close ties that often exist between these businesspersons and the Chinese state suggest the possibility that such funding is a way for the Chinese government to influence teaching and research on China abroad. In many cases, with the exception of endowed chairs, the donations are not tied to the study of China. But in some cases they are (see Sharma 2016).

Canada has never played in this league. Nevertheless, for roughly 40 years, the Government of Canada operated a rather modest program of cultural diplomacy that included financial support for Canadian studies abroad. It appeared to have played an important role in encouraging the proliferation of Canadian studies associations in countries across the world, as well as an increase in the number and activities of centers and programs for Canadian studies abroad. An important part of this program involved financing foreign academics, researchers, and students who wished to visit Canada for purposes relating to their research or teaching. Despite the rather small sums of money spent on this program—its annual budget never rose much above about US$4 million— and the fact that it was judged by a number of evaluations to be quite cost-effective, it was terminated in 2012.

Although this Canadian government support was ended, Canadian studies abroad have continued. Indeed, as the subsequent chapters explain, Canadian studies abroad preceded the financial encouragement of the Canadian government and will doubtless continue without this support. Nevertheless, the impact of the 2012 decision has not been insignificant, affecting Canadian studies in some countries more than in others. Moreover, there is the question of why, at a moment in history when some of the world's countries were increasing their investment in cultural diplomacy and others, such as the United States, were at least holding steady,[2] the Canadian government would decide to turn its back on this tool of soft power. How and why the Canadian government came to embrace Canadian studies abroad as a tool of cultural diplomacy, and why it terminated this support in 2012, is the story of this chapter.

Projecting Canada Abroad: From the Massey Commission (1951) to the Symons Report (1975)

In 1942, Canadian journalist Bruce Hutchison published a book entitled, *The Unknown Country: Canada and Her People* (Hutchison 2010, first published in 1942). "It is written in the belief," says Hutchison in the introduction, "reinforced by much traveling among them, that Canadians and Americans really know very little about Canada; that

Canada is, among the important nations of the world, the least known in its real content; that the future relations between Canada and the United States will inevitably form one of the basic factors of world politics; and that these relations are widely misunderstood and often misrepresented" (Hutchison 2010). The idea was to make Canada better known to its American neighbors and wartime ally. It is perhaps ironic that it took an American publisher, the Coward-McCann imprint of New York-based G.P. Putnam's Sons, to take make this book available to readers on both sides of the border. The book did well in the United States. In Canada, it not only sold well and earned Hutchison the Governor-General's Award for Non-Fiction, it became a sort of rallying point for those in English Canada's cultural and political elites who felt that Canada had reached a level of maturity and importance such that its story deserved to be known by the world, to say nothing of Canadians themselves.

This sentiment led to the 1949 creation of the Royal Commission on National Developments in the Arts, Letters and Sciences, better known as the Massey Commission (1949–1951). The Commission's report included a chapter on the projection of Canada abroad that began with this declaration: "Ignorance of Canada in other countries is very wide-spread" (253). After acknowledging the handful of programs and initiatives undertaken by the Canadian government to dispel some of this ignorance,[3] the Commission turned its attention to what it argued to be the important, and in the case of Canada, largely neglected role that cultural diplomacy could play in the pursuit of foreign policy objectives. "Canada," the Massey Report states, "is out of step with the rest of the world. For good or ill, information and cultural matters are not becoming more and more an essential part of foreign policy" (263). In terms of both spending and the deliberateness of their efforts to project knowledge and ideas about their country to populations abroad, such countries as Great Britain, France, and the United States were judged by the Commission to be light years ahead of Canada. "The great need," the Report concludes, "is for financial support and for consolidation of effort" (267). Neither of these failings would be addressed in a serious manner until the 1970s.

The reasons for Ottawa's failure to take seriously what the Massey Report characterized as widespread ignorance of Canada abroad must include, at the top of any list, Canada's federal system of government, differences between French and English Canada over what image of the country should be projected abroad, and a lingering colonial mentality that continued to exist in some influential cultural quarters until the late 1960s. As a practical matter, much of what other countries were doing in order to make themselves known and to project an image abroad, and that the Massey Commission admired, fell under the authority of Canada's provincial governments. The country's comparatively decentralized model of federalism guaranteed that, at a minimum, provincial cooperation would be required in such matters as international student and teacher exchanges. In matters of culture more generally, section 92(16) and section 93 of the Constitution Act, 1867 appeared to provide the basis for the primacy of the provinces in matters of education and culture. Thus, while only Ottawa had the authority to enter into agreements with other sovereign states and their representative bodies, it was already clear in Canada that this power did not extend to the implementation of the terms of these agreements if the subject matter fell under provincial jurisdiction.[4] The Massey Report seemed to think that this was not a serious obstacle to a much greater federal role in the field of cultural and especially educational exchanges (265). The commissioners were, however, quite wrong on this point. They would soon be reminded of what some provinces believed to be their exclusive or at least primary jurisdiction in such matters.

The reminder was delivered in 1956 by Quebec's Commission of Inquiry on Constitutional Problems, popularly known as the Tremblay Commission. Its report insisted on the cultural sovereignty of Quebec and was categorically opposed to what were seen as federal intrusions in matters of education and culture. The Massey Report had been remarkably tone deaf when it came to Quebec's objections to the much greater role that it recommended for Ottawa in cultural matters at home and abroad. This deafness had various causes. One was surely the centralist bias that had been gaining strength in Canada's English-speaking elite from the Great Depression, so evident in the centralizing recommendations on public finances of the Royal Commission on Dominion-Provincial Relations (1937–1940). This bias gained momentum during World War II due to the exigencies of wartime planning and mobilization under the War Measures Act. It did not abate at the War's end. On the contrary, there was a widespread sense among Canada's English-speaking leaders that Canada had earned a place among the middle powers of the world and that its voice should be heard abroad. This voice would, of course, be Ottawa's. Those engaged in the Massey Commission were, as Zoe Druick observes, Canadian nationalists in their sympathies, but they were also internationalist (Druick 2006: 8). They believed that intercultural relations should be harnessed to foreign policy. This was a view that was bound to encounter opposition in predominantly French-speaking Quebec, where a greater role for Ottawa in cultural matters was seen as a threat to the province's cultural sovereignty.

The third factor that stood in the way of the much more aggressive projection of Canada abroad that the Massey Commission recommended was the unresolved tension that existed until the late 1960s about what image of Canada should be projected. The idea of Canada as a Commonwealth country, a country whose Britishness was still an important marker of identity and difference from the United States remained influential. It was evident during the prime ministership of John Diefenbaker (1957–1963), in the Flag Debate of 1964, and in Canadian philosopher George Grant's influential *Lament for a Nation* (1965), in which a sort of nostalgic regret for the passing of Toryism and Canada's British identity can be heard (see Rutherford 2005: 201). This soon would be a rather marginal image of Canada, as changing patterns of immigration and the irresistible forces of Americanization rendered it untenable.

Thus, a decade after the Massey Report's call for the robust projection of Canadian culture abroad, little of real consequence had happened. The amount of money spent on such activities was pathetically small, the efforts of such federal bodies as the Department of External Affairs, the CBC, the National Film Board, the National Gallery, and the Canadian Council for the Arts were uncoordinated, and in no serious manner was cultural diplomacy integrated into the larger picture of Canadian foreign policy.[5] As Mary Halloran writes, "the work remained improvisational in nature, the resources allocated comparatively scarce, and an overall strategy non-existent" (Halloran 1996: 2).

Improvisational aptly describes Ottawa's increased spending on cultural diplomacy in France and the French-speaking regions of Belgium and Switzerland during the Pearson government of the 1960s. After years of being wary of closer cultural ties with France (Meren 2013), the Quebec government of Jean Lesage embraced and expanded Quebec–France cultural and academic exchanges. Ottawa reacted by increasing its spending on cultural relations with francophone countries from about CAN\$250,000 in 1963 to CAN\$1million by 1965. Domestic politics and the fear that Quebec might come to be seen as the only genuine voice abroad of French Canada stirred Ottawa to action.

Modest in scale and unconnected to the broader goals of Canadian foreign policy, limited efforts to project Canada abroad virtually ignored research and teaching on Canada by foreign academics. Despite this neglect, and as described in the subsequent chapters of this book, teaching and research on Canada had taken root in many countries of the world. Direct and systematic support from the Canadian government did not begin until 1975 when Ottawa contributed CAN$250,000 to finance the Centre for Canadian Studies and the Chair in Canadian Studies at the University of Edinburgh.[6]

It is at this point that one can say that Canadian studies abroad—teaching, research, academic meetings, publications, and outreach activities conducted outside of Canada and supported by the Canadian government for the express purpose of increasing knowledge about Canada—was harnessed to Canadian foreign policy. The Liberal government's 1970 White Paper, *A Foreign Policy for Canadians*, had made a number of albeit brief references to the importance of increasing Canada cultural relations with the other countries, particularly with Western Europe. Influenced by the wave of anti-Americanism that was cresting in Canada in the early 1970s, the White Paper proposed this greater investment in cultural diplomacy as a counterweight to American cultural influence:

> Canada has compelling reasons for developing relations in the fields of culture and communication beyond the North American continent, and especially with Europe. There are the needs of its bilingual society and the desirability of diversifying contacts in Europe as a complement to American influences....The particular needs of French-speaking Canadians, principally in Quebec, have prompted provincial governments to seek contacts in the *francophone* world, especially in France, but the Federal Government has become much more extensively involved in international cultural programmes in order to provide a national framework for the cultural aspirations and interests of all Canadians. The Government recognizes that information and cultural relations have become a very important element in Canada's foreign policy and that Europe is the most important area for the intensification of those relations. (Canada, Department of External Affairs 1970a: 28)

There is no mention of direct support for teaching and research on Canada. Instead the White Paper includes an already tired catalog of the several uncoordinated activities for the projection of Canada abroad that could have been drawn directly from the pages of the Massey Report. The 1970 White Paper's section on Canada's relations with Pacific countries also suggests that more should be done in the way of cultural relations, including educational exchange agreements with Asian countries. The entire rather short discussion is framed in terms of the economic benefits expected to flow from this projection of Canada in Asia (Canada, Department of External Affairs 1970b: 22–23).

In the end, there was little in the 1970 White Paper that would have led one to anticipate that Ottawa would soon view Canadian studies abroad or cultural diplomacy more generally as important tools of foreign policy. The mentions of these were too few and too brief and fell far short of the ambitious approach that the Massey Report had recommended 20 years earlier. But the times were ripe for change. Canadian nationalism and the idea that Canadian studies warranted a more serious place in Canadian education led to the creation of the Commission on Canadian Studies, launched by the Association of Universities and Colleges of Canada in 1972 under the direction of former Trent University president Tom Symons. Its 1975 report, *To Know Ourselves*, generally referred to as the Symons Report, included a very detailed examination of the state of Canadian studies abroad. The Report's tone was harsh in what it judged to be Ottawa's general failure to support such efforts or to truly recognize their value for Canadian foreign policy. It made 41 detailed recommendations for the remediation of these failings.

The Symons Report deserves to be thought of as the Massey Report of its times. Like the Massey Report two decades earlier, it became the center of the conversation on Canadian identity, and what governments and universities ought to do to make that identity and the factors that shaped it known to Canadians and to the world. The Symons Report's conclusions on the state of Canadian studies abroad were rather bleak:

> [W]hile teaching about Canada in universities outside the country is at present limited and generally inadequate, more is going on than might have been expected. However, academic activity relating to Canada and academic knowledge of Canadian affairs outside this country are rarely coordinated in comprehensive programs. Nor, with just a few recent exceptions, have courses about Canada offered abroad received any significant support and encouragement from Canadian sources. Consequently, attention to Canadian affairs in courses at universities outside Canada is

fragmentary and seldom firmly integrated into the curriculum. In most instances where universities abroad devote any attention to this country, they study Canada not as a distinct nation but as a part of North America or of the Commonwealth or of the Francophone community. In such cases Canadian content is often marginal or incidental. Even where Canadian studies do exist as such, they are frequently on haphazard footing. In many instances they have resulted from the personal initiative of an expatriate Canadian teaching abroad who has persuaded his colleagues to allow him to teach something on Canada....

For the most part, the universities located in countries with which Canada has close economic and cultural ties have been no exception to this general pattern. They have tended to view Canada as being either not sufficiently different from their own country, or not sufficiently exciting, to merit special study; or they have simply considered Canada to have no importance except, occasionally, as an extension of the United States. (Symons 1975: 2)

The Report placed the blame for what it characterized as a lamentable and totally unnecessary state of affairs squarely on the shoulders of the federal government. Its judgment pulled no punches:

...[T]he inadequacy of Canada's programme of external academic liaison is a reflection of a wider problem, namely, that Canada does not place any kind of priority upon her cultural relations with other countries; that Canada stands alone among the world's industrialized nations in lacking a well-developed policy regarding her cultural relationships with foreign countries; that the mechanisms in Canada for conducting external cultural and academic relations are, in the words of more than one brief, 'half a century out of date' in terms of current international practice; that Government support for Canadian external cultural relations, and within these for Canadian studies abroad, has been meagre, haphazard and arbitrary; that such support as has been given has often been weakened by a lack of co-ordination in the planning of policy and in the implementation of programs; and that there has been a regrettable failure to sustain worthwhile initiatives and to promote new opportunities. (Symons 1975: 7)

The Report did not hesitate to add a bit of shame to this indictment: "Foreign Governments and private interests outside Canada have done more to promote Canadian studies abroad than has the Canadian government itself" (Symons 1975: 6).

INTEGRATING CANADIAN STUDIES INTO FOREIGN POLICY

A year before the 1975 release of the Symons Report, Ottawa created the Academic Relations Section within the Department of External Affairs (DEA). Its role, as described by an official within DEA, was "to develop an informed awareness and a more balanced understanding of Canada…and to facilitate the development of more productive contacts and cross fertilization between Canadian and foreign scholars" (Graham 1976: n.p.). The Canadian Studies Abroad Program (CSAP) immediately became the cornerstone of the Academic Relations Section's activities. The budget for CSAP and other federal investments in international cultural relations increased steadily over the next decade. It remained, however, pathetically small in comparison to what was spent by many other countries. Trilokekar reports that in 1983 Ottawa spent about CAN$7 million on international cultural relations, compared to CAN$127 million spent by Britain, CAN$340 million spent by France, and CAN$200 million spent by West Germany (Trilokekar 2007). In 1983, the United States spent over CAN$120 million on the Fulbright Program alone (United States, Government Publishing Offices 1983). To express this a bit differently, Canadian per capita spending on international cultural relations in 1983 was CAN$0.27, compared to $6.1 for France, $3.3 for West Germany, and $2.3 for the UK. Per capita spending on the Fulbright Program alone in the US was about CAN$0.51. If spending on the US Information Agency that year is included, the per capita figure rises to about CAN$3.3.

Ottawa's spending on international cultural relations peaked in the mid-1980s. The total budget of the Culture, Public Affairs, and Information Bureau within DFAIT grew to roughly CAN$25 million by 1984. Of this, the Academic Relations Section accounted for CAN$5.7 million, most which went to the support of foreign academics, programs, and centers studying Canada (Canada, Task Force on Program Review 1986: 199). As Trilokekar writes, "The CSAP appealed to senior officials [in DFAIT] as a useful and effective tool to project Canada's image abroad and raise its profile among international decision-makers. The program was also perceived as a less direct and intrusive [international education] approach, as it did not challenge provincial jurisdictional authority nor institutional autonomy or academic freedom" (Trilokekar 2015: 6).

The 1984 election of the Conservative Party under the leadership of Brian Mulroney saw the launch of the first comprehensive review of federal spending ever undertaken. Here is what the review said about the Academic Relations programs operated by the Department of External Affairs:

> The study team believes that serving Canada's foreign policy interests is too broad and vague to suffice as an objective giving direction and purpose to a program....A clarification as to the program's mandate and objectives, in order to emphasize the promotion of Canada as a field of academic study, would enable more effective utilization of the budget. (Canada, Task Force on Program Review 1986: 270)

The Task Force's main criticism of what External Affairs was doing through Canadian studies abroad involved what it saw as a lack of focus and a need for "a more precise set of objectives to be developed" (271). Otherwise the evaluation, although rather brief and lacking detail, was quite positive. Indeed it suggested that Canada should be doing more to "promote the cultural and academic understanding of Canada abroad" (269). It chided Ottawa for not providing scholarship opportunities to the nationals of some countries at a level equal to those provided to Canadians wanting to study in those countries. It also suggested that Canadian studies abroad and scholarship opportunities to study in Canada should be broadened beyond the United States and Europe so that "Canada's increasing interest and relationship with other nations be reflected" (270). The evaluation concluded by stating that, "The development of academic studies on Canadian matters by non-Canadians is clearly an integral component of promoting the international interests and stature of Canada" (270).

The program review exercise carried out under the Conservative government of Brian Mulroney was criticized by some as the work of "amateurish outsiders" that was doomed to be torpedoed by wily bureaucrats (Wilson 1988). A more accurate assessment is probably that of Ian Greene, who argues that what is widely conceded to have been the rather negligible impact that the exercise had on federal spending priorities was mainly due to politics: "The cabinet had decided that programs needed to be cut more or less equitably across the regions, also taking into account the relative strength of the Conservative Party in each region" (Greene, n.d.). This was not good news for the Academic Relations

Division of External Affairs or for its Canadian Studies Abroad Program. It meant that the positive assessment of the Task Force and its clear support for a greater investment in cultural diplomacy would be submerged under the usual political considerations influencing government's spending decisions.

Spending on international cultural relations in general and on Canadian studies abroad in particular did not decrease significantly until 1991, a decline that continued after the election of the Liberal Party in 1993. This reversal of the trajectory of spending growth that had occurred from the mid-1970s to the mid-1980s attests to the fact that the idea that cultural diplomacy and, as an important part of this, Canadian studies abroad, were more than interesting luxuries on the margins of the essential tool kit of foreign policy never really achieved much acceptance among Canadian political elites. This was quite different from the situation in Britain, France, Germany, Japan, Sweden, and the United States, to mention only some of the more notable cases of countries that had long made significant investments in cultural diplomacy and believed that it could be used as a tool for the promotion of national interests and the projection abroad of a country's values. Indeed, data for 1990 compiled by an economist for the Special Joint Parliamentary Committee on Canadian Foreign Policy found that when all forms of state promotion of cultural exports were taken into account, Canada lagged far behind its European partners. It was estimated that the Canadian government spent $4.90 per person, compared to $26.58 in the case of France, $18.00 in the case of West Germany, and $16 per person in the UK.[7]

Before explaining why Canadian decision-makers remained out of step with their counterparts in these other countries, it is worth mentioning that all of these other countries were better known internationally than was Canada. Even Sweden, with a population less than one-third of Canada's, was known for Abba, Volvo (which now has a Chinese owner but is still widely associated by people throughout the world with Sweden), social democracy at home and a generous policy of developmental assistance and humanitarianism abroad. The ideas that foreign populations and decision-makers have about a country, particularly about a free and open country that does not control all of the institutions that create and project ideas and images about itself, are not shaped exclusively or even primarily by the activities of governments. To put this differently, even without the US Fulbright Program, the British Council,

Alliance Française, or the Japan Foundation, foreign populations will still know about these countries. Whether what they think they know is accurate is, of course, another matter and much of public diplomacy may be targeted at correcting what governments believe to be misperceptions and inaccurate information (see chapter 6 in Brooks 2016).

Canada is not and has never been in a position where its political leaders could assume that the populations and decision-makers in those countries with which it has important ties of trade or other shared interests and concerns know very much about their country. Canada remains—and Canadians are incredulous when they hear this, having been told so often by their political and opinion leaders that the world pays close attention to their country and admires its institutions, values, and accomplishments—largely the "unknown [but liked] country" that Bruce Hutchison called it in the mid-twentieth century. Nowhere is this more true than in the United States, Canada's major trading partner. Canadians cannot simply assume that the world will know more than the usual tropes about their country: that it has a vast territory and a relatively small population; it is northern and rather cold for much of the year; it is a wealthy democracy; and it has as its neighbor the world's most powerful country.

Those who belong to the international community of Canadianists know that Canada does indeed remain a largely unknown country. My own experience has confirmed this on countless occasions. I have taught Canadian politics to hundreds of American university students over the years, almost all of whom were surprised to learn that Canada is and long has been their country's major trading partner and main source of foreign energy imports (those who knew usually were Canadian citizens or had Canadian family!). When I taught Canadian politics in Paris for nine months in 2007–2008, during which time I watched the French *télé-journal* every evening, I heard precisely two stories about Canada. One involved the collapse of an arena roof in Quebec under the weight of the snow that had accumulated. The other was prompted by Canadian Governor-General Michaëlle Jean's visit to Paris. That was all. That same year I traveled to Warsaw to give a talk on immigration and Canadian labor markets to a group of academics and senior students. Among them were some who may have heard about Canada's policy of multicultural-ism, but they were very definitely in the minority.

Some might say that if the populations of other countries do not know much about Canada, at least what they think they know is not negative. Indeed, Canada does rather well on international surveys asking national populations how favorably they view other countries.[8] But this may not be enough. In the international competition for foreign students, Australia does considerably better than Canada. The reasons might have to do with factors, such as climate, that would not be changed by a robust program of cultural diplomacy that includes Canadian studies abroad. But perhaps some would. Canada is also in competition with other developed countries for highly educated and skilled immigrants. If all they know about Canada is that it is vast, rather cold and next to the United States, this may prove less motivating than a more richly textured story about a place in which immigrants might wish to build new lives. When issues of trade, cross-border environmental management, or border security arise between Canada and the United States and Congress or state legislatures are holding hearings, is it not at least possible that experts at American universities and think tanks who have visited, studied, and perhaps even written and taught about Canada might function as knowledge ambassadors between American law-makers and the largely unknown country to the north? In short, when it comes to the world's knowledge of Canada, it has always been prudent to presume that this is not very extensive.

Returning to the question of why the Canadian government's investment in Canadian studies abroad reached a plateau in the 1980s and then began a slow but steady decline in real terms until finally being terminated in 2012, a number of reasons may be identified. Foremost among them was uncertainty over the goals of Canadian foreign policy and whether and how cultural diplomacy, including Canadian studies, could be made to serve these goals. This uncertainty has existed from the foreign policy review that took place under Prime Minister Pierre Trudeau in 1970. The 1970 White Paper, *Foreign Policy for Canadians*, was positive about the contribution that cultural diplomacy could make to the achievement of Canadian interests, making mention of its potential in the volumes of the White Paper on Europe and on the Pacific. At the same time, however, the White Paper said relatively little on this subject and a plan for Canadian studies abroad was wholly absent. Also absent was any mention of cultural diplomacy with the United States, an omission that can only be explained in the context of the anti-American sentiment that was so evident during the first several years of the Pierre Trudeau government. This omission was especially ironic in view of the flurry of Canadian studies activity that was taking place in the United States at that moment, including the 1971 creation of the Association for Canadian Studies in the United States (ACSUS). When the Academic Relations Division of DEA was established in 1974 and CSAP was launched, these initiatives were at least consistent with the 1970 White Paper's acknowledgment that cultural diplomacy ought to assume a greater role in Canadian foreign policy. At the same time, however, these developments may well have owed more to the activities of American, British, and French Canadianists, unprompted and in the main unsupported by the Canadian government, than to a new enthusiasm in DEA and the Trudeau government for cultural diplomacy. In any case, a beachhead had been established and modest support for Canadian studies abroad, including support for a growing number of Canadian studies associations in Europe and Asia, increased over the next decade.

The 1995 foreign policy review under Liberal Prime Minister Jean Chrétien formally recognized international cultural relations as one of the three pillars of Canadian foreign policy.[9] Although this seemed to promise a more prominent role for cultural diplomacy, the reality was otherwise. Spending on international cultural relations declined during the mid- to late-1990s. It was low-hanging fruit during a period marked by federal budget cuts. As Graham writes, "the cultural and academic budgets…[were] always seen as easy targets by senior DFAIT management, who still regarded these as peripheral to Canadian foreign policy objectives" (Graham 1999: 140).

Ten years later, the government of Paul Martin launched another review of Canadian foreign policy. It report, *A Role of Pride and Influence in the World* (2005a), suggested a more robust role for cultural diplomacy in its various forms. This would be part of what the report called a new diplomacy adapted to the realities of a globalized world. "[F]ostering academic and professional partnerships between Canadian and foreign counterparts takes on added significance. Showcasing Canadian artistry and innovation in the world will cultivate long-term relationships, dialogue and understanding abroad. These activities have taken on a new significance as modern diplomacy increasingly trades on established credibility" (29). The report promised to "Expand the international public diplomacy program" (29). Although there was no specific mention of Canadian studies abroad, the manner in which cultural diplomacy and public diplomacy more broadly were framed in the report suggested that the value of such activities was obvious and recognized.

The recommendations of the Martin government's 2005 report were strongly supported by outside evaluations that had been contracted as part of the review process. The evaluation of International Academic Relations programs was fulsome in its praise for cultural diplomacy initiatives. It was, however, somewhat more reserved in the specific case of the Canadian Studies Abroad Program and the Scholarship Program, the latter providing financial support to foreign scholars studying in Canada. In retrospect, it is apparent that potential storm clouds were on the horizon as may be seen in this excerpt from the evaluation:

> In general we found both programs to have a firm rationale. They both supported the foreign policy objectives of Foreign Affairs and International Trade Canada, especially those objectives related to the third pillar. With respect to their effectiveness we found that the two programs generated a significant number of outputs, which are documented (elaborated) in the study. In addition we found that there is a great deal of emerging and anecdotal evidence that would indicate that these programs have had important effects in influencing people and institutions in a wide variety of countries. Unfortunately, the programs do not systematically capture the data related to outcomes and impact... . [M]ore needs to be done in the areas of strategy development, monitoring and building a results-oriented culture. (Canada, DFAIT 2005b: n.p.)

As it happened, however, the Martin government was out of power within a year of this evaluation and the foreign policy review that prompted it.

The storm clouds that hinted at the 2005 evaluation of Canadian studies abroad became more menacing under the Conservative government elected in 2006. In the 2009–2010 Departmental Performance Report of DFAIT, the Third Pillar of Canadian foreign policy that had been announced in 1995 had virtually disappeared. References to public diplomacy in this 100-page report are very few. When it is mentioned at all, it is in a very short-term and goal-specific manner, such as this comment on preparations for the 2010 G-8 Summit held in Toronto and Huntsville: "[DFAIT] conducted an extensive advocacy and public diplomacy campaign targeted to Canadian and international academia, businesses, government, labour and civil society to build support for G-8 Summit priorities, in particular the signature initiative on maternal and child health" (Canada, DFAIT 2010: 41). There is no mention anywhere in this document of cultural diplomacy, much less of the Canadian Studies Abroad Program (renamed the Understanding Canada Program in 2008).

In summary, references to cultural diplomacy appeared in every major review and evaluation of Canadian foreign policy from 1970 until these references disappeared in the 2009–2010 evaluation of DFAIT. Canadian studies abroad was often mentioned in these reviews, usually in a manner suggesting that it supported the goals of Canadian foreign policy and that current investments in such activities should be bolstered. But the assessment of Canadian studies abroad was not always positive. The 2005 evaluation of DFAIT's International Academic Relations Programs raised doubts about the measurement of impacts and referred to the need for a "results-oriented culture." The failure of the 2009–2010 departmental review to even mention Canadian studies abroad was a telling indication of how vulnerable it had become.

Thus, after four decades during which Canadian studies were on the radar screen of Canadian foreign policy, it no longer produced even a blip. Individuals close to what was now called the Understanding Canada Program believed in its value and also realized that they needed to be able to demonstrate that it produced measurable positive outcomes. DFAIT commissioned the International Council for Canadian Studies (ICCS) to provide data on the state of Canadian studies abroad, including the scale and types of activities undertaken, the composition of the international Canadian studies communities, the influence of these communities beyond academe, the relationship of this influence to the goals of DFAIT and the Canadian government, and how effective the Understanding Canada Program was in leveraging other financial and non-financial forms of support for Canadian studies abroad (International Council for Canadian Studies 2011). In short, ICCS was to measure how much bang, and what sort of bang, the Canadian government got for its buck. In order to do this, ICCS carried out three surveys. One was sent to the 35 national and regional associations for Canadian studies around the world. The second was sent to Canadian studies centers and programs abroad. The third was sent to individual professors engaged in Canadian studies through their teaching, research, or publishing.

Before the ICCS study was commissioned, there already had been intimations that the Conservative government of Stephen Harper was not enthusiastic about cultural diplomacy. The language of the Third Pillar of Canadian foreign policy, launched during the Chrétien government and continued during Paul Martin's two years as prime minister, was strikingly absent during the Harper years. It was not that the Conservative government believed that public diplomacy was ineffective. In fact it spent millions of dollars on carefully targeted advertising campaigns in the United States, most of it in relation to the Keystone-XL Pipeline proposal that was vigorously opposed by some environmental and Native groups on both sides of the Canada–US border. Cultural diplomacy, however, appeared to be another matter.

Nevertheless, there was guarded optimism among the community of Canadianists abroad and those in Canada who believed in the value of the Understanding Canada Program. It was optimism based on their firm conviction that a simple cost-benefit analysis, looking merely at how much the government spent on the program and the returns this generated for the economy, would sweep aside any financial doubts about the program. I recall a conversation that I had in 2010 with a very prominent Canadianist who provided such data for the ICCS study. He was certain that the numbers spoke for themselves and that they would convince politicians looking to cut inefficient and unnecessary spending.

Had spending efficiency been the goal, my European colleague surely would have been right. But this was not the reason why the Understanding Canada Program was terminated by the government in 2012. Before explaining why this decision was taken, the main findings of the internal report carried out by ICCS in 2011 and communicated to officials in DFAIT deserve to be summarized. Here are some of the most salient points.

- The network of Canadian studies abroad at the time of this survey was impressive. It included 25 national associations for Canadian studies, 5 multinational associations, several regional networks for Canadian studies, and more than two dozen specialized associations or groups linked to some of these national associations. Their combined non-Canadian membership was estimated be close to 6000 persons. If even one-third of these individuals included Canada in some part of their teaching or research—probably a very conservative assumption—that would still represent quite a significant population of active Canadianists abroad.
- About one-third of the Canadianists surveyed indicated that an award received through the Understanding Canada Program (or during the years when it was called the Canadian Studies Abroad

Program) provided them with the motivation to become involved in Canadian studies. In some parts of the world where the roots of Canadian studies are not as deep as in, say, Britain, France, or the United States, the figure was much higher. In Latin America it was 78% and among Canadianists in the Asia Pacific region it was 66%.

- The prospect of a reduction in funding from the Canadian government for the Understanding Canada Program alarmed most national associations, programs, and centers. Interestingly, the possibility that this funding might be eliminated entirely was not even contemplated by the ICCS questionnaire. Had it been, the alarm bells doubtless would have sounded much louder. About half of all the associations surveyed said that cutbacks would lead to "major reductions" or "cancellations" of courses on Canada or that included an important Canadian component. A similar pattern of responses was found when associations were asked about the likely impact of funding cuts on research. About 60% of associations believed that cutbacks would result in a major reduction in their membership. "The stark negative prognostications...assuming cuts were to be made, make it justifiable," concluded the ICCS report, "that the community sees DFAIT's programming as highly relevant and even critical to its existence" (ICCS 2011: n.p.).

- The impact of the international community of Canadianists outside their classrooms, academic journals, and conferences was found to be quite extraordinary. The ICCS survey found that many Canadianists were interviewed by their national media, consulted by their governments, or gave public lectures on Canadian subjects.[10] The number of books and articles, scholarly and non-scholarly, published by this community was very large. The 507 individuals who responded the ICCS survey together had published over 300 books and over 1700 articles related to Canada over the preceding three years.

- Linkages between foreign Canadianists and their colleagues in Canada were found to be extensive. Almost half of European Canadianists and about 40% of those in the United States and the Asia Pacific region indicated that their home institutions had formal linkages with Canadian universities.

- Based on estimates provided by the associations and centers for Canadian studies, as well as those from individual professors, it was calculated that their combined expenditures on goods and services in and from Canada was in the area of CAN$70 per year. The Understanding Canada Program, whose budget at the time was about $5.5 million, cannot be credited for all this activity. But it is undeniable that it was the reason for many of the purchases of books, films, CDs, and visits to Canada, and that without the leverage that Understanding Canada awards provided, much of this spending would not have happened. "[T]he Understanding Canada: Canadian Studies program [is] essentially self-funding," observes the ICCS report. "It is doubtful," it adds, "that any other Canadian government program can make such a claim" (ICCS 2011: n.p.).

A more supportive report based on sound methodology and, where estimates or assumptions were required, tending to the conservative side, would have been hard to imagine. Moreover, there is no doubt that the Understanding Canada Program had friends within DFAIT. In the end, however, it did not matter how far up the departmental food chain this report rose nor how convinced the foreign affairs bureaucrats were that this program provided significant value for money. Decisions about what to cut announced in the Conservative government's 2012 budget were made in the Prime Minister's Office. On 1 May 2012, it was announced that the Understanding Canada Program was being phased out. In fact, however, its termination was immediate in the sense that no new awards could be made under the program.

It Was Never About Saving Money

The official announcement of that the Understanding Canada Program was terminated referred to "the current fiscal context" as the basis for this decision. In light of the information provided to DFAIT in the 2011 ICCS report, this is more than a little improbable. A much more likely explanation is that the decision was driven principally by ideology and mistrust of the academic community, in Canada and abroad, and of their patrons in the federal bureaucracy. The same mistrust and unacknowledged ideological reasons that resulted in the elimination of Statistics Canada's long-form census also doomed the Understanding Canada Program.[11] Both were viewed as programs that tended to produce data, studies, and interpretations favorable to a liberal ideological orientation, a statist approach to the framing and resolution of policy issues, and the celebration of a sort of multicultural and post-colonial understanding of Canada and its history. Through such programs the Canadian government provided, if I may borrow a term from Article III, section 3 of the US Constitution, aid and comfort to the enemy. The enemy were those who shared a particular world view that tended to be unsympathetic and even hostile to conservative ideology and to what might be described as a more traditional understanding of Canada.

In addition to the termination of the long-form census and the Understanding Canada Program, the 2012 federal budget also made major cuts to Library and Archives Canada. This is a program that is crucial to the work of those in the interdisciplinary field of Canadian studies. These cuts prompted Trent University history professor John Wadland to contact his Conservative MP, Dean Del Mastro. Wadland's vigorously expressed objection to what he saw as the evisceration of Canadian studies at home and abroad elicited this response: "I am fascinated by Canadian history. I just don't like revisionist history" (Wadland 2014: 1). Del Mastro's response captures, I believe, what Canadian Conservatives and conservatives found to be fundamentally objectionable about government spending on such programs as Understanding Canada. Such programs channeled taxpayer dollars to activities that, in the main, supported a view of Canada that was antithetical to conservative viewpoints and that tended to be critical of the Conservative Party of Canada and the values and interests that it represented. The Harper government had made very clear that it preferred a representation of Canada that placed more emphasis on Canada's military history, the country's historical connection to Britain, and such historical figures as Prime Ministers John A. Macdonald and Wilfrid Laurier and less on what I would call the Charter vision of Canada, with its emphasis on group rights, accommodation of cultural differences, and the values associated with contemporary communitarianism.

What if, however, the Conservatives were right? We should at least be open to the possibility that some government spending, including on cultural diplomacy, may systematically be tilted toward certain ideological perspectives and opposed to others. It is not obvious, however, that this was the case. The ICCS maintained a bibliography of foreign publications and theses on Canada for countries and regions across the world.[12] For the period from 1980 to 2000, this bibliography includes 921 entries from the United States and 868 from Europe. Within Europe, 157 were published in France and 227 in the UK. I will not pretend to have paid careful attention to all of the entry titles, much less to have drilled a bit deeper to find what lies beneath them. Nevertheless, a perusal of the ICCS bibliographies—and I would invite anyone with the necessary patience to replicate this exercise—makes clear that there is no particular ideological bias in what was written about Canada in these countries, only a part of which had been supported in some manner or other by Canadian government funding.

But as Canadian historian Ramsey Cook has suggested, the problem might not have been, or at least not chiefly, the Canadian government's belief that the Understanding Canada Program was giving aid and comfort to the ideological enemy. In a 2013 interview in which he was asked about the Conservative government's approach to Canadian history, Cook said, "I think the problem is that governments, when they interest themselves in history, they already have answers for what they believe Canadian history is, whereas trained historians ask questions about the past. We have questions, but they have answers, which means they have an agenda" (quoted in CBC 2013).

Cook argued that the government sought a reorientation of how Canadian history was represented and interpreted in order to align these representations and interpretations more closely with its political agenda. Academic freedom was not, in the government's view, producing this outcome. The same reasoning surely applied when the Conservative government trained its sites on support for Canadian studies abroad. The government never had any direct control over who received funding to teach, organize a conference, do research, or carry out any other activity funded by the Understanding Canada Program. It is doubtful that anyone involved in the decision to terminate this program even looked at the content of the "deliverables" whose production was supported by this program. The fact that the government had no direct influence on these funding decisions,[13] coupled with its mistrust of the academic community, was enough to seal the fate of the Understanding Canada Program.

This might not have happened, however, if the program had had influential champions. But it did not, nor did it ever have politically influential champions from its beginnings in the mid-1970s. Figure 1.1 shows the constellation of interests linked either directly or indirectly to support for the Understanding Canada Program. While we might wish to argue that all Canadians were beneficiaries of this modest program, this is too indirect and diffuse an interest to matter politically for reasons

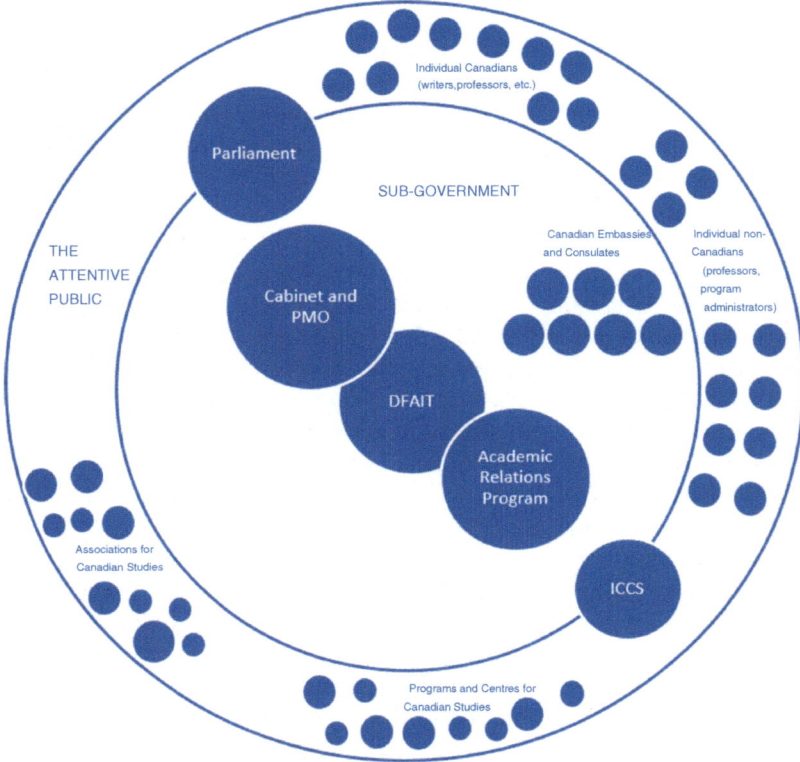

Fig. 1.1 The Canadian studies abroad community

that are well known to students of public policy (Olson 1965). Those stakeholders most aware of the program and most directly benefited by it are closest to the diagram's center. They included foreign academics whose research, teaching, publishing, or community engagement involved Canada to some degree, and the national and regional associations of Canadian studies to which they belonged. Foreign centers and programs of Canadian studies were also important beneficiaries, as were the small number of DFAIT officials directly connected with the program and cultural affairs officials at Canadian embassies and consulates. ICCS, which administered parts of the program, was also a beneficial stakeholder. Finally, I have included those Canadian academics and university centers or programs that had—and many continue to have—links to the Canadian study community abroad.

I have omitted from this policy community the Canadian studies community in Canada, notwithstanding that many prominent voices in this community were raised in vigorous opposition to the 2012 termination of the Understanding Canada Program. In fact, however, the relationship between the Canadian studies community abroad and the Canadian studies community in Canada was not always close. When in the mid-1970s the Department of External Affairs began to invest more systematically in Canadian studies abroad, nationalist voices were heard objecting to Canadian money being channeled to non-Canadians, outside the country, to facilitate their teaching and research on Canada. These nationalist academics were particularly irked when this support went to the United States. Those whose criticism was not purely or principally an expression of their anti-Americanism objected to the very idea that Canadian studies undertaken outside of Canada should receive government support. Ged Martin, who perhaps deserves to be thought of as the father of Canadian studies in the UK, recalls this early opposition: "Within Canada, a few overblown egos...vocally resented any diversion of funding that they saw as rightfully theirs" (Martin 2010: n.p.). The resentful tone became more muted over time, but no serious cooperation developed at the institutional level between the domestically-focused Association for Canadian Studies, created in 1973, and the internationally-focused ICCS, created in 1981. "It is perhaps unsurprising," observed David Cameron in a review of Canadian studies written in the mid-1990s, "that in the early years of their joint existence the two associations have experienced some tension and occasional difficulties in working out their relationship with one another" (Cameron 1996: 133). The tension may have faded as time went on, but ACS never became a champion of Canadian studies abroad.

I have also omitted provincial governments from this policy community, notwithstanding that their constitutional responsibilities for education and local culture are such that one might have expected them to be interested stakeholders in the form, delivery, and fate of Canadian studies abroad. For the most part, however, this has not been the case. They have been much more interested in issues involving the internationalization of education, including study abroad programs and student and faculty exchanges, scholarships, and the recruitment of foreign students (see Trilokekar 2007, 2015).

The voices that leaped to the defense of the Understanding Canada Program might best be described as culturally prominent but not politically influential. Among them were such writers as Margaret Atwood,

Neil Bissoondath, and Jane Urquhart. Not only did their voices lack political heft, they were heard after the decision was announced, when there was virtually no chance that the government would reconsider its decision. Finally, many of the voices raised in opposition to the government's decision were not even Canadian. York University professor Colin Coates, director of the Canadian Studies Network, started an online petition that eventually had more than 2200 signatures. The vast majority who signed were non-Canadians, presumably foreign academics who may in some manner have benefited for the Understanding Canada Program (Robarts Centre 2012). As much as those convinced of the value of Canadian studies abroad might like to believe otherwise, the indignation of those who voiced their opposition to the Conservative government's 2012 decision caused only a slight and rather brief ripple on Canada's political waters.

Life After the Understanding Canada Program

Change is often greeted with alarm and its consequences may be difficult to predict. With the passage of time, it is clear that the sky did not fall after the termination of DFAIT's Understanding Canada Program. In the words of Jean-Michel Lacroix, the dean of Canadian studies in France, "Canadian studies existed before the support of the Canadian government and will continue without its support" (personal correspondence, 2017). Asked about the impact that the 2012 termination of financial support from the Canadian government has had on the activities of the British Association of Canadian Studies, its president, Tony McCulloch, replied in the tradition of the stiff upper lip: "The core activities of BACS—the annual conference, the British Journal of Canadian Studies, the network of specialist groups, the website and the newsletter have all continued…" (ICCS 2016).

In the country chapters that follow, the impacts of Ottawa's 2012 decision to end support for Canadian studies abroad are part of the story told by each of the contributors to this book. These impacts vary quite significantly, ranging from devastating to inconvenient. But even in those countries that have very robust Canadian studies networks that were established before the mid-1970s, when the Canadian Studies Abroad Program was launched, the level of activity has fallen off and the inducements for scholars to enter or remain in the field have weakened.

A sense of the nature and scale of these impacts may be gleaned from the results of a survey carried out by ICCS in 2015. Questionnaires were sent to all national ICCS member associations (23) and associate member associations (5). Responses were received from 20 of the 28 associations. One of the questions asked was, "What has been cut from your association activities since 2012?" Six of the twenty responding associations did not answer this question. They included such national and regional associations as the Central European Association for Canadian Studies, the Korean Association for Canadian Studies and the Association for Canadian Studies in Ireland, all of which are countries where the loss of Canadian government funding would have been felt more deeply than in the case of some of the larger national associations. The responses from the 14 associations that answered this question mentioned a wide range of effects, including the following:

- loss of full- or part-time administrative staff;
- reduction in the number of conferences and other events, visits from Canadian academics and writers, and in the number of visits to Canada by foreign Canadianists and students interested in studying Canada;
- no new purchases of Canadian books;
- cancellation of prize competitions for best paper on Canada;
- decline in association membership;
- fewer opportunities for collaboration with Canadian academic colleagues and with Canadian embassies and consulates;
- decrease in activity at Canadian studies centers and programs, some continuing to exist in name only; and
- termination of some journals of Canadian studies.

These were some, but not all, of the consequences identified by survey respondents. A separate survey of Canadianists in the United States was carried out in 2013, the results of which are discussed in Chapter 2.

These impacts obviously matter for the direct stakeholders in the Canadian studies abroad community. But do they matter for Canada and Canadians? If the benchmark against which we judge the value of a country's efforts to project itself abroad is whether such efforts can be shown to have advanced one iota the interests and values of the country making this investment, can we confidently state that the achievement of these values and interests has been impaired by the termination of government support for Canadian studies abroad?

We cannot answer this question with any certainty. Measuring the effectiveness of diplomacy, whether state-to-state or public, is an elusive enterprise. Even when the diplomatic intervention is widely celebrated as a sort of *coup*, as was President Obama's famous speech at Cairo University in June 2009, we cannot know that it moved the needle of public and elite opinion in the populations it targeted in ways or to a degree that advanced the goals of American foreign policy (Seib 2010; Brooks 2016). Moreover, while some believe that a country's standing in the eyes of other populations, or at least their leaders, is linked causally to its international influence, others are dubious (APSA 2009).[14]

A mistake that is often made by those who search for evidence that public diplomacy, including cultural diplomacy, made a difference is to train one's eyes too low, focusing on the immediate, the near horizon. Such diplomacy needs to be thought of as a long-term investment in generating and maintaining knowledge and interest in the country, making it more likely that when issues arise in that country's relations with others or when something occurs domestically that captures the world's attention, the country has interpreters abroad. Not official spokespersons, but local experts who can tell their country's leaders, media and citizens what is happening and how to make sense of it. When it appeared as though Quebecers might vote to separate from Canada in 1995, this was the role that hundreds of Canadianists played in countries from the United States to Japan. "In years ahead," writes Ged Martin, "Canada might face some other crisis of national unity or continental hegemony. It would be sad if Ottawa went knocking on doors to find interpretive friends, only to find that they could no longer contribute" (Martin 2010).

Help in crisis management is certainly useful. When the normally cordial relations between Canada and the United States crossed a rocky patch in 2003–2004, the two governments disagreeing over the War in Iraq, continental missile defense, and border security (Cellucci 2005), the fact of having hundreds of Canadianists in the United States helped in explaining to the American media and to law-makers in that country what many thought to be puzzling positions on the part of their northern neighbors. But crisis and conflicts aside, having a network of Canadian experts across the world is perhaps the most effective way to ensure that Canada's story, or indeed stories, are told. The stories that these Canadianists tell may not always be sympathetic, although there is abundant evidence showing that they are (CBC 2012). But without these many story-tellers interpreting Canada to the world, what Bruce Hutchison once described as "the unknown country" could become so once again.

This begs an important question: does it matter whether Canada's stories are known and whether there are people in other countries who are motivated to tell them? One at least has to concede the possibility that the loss to the rest of the world would not be so great, although most Canadianists and most Canadians would surely disagree. There is no doubt, however, that the loss to Canada would be considerable. Cumulatively, these stories about Canada's people, values, history, role on the world stage, and achievements constitute Canada's cultural capital. Unlike GDP or technology patents per capita, defense spending, or the number of embassies and consulates a country has throughout the world, there is no metric that allows one to say definitively, "Here is the value of our cultural capital." But as the British Council observes in its 2017 report, *The Art of Soft Power*, "[Cultural capital is] based on the attractive qualities—the ideas and values, together with the behaviour, credibility and moral authority—of the agent. In this way, questions such as how [a] society is organized, its fundamental value system, and the (foreign and domestic) policies its government pursues, all affect [its] capacity to generate Soft Power... . [It] is the cumulative, long-term bank of national assets, moral and cultural, which predispose people to listen to a country" (British Council 2017: unpaginated).

Countries that have robust hard power capacities may decide that these are sufficient in order to get others to listen, although their leaders may know and take seriously Machiavelli's dictum that it is better to be loved than to be feared. For countries like Canada, however, which are not able (or even inclined) to rely on military might, economic muscle, and sanctions of various sorts in order to achieve their foreign policy objectives, getting others to listen may depend on their country's image. Building and maintaining a positive image is not something that can simply be assumed. In their small way, the thousands of researchers, teachers, and students in countries throughout the world who have studied Canada contribute to this image and thus to Canada's cultural capital abroad.

Notes

1. There is not much evidence to support his claim. In the 10 years after he made this statement the value of trade in goods and services between the US and China increased from US$63 billion to US$341 billion and the value of American investment from just under US$2 billion to roughly US$55 billion. In the case of Canada–China trade, this increased from CAN$8.7 billion to CAN$42.1 and Canadian investment in China from CAN$419 million to CAN$2.1 billion. It seems that national image is far from the whole story when it comes to such matters.

2. In March 2017, the Trump administration proposed major cuts to public diplomacy spending by the State Department (https://www.nytimes. com/2017/03/16/us/politics/trump-budget-cuts-state-department. html?_r=0). At this writing it remains to be seen what the precise nature and scale of these cuts might be.

3. These involved mainly the activities of the CBC, the Canadian Government Motion Picture Bureau and its successor, the National Film Board.

4. The key court ruling on this jurisdictional matter was *The Labour Conventions Reference (1937)*. http://www.bailii.org/uk/cases/UKPC/ 1937/1937_6.html.

5. The lack of coordination between agencies of the federal government is described by Elizabeth Diggon's interesting account of the very different goals and responses to Canadian participation in the São Paulo and Venice art biennials during the 1950s. *The Politics of Cultural Power: Canadian Participation at the Venice and São Paulo Biennials, 1951–1958*, Queen's University, 2012: 37–46.

6. The fact that the Minister of External Affairs at the time was Alan MacEachern, a Nova Scotian proud of his Celtic heritage, might have had some influence on the choice of where to make this first major investment. Chairs and centers already existed in the United States at Harvard, Yale, Duke, and Maine, but they were created and sustained by some combination of university and private funding.

7. The economist who produced these estimates, whose name is given simply as Chartrand in the minutes of the Committee's proceedings, defined state investment in cultural exports very broadly to include, "…money spent by countries to export their cultural products or to invest in their cultural activities, culture [including] education, science and the arts." Special Joint Parliamentary Committee, "Reviewing Canadian Foreign Policy," May 12, 1994, pp. 10–11.

8. Gallup regularly publishes the results of such surveys. http://www.gallup. com/poll/1624/perceptions-foreign-countries.aspx.

9. The three pillars included the promotion of prosperity and employment; the protection of national security within a stable global framework; and the projection of Canadian values and culture.
10. See also the survey data reported in Chapter 2 on Canadian studies in the US.
11. This decision and the reaction to it is examined in Munir A. Sheikh, "Good government and Statistics Canada: The need for true independence," *Academic Matters: OCUFA's Journal of Higher Education.* http://academicmatters.ca/2013/05/good-government-and-statistics-canada-the-need-for-true-independence/. The Liberal government announced the reinstatement of the long-form census in November 2015.
12. This is one of many ICCS activities that was stopped due to the termination of funding that had been provided through the Understanding Canada Program. http://iccs-ciec.ca/asppages/results_ftp.asp.
13. The Conservatives had introduced rather loose requirements in 2006 when it established priority themes for funding. These included peace and security, Canada–US bilateral issues, economic competiveness, democracy and human rights, management of diversity, and the environment and energy. It was hard to see where Alice Munro, Margaret Atwood, or Inuit throat-singing would fit under this list of priorities.
14. This report of the American Political Science Association came down strongly, but not unanimously, in support of the claim that there exists a positive and causal correlation between a country's standing in the world and its influence. There were prominent dissenters among those political scientists who participated in this task force.

References

American Political Science Association. 2009. U.S. Standing in the World: Causes, Consequences, and the Future. http://www.apsanet.org/Portals/54/APSA%20Files/publications/TF_USStanding_Long_Final5.pdf.

Arndt, Richard T. 2005. *The First Resort of Kings: American Cultural Diplomacy in the Twentieth Century.* Dulles: Brassey's.

British Council. 2017. *The Art of Soft Power*, December. https://www.britishcouncil.org/organisation/policy-insight-research/art-soft-pwer.

Brooks, Stephen. 2016. *Anti-Americanism and the Limits of Public Diplomacy.* New York: Routledge.

Cameron, David. 1996. *Taking Stock: Canadian Studies in the Nineties.* Montreal: Association for Canadian Studies.

Canada, Department of External Affairs. 1970a. *Foreign Policy for Canadians,* Volume on Europe.

Canada, Department of External Affairs. 1970b. *Foreign Policy for Canadians*, Volume on Pacific countries.

Canada, Department of Foreign Affairs and Trade. 2005a. *A Role of Pride and Influence in the World*.

Canada, Department of Foreign Affairs and Trade. 2005b. Evaluation of the International Academic Relations Program, July (n.p.). http://www.dfait-maeci.gc.ca/about-a_propos/oig-big/2005/evaluation/relation_academic-academique.aspx?lang=eng.

Canada, Department of Foreign Affairs and Trade. 2010. 2009–10 Departmental Performance Report. http://www.tbs-sct.gc.ca/dpr-rmr/2009-2010/inst/ext/extpr-eng.asp?format=print.

Canada, Royal Commission on Dominion-Provincial Relations. 1940. *Final Report*.

Canada, Royal Commission on National Developments in the Arts, Letters and Sciences. 1951. *Final Report*.

Canada, Task Force on Program Review. 1986. *Economic Growth: Culture and Communications*, August. Ottawa: Minister of Supply and Services Canada.

Canadian Broadcasting Corporation. 1996. *What Border? The Americanization of Canada*. First Broadcast, June 4.

Canadian Broadcasting Corporation. 2012. How the World Sees Canada: Knowledgeable People Give Their Views, July 1. http://www.cbc.ca/news/canada/how-the-world-sees-canada-1.1130322.

Canadian Broadcasting Corporation. 2013. Scholars, Authors, Wary of Government Review of Canadian History. *CBC News*, June 16. Canadian Broadcasting Corporation. http://www.cbc.ca/news/canada/scholars-authors-wary-of-government-review-of-canadian-history-1.1377912.

Cellucci, Paul. 2005. *Unquiet Diplomacy*. Toronto: Key Porter Books.

Cull, Nicholas. 2006. Public Diplomacy Before Gullion: The Evolution of a Phrase. *USC Center on Public Diplomacy Blog*, April 18. https://uscpublicdiplomacy.org/blog/public-diplomacy-gullion-evolution-phrase.

Druick, Zoë. 2006. International Cultural Relations as a Factor in Postwar Canadian Cultural Policy: The Relevance of UNESCO for the Massey Commission. *Canadian Journal of Communication* 31 (1). http://www.cjc-online.ca/index.php.journal/issue/view/114/showtoc.

Fulbright, William J. 1989. *The Price of Empire*. New York: Pantheon.

Graham, John. 1976. Recent Growth of Interest in Canadian Studies Abroad. *International Perspectives: Journal of Foreign Policy*, n.p.

Graham, John. 1999. Third Pillar or Fifth Wheel? International Education and Cultural Foreign Policy. In *Canada Among Nations: A Big League Player*, ed. Fen Osler Hampson, Michael Hart, and Martin Rudner. Toronto: Oxford University Press.

Greene, Ian. n.d. Lessons Learned from Two Decades of Program Evaluation in Canada. http://www.yorku.ca/igreene/progeval.html.

Goff, Patricia. 2017. Cultural Diplomacy. *Oxford Bibliographies*, April 27. http://www.oxfordbibliographies.com/view/document/obo-9780199743292/obo-9780199743292-0202.xml.

Halloran, Mary. 1996. *Cultural Diplomacy in the Trudeau Era, 1968–1984.* Ottawa: DFAIT.

Hutchison, Bruce. 2010, first published in 1942. *The Unknown Country: Canada and Her People.* Toronto: Oxford University Press.

International Council for Canadian Studies. 2011. *Brian Long Report.* Internal Document Commissioned by DFAIT.

International Council for Canadian Studies. 2016. Report on Activities of Member and Associate Member Associations. http://www.iccs-ciec.ca/iccs-reports.php.

Japan Foundation. 2016. Annual Report, 2015–2016. http://www.jpf.go.jp/e/about/result/ar/2015/pdf/dl/ar2015e.pdf.

Martin, Ged. 2010. Review of *Canadian Studies in the New Millennium*, ed. Patrick James and Mark Kasoff. Toronto: Published in 2008 by the University of Toronto Press. http://www.gedmartin.net/other-reviews-on-canadian-topics/211-patrick-james-and-mark-kasoff-eds-canadian-studies-in-the-new-millennium.

Meren, David. 2013. *With Friends Like These: Entangled Nationalisms and the Canada-Quebec-France Triangle, 1944–1970.* Vancouver: University of British Columbia Press.

Nye, Joseph. 1990. *Bound to Lead: The Changing Nature of American Power.* New York: Basic Books.

Nye, Joseph. 2010. Soft Power and Cultural Diplomacy. *Public Diplomacy Magazine*, June 1. http://www.publicdiplomacymagazine.com/soft-power-and-cultural-diplomacy/.

Olson, Mancur. 1965. *The Logic of Collective Action: Public Goods and the Theory of Groups.* Cambridge: Harvard University Press.

Quebec, Commission of Inquiry on Constitutional Matters. 1956. *Final Report.*

Redden, Elizabeth. 2015. New Money for Japanese Studies. *Inside Higher Ed*, May 19. https://www.insidehighered.com/news/2015/05/19/japanese-government-gives-15-million-us-universities-endowed-professorships-japanese.

Rivera, Tim. 2015. Distinguishing Cultural Relations from Cultural Diplomacy: The British Council's Relationship with Her Majesty's Government. USC Center on Public Diplomacy. https://uscpublicdiplomacy.org/sites/uscpublicdiplomacy.org/files/useruploads/u33041/Distinguishing%20Cultural%20Relations%20From%20Cultural%20Diplomacy%20-%20Full%20Version%20%281%29.pdf.

Robarts Centre for Canadian Studies. 2012. Update on the Petition Against the Cuts to Canadian Studies Programmes and Associations Outside of Canada, York University. http://robarts.info.yorku.ca/2012/07/update-on-the-petition-against-the-cuts-to-canadian-studies-programmes-and-associations-outside-of-canada/.

Rutherford, Paul. 2005. The Persistence of Britain: The Culture Project in Postwar Canada. In *Canada and the End of Empire*, ed. Phillip Buckner. Vancouver: University of British Columbia Press.

Seib, Philip. 2010. *Public Diplomacy and the Obama Moment*, vol. II, no. 3. Layalina Productions, March. http://www.layalina.tv/wp-content/uploads/2014/07/2010-Mar-Philip-Seib.pdf.

Sharma, Yojana. 2016. Universities Warned on 'Pressure' from Chinese Donors. *University World News*, June 7. http://www.universityworldnews.com/article.php?story=20160915134221500.

Symons, T.H.B. 1975. *To Know Ourselves: The Report of the Commission on Canadian Studies*, vol. II. Ottawa: Association of Universities and Colleges of Canada.

Trilokekar, R.D. 2007. *Federalism, Foreign Policy and the Internationalization of Higher Education: A Case Study of the Department of Foreign Affairs*. PhD thesis, York University.

Trilokekar, Roopa Desai. 2015. From Soft Power to Economic Diplomacy? A Comparison of the Changing Rationales and Roles of the U.S. and Canadian Federal Governments in International Education. Center for Studies in Higher Education, University of California, Berkeley. http://www.cshe.berkeley.edu/publications/soft-power-economic-diplomacy-comparison-changing-rationales-and-roles-u-s-and-canadian.

United States, Government Publishing Office. 1983. Public Law 98-164, November 22. https://www.gpo.gov/fdsys/pkg/STATUTE-97/pdf/STATUTE-97-Pg1017.pdf.

United States, Department of State. 2017. Study of the US Institutes for Scholars. https://exchanges.state.gov/non-us/program/study-us-institutes-scholars.

Wadland, John. 2014. Canadian Studies at 50: An Address to the Peterborough Historical Society. http://www.peterboroughhistoricalsociety.ca/userfiles/file/John%20Wadland%20Remarks.pdf.

Wilson, V.S. 1988. What Legacy? The Neilsen Task Force Program Review. In *Conservatives Heading into the Stretch*, ed. Katherine Graham, 23–47. Ottawa: Carleton University Press.

CHAPTER 2

Getting on the American Radar Screen: The Growth, Achievements, and Limitations of Canadian Studies in the United States

Stephen Brooks

INTRODUCTION

It is a rare Canadian who does not believe that Americans tend to be woefully ignorant when it comes to their northern neighbor. For the most part, Canadians are right. Columbia University historian John Bartlett Brebner, one of the founders of Canadian studies in the United States, expressed this sentiment in his well-known aphorism about Canadian–American relations. "Americans are benevolently ignorant about Canada," he observed, "while Canadians are malevolently well informed about the United States" (Brebner 1945: 3). Many Canadians react to this ignorance with puzzlement and resentment. Why don't they know that we have been their largest trading partner for decades[1] and that Canada has long been the United States' major supplier of energy? Do they know that thousands of Canadians fought and died in World War I and II and in the Korean War, that a Canadian invented

S. Brooks (✉)
Department of Political Science, University of Windsor,
Windsor, ON, Canada

© The Author(s) 2019
S. Brooks (ed.), *Promoting Canadian Studies Abroad*,
Palgrave Macmillan Series in Global Public Diplomacy,
https://doi.org/10.1007/978-3-319-74027-0_2

the modern concept of United Nations peacekeeping, and that we—not Americans!—won the War of 1812? Every Canadian will have heard and perhaps even expressed such frustrations.

So it may come as a surprise to Canadians to learn that some Americans have paid quite a lot of attention to their country. Indeed, some of the most astute, enduring, and influential analyses of Canada and Canadians have been written by Americans. Among these are Massachusetts historian Francis Parkman's multi-volume *France and England in North America* (1865–1892), University of Chicago sociologist C. Everett Hughes' *French Canada in Transition* (1943), several of sociologist Seymour Martin Lipset's books, beginning with his *Agrarian Socialism* (1950), and John Hopkins political scientist Charles Doran's *The Forgotten Partnership* (1985). Those familiar with the study of Canada in the United States know that many other seminal books on Canada could easily be added to this list.

Canadians might be even more surprised to learn that by the early years of the twenty first century, there were hundreds of professors in the United States teaching courses about Canada or that included some significant Canadian content. Attendance at the biennial conferences of the Association for Canadian Studies in the United States (ACSUS) often reached 400–600 persons during this period. The community of Canadianists in the United States was generating hundreds of publications every year, supervising graduate theses on Canada, giving media interviews on issues relating to Canada and Canadian–American relations, and even providing expert opinion to federal and state lawmakers in the United States.

For all this activity, however, Canada remains what Bruce Hutchison once called the "unknown country" (Hutchison 1942). The Canadian studies community in the United States is the largest and most active in the world, and yet most of the time Canada struggles to get onto the American radar screen and to be known beyond the usual tropes of hockey, maple syrup, and snow.[2] Canadians should not imagine that their country is the only one to suffer this fate. A 2016 National Geographic survey confirmed that even university-educated Americans typically do poorly on questions about foreign relations, world geography, and global issues (Little 2016). Moreover, it may not matter whether the average American in Akron or Denver knows that Ottawa is Canada's capital, that Alice Munro is the only Canadian to have won the Nobel Prize for Literature, and that some components in the Chrysler Pacifica, assembled in Windsor, Ontario, have crossed the Ambassador Bridge between Windsor and Detroit—the busiest border crossing in North America—five or six times before that vehicle rolls off the assembly line. *It may matter*, however, if too few persons who influence public opinion and who make and implement policy in the United States know the importance of Canada to the United States and something about their neighbor's values and institutions.

This chapter examines the development of Canadian studies in the United States. The analysis is guided by five questions. Who is engaged in Canadian studies? What are their motivations? What activities are undertaken and what organizations for Canadian studies exist? What consequences have resulted from these activities and organizations? Finally, in what ways did the support of the Canadian government influence the Canadian studies community in the United States and how has the withdrawal of that support affected the community?

I have found it useful to describe the historical development of Canadian studies in the United States using a model developed by Paul Pross in his work on interest groups (Pross 1992). Pross argues that interest groups and their prospects for influence may be understood in terms of their degree of institutionalization. At one end of this continuum are what he calls nascent groups. These generally are single-issue, ad hoc groups that arise in response to a particular event and that have little in the way of resources or direct access to policy-makers. At the other end of the continuum are fully institutionalized groups that are active on a range of issues relevant to their members' interests, have large and/or powerful memberships and permanent professional staffs, and have regular and routine access to those who make and implement policy. Between these poles there are intermediate stages. Interest groups may, Pross argues, evolve from a less to a more developed stage of institutionalization. Or they main remain at one of the stages on the continuum.

Table 2.1 is an adaptation of Pross's model to the analysis of the Canadian studies community in the United States. I will argue that this community has evolved through all four stages of development since its earliest roots in the 1800s to the present day. I will also argue that the robust institutionalized condition of Canadian studies that developed in recent decades has suffered an important setback since the termination in 2012 of the Canadian government's financial support. The chapter concludes with a discussion of whether and how this decline in Canadian studies activities has or may yet affect Canada's relationship with the United States.

Table 2.1 Stages of development of Canadian studies in the United States

Nascent	Fledgling	Mature	Institutionalized
• Writers (Thoreau, Howells, London, etc.) • Scholars (Parkman) • Graduate theses on Canada • Canadian Club of Harvard	• Scholars (C. Everett Hughes, Seymour Martin Lipset, James T. Shotwell, John Bartlet Brebner, etc.) • Conference on Canadian–American Affairs, 1935–1941 • Carnegie Series on Canada–US relations • Multiplication of private sector initiatives: foundations and business associations • State Department interest in promoting greater economic integration with Canada	• Emergence of centers, institutes, programs, and chairs of Canadian studies • Proliferation of seminars, conferences, publications • Prominent role played by American foundations • New generation of leadership in Canadian studies	• ACSUS created in 1971 • Canada included under Title VI of the U.S. Higher Education Act • Fulbright Program extended to include Canada • Canadian studies abroad grants • Rapid and dramatic proliferation of centers, institutes, and programs • Americans Review of Canadian Studies • Creation of regional associations • Emergence of a communal identity as Canadianists
1850	1920s–1950s	1960s	1971–2012

THE NASCENT STAGE: VISITORS, LONE SCHOLARS, AND CANADIAN EXPATS

The study of Canada predated anything that could be called Canadian studies in the United States. The same may doubtless be said of any country in which a community of Canadianists has emerged. Before there are conferences and seminars held on a regular basis, a community of researchers and teachers, associations and grant opportunities—the hallmarks of a regional studies community—there are the field's pioneers. They publish the first books or articles, teach the first courses, and give the first public lectures.

Prominent among these pioneers are those who travel to a country with the intention, or who form the intention while there or afterward, of explaining that country's customs, values, institutions, geography, and so on to their compatriots. Although he was not the first, Alexis de Tocqueville is the archetype and surely the best-known case of the visitor who interprets a foreign place to his countrymen. The United States of the nineteenth century was a magnet for such visitors from Great Britain, France, Germany, and other countries. Some of them, including Tocqueville, spent some of their time in British North America or, after 1867, in Canada. Canada did not, however, attract very much in the way of scholarly attention from its southern neighbor.

The great exception to this rule was Francis Parkman. His multi-volume *France and England in North America* interpreted the clash between the French and English, epitomized in the persons of James Wolfe and Louis-Joseph de Montcalm, as an epic struggle between an ascendant modernist liberal civilization and a feudal model of society whose time had passed. Leaving aside questions that more recent generations of historians have raised about Parkman's scholarship, his analysis of the nature and fall of New France was influential well into the twentieth century and, more than any other book, made this period in Canadian history known to English-speaking readers.

Although few American scholars paid any serious attention to Canada and its history, some important writers provided their American readers with interpretations of their northern neighbor. One of them was William Dean Howells. Editor-in-chief of *The Atlantic Monthly* from 1866 to 1906, Howells' novels, *Their Wedding Journey* (1872) and *A Chance Acquaintance* (1873) are set in the region straddling the St. Lawrence. In the realist fiction style of such contemporaries as Theodore

Drieser and Stephen Crane, Howells believed that "It is the business of the novel to picture the daily life in the most exact terms possible, with an absolute and clear sense of proportion" (Howells 1902: 294). In the two novels mentioned above, Howells provides a wealth of observation and commentary on differences between Canada and the United States.

A generation earlier Henry David Thoreau offered New England readers his own observations and interpretations of Canada, mainly of Montreal and Quebec City, in articles published in *Putnam's Monthly* in 1853. Canada, Thoreau told his readers, was a rather backward place due to the combined influence of feudalism in French Canada and remnants of aristocratic thinking in English Canada. Canadian society seemed to him rather old in its ways, more European than American. "It is said," Thoreau wrote, "that the metallic roofs of Montreal and Quebec keep sound and bright for forty years in some cases. But if the rust was not on the tinned roofs and spires, it was on the inhabitants and their institutions." Someone of a democratic disposition, Thoreau observed, was unlikely to feel easy in what he characterized as the statist culture of Canada: "[I]n Canada you are reminded of the government every day. It parades itself before you. It is not content to be the servant, but will be the master..." (Thoreau 1850).

American readers were already predisposed to accept this unflattering view of Canada, common as it was in American fiction set in Canada. As James Doyle writes, such fiction "denounced [British imperialism], along with provincial submissiveness and lack of initiative, French Roman Catholicism and northern primitivism..." (Doyle 2006). These fictionalized accounts would have provided one of the main sources of ideas about values, institutions, and politics in Canada.

All of the foregoing adds up to rather meager beginnings in the study of Canada. They were not, however, insignificant and they were accompanied by a couple of other developments that prefigured the emergence of what may properly be called Canadian studies in the United States. One of these involved graduate work on Canadian subjects carried out at American universities. Until well into the twentieth century, it was typical for English-speaking Canadians with doctoral ambitions to pursue their studies in the United States or England. University of Toronto historian George Brown compiled a list of doctoral theses completed in Canada, Great Britain, and the United States dealing with Canadian subjects in the fields of economics, history, and political science during the three to four years prior to 1928. Based on the replies that he received,

Brown found that 53 had been completed in the United States, 10 in Canada, and none in Britain. Harvard, Columbia, Chicago, and Yale accounted for most of these doctoral theses on Canada. Although data for the period before the 1920s have not been collected in a similarly systematic manner, nor does it exist for doctoral research on Canada in other disciplines, it seems very likely that such data would tell a similar story. Advanced graduate research on Canada was being carried out by the early twentieth century. Most of it, however, was being carried out in the United States.[3]

Those engaged in this graduate research appear to have been mainly Canadians. Some, including such prominent scholars as Harold Innis (University of Chicago, 1920), W.A. Macintosh (Harvard, 1922), A.R.M. Lower (Harvard, 1927), Charles Perry Stacey (Princeton, 1933), and J.M.S. Careless (Harvard, 1950) returned to Canada where they taught and carried out research over the course of their careers. Others, including John Shotwell (Columbia, 1900), William Bennett Munro (Harvard, 1906), Jacob Viner (Harvard, 1922), and John Bartlett Brebner (Columbia, 1927) remained in the United States for most or all of their careers. These Canadian expatriates would be crucial to the development of a more purposeful and organized approach to the study of Canada in the United States.

It is very likely that many, if not most of these Canadians trained at Columbia, Harvard, and other American universities would have been glad of the opportunity to return to careers in Canada. But as Carl Berger observes, the Canadian university system was too small to provide enough places for them. In addition, Berger argues, "in some quarters there existed a preference for Englishmen, or at least for Canadians educated in England, a snobbish opinion of the allegedly fact-grubbing, over-specialized and unpolished products of the American seminars" (Berger 1972: 34).

A special word needs to be said about the role that Harvard played during this nascent stage in Canadian studies. During the nineteenth century, Harvard was a magnet for Canadians, particularly from the Maritimes, who wished to pursue careers in the liberal professions. In 1890, the Canadian Club of Harvard was created and it continues to exist today. The Club's first annual report included a list of the 448 Canadians who had studied at Harvard between 1804 and 1890. The vast majority did their degrees in law or medicine. Ten did graduate studies. The Harvard Club originally was conceived as "a means of re-union for Canadian students in the University, and to facilitate the acquisition of information by students in Canada desirous of pursuing advanced courses in this University" (Harvard, 1890). The Club's social activities soon came to include talks by prominent Canadians visiting Boston and occasionally by Canadians teaching at Harvard. Although not intended to serve as a forum for the dissemination of information about Canada to Americans, the Canadian Club deserves to be thought of as the first and oldest continuous organization for the discussion of Canada at an American university. It has had many illustrious alumni, including Prime Minister Mackenzie King (MA, 1898; PhD, 1908), in whose name a chair in Canadian studies at Harvard would be created in 1967.

The Fledgling Stage: Founders, Scholars and Patrons

The decades of the 1920s and 1930s saw the transition from the nascent to the fledgling stage in Canadian studies in the United States. The lonely efforts of a rather small number of scholars studying Canada increased during these decades and would continue to grow during the 1940s and 1950s. "By the mid-1930s," writes Carl Berger, "there were more courses in Canadian history being taught in the United States than in Canada" (Berger: 34).

In addition to this quantitative change an important qualitative transformation also took place during the period from the 1930s through the 1950s. Prior to these years, Francis Parkman's history of the fall of New France stood almost alone as a case of serious scholarship that would influence subsequent generations of those who studied Canada. In the early to mid-twentieth century, it would be joined by sociologist Everett C. Hughes' *French Canada in Transition*, John Bartlett Brebner's *North American Triangle* and several of the other books in the Carnegie Series on Canadian–American Relations, R. Taylor Cole's *The Canadian Bureaucracy*, and Seymour Martin Lipset's *Agrarian Socialism*.

It was during this period that a quickening took place in the study of Canada in the United States. One of the main causes of this accelerated interest in Canada was economics. By the eve of the Great Depression, Canada and the United States had become each other's major trading partner. During the post-World War II years, the importance of Canada as a market for exports, a source of imports, and a location for direct investment by American companies increased sharply. Moreover, Canada's role as a defense partner of the United States, a partnership that began with the 1940 Ogdensburg Declaration and the creation of a Joint Board of Defense between Canada and the United States, was reinforced by cooperation during World War II. Canada's strategic importance to the United States became even more significant during the Cold War. The North American Air Defense Command, including the string of Dew Line radar stations across Canada's Arctic, became the cornerstone of this continental defense integration.

An overly simple but not inaccurate characterization of the drivers during the fledgling stage of Canadian studies in the United States might go like this. American academics, especially those born in Canada, had the interest. Some segments of the American business community and major philanthropic foundations had both interest and money. The State Department, for its part, was happy with the general direction that was evident from the conferences, research, and publications produced by this combination of academic entrepreneurship and corporate money, but stayed on the sidelines.

Financed by the Carnegie Foundation for International Peace, the four conferences that took place at St. Lawrence University in Canton, New York, and Queen's University in Kingston, Ontario between 1935 and 1939 are rightly seen as a major step in the development of Canadian studies. A total of 422 participants, about half of whom were academics, attended at least one of the conferences. The remaining attendees included business people, lawyers, journalists and some political party and public officials. In retrospect, these conferences were the prototype for the hundreds of conferences, roundtables, and other forums that would be organized in subsequent decades on the national and regional levels, bringing together those who study and carry out research on Canada with business leaders and government officials.

Before agreeing to finance this series of conferences on Canadian–American relations, the Carnegie Endowment had already committed to support the publication of a large series of books by academics on both sides of the border. Canadian-born and Columbia-trained historian John Shotwell was the Director of the Division of Economics and History at the Carnegie Endowment and became the editor of what ultimately was a 25-volume series on various aspects of Canada–United States relations. As Carl Berger writes, "The whole project was initiated, largely supervised, and partly written by Canadian-born scholars in the United States aided by scholars who were American-trained and living in Canada" (Berger: 36).

With few exceptions, the persons involved in the Carnegie project believed that the histories and destinies of Canada and the United States were intimately and inextricably intertwined and that greater North American integration was both desirable and inevitable.[4] It is, therefore, more than a little ironic that what would become in Canada the two most influential volumes in the Carnegie series on Canadian–American relations, Harold Innis' *The Cod Fisheries* (1940) and Donald Creighton's *The Commercial Empire of the St. Lawrence* (1937), ran strongly against the grain of this interpretation. This had everything to do with the wave of Canadian nationalism or, to put it more frankly, anti-Americanism that gained momentum in the 1950s. Thus, at the same time as the Carnegie project marked a major advance in Canadian studies in the United States, it would also sow the seeds of an important division between American academics studying Canada, many of whom were Canadian-born, and some of their Canadian-based colleagues.

This division was not only a matter of a tendency south of the border to subscribe to continentalist interpretations of Canadian development versus a nationalist narrative to the north. The difference also had to do with the question of the *goals* of Canadian studies in the United States. It would not take long before Canadian nationalists came to see the prevailing interpretation of Canadian–American relations expressed in the Carnegie series, including Brebner's *North American Triangle,* as indicative of American intellectual imperialism. The fact that the funding for the Carnegie book series and conferences came from a major American foundation and that the endeavor and its continentalist conclusions were applauded by American business just confirmed the suspicions of Canadian nationalists.

This would have and ultimately did surprise and disappoint some of those who, through their involvement in the Carnegie project, deserve to be thought of as the founders of Canadian studies in the United States. "In their view," writes Maria Tippett, "nothing could be plainer than that things were being done which would otherwise not be taking place....Few, in consequence, would have argued with what Columbia University professor R.M. MacIver told the Carnegie-sponsored conference...in 1937: 'Canada,' he asserted, 'can work together freely with the United States in the building of a greater continental culture, yet at the same time, within that larger co-operation, can retain, may develop, her self-hood as a distinct nation'" (Tippett: 153–154). Far from being the banker of American cultural imperialism, Shotwell, MacIver, Brebner, and other key figures in this project saw the Carnegie Endowment's support as being motivated by the liberal internationalism that was ascendant at that moment in history. What could be wrong with investing in a better understanding of a longstanding and increasingly important relationship between two neighbors? Canadians certainly were not putting any money toward this endeavor.

Few Canadians and too few Canadian academics know or care to acknowledge that money provided by such American foundations as the Carnegie Endowment, the Rockefeller Foundation, the Ford Foundation, and the William H. Donner Foundation made possible much of the cultural life that developed in Canada in the first half of the twentieth century. This is a subject that has been examined in meticulous detail by Maria Tippett in her book, *Making Culture*, and in Jeffrey Brison's *Rockefeller, Carnegie, and Canada*. Canadian universities were among the beneficiaries of these American foundation grants at a time when, according to Acadia University professor Walter Abell, "there was none other to call upon" (quoted in Tippett: 147). Dependence on American foundation money for much of what happened in the arts and social sciences in Canada continued until the creation of the Canada Council in 1957.

Led by nationalist historians Harold Innis and Donald Creighton, neither of whom was above accepting American foundation money to support their own work, the years that produced the Royal Commission on National Development in the Arts, Letters and Sciences (1951) and the Royal Commission on Canada's Economic Prospects (1956) were ones that looked suspiciously on what was increasingly seen as American imperialism in all its alleged forms. Thus, far from acknowledging and celebrating American financial support for the study of Canada or the fact that Canadians in the hundreds received graduate training at American universities and that courses on Canada or that included material on Canada were taught in the United States, these were interpreted by Canadian nationalists as part of an insidious design for American cultural hegemony across the continent. This belief has never been expressed as forthrightly as by the University of Toronto's James Eayrs. At a conference held at the newly established Center for Canadian Studies at Johns Hopkins University, Eayrs perhaps thought to entertain his hosts by comparing them to imperialists of old: "Whom imperialists would exploit they first submit to anthropological investigation. Lineal descendants of the Royal Colonial Institute and the Comité de l'Afrique française are the chair of Canadian Studies at Harvard, and the Center for Canadian Studies at Johns Hopkins University – one at each end of the Bowash corridor of power" (quoted in Thomson and Swanson 1970: 3).

This conviction that American academic interest in Canada and money provided by American sources in support of the study of Canada and Canadian–American relations must reflect an imperialistic outlook and possibly be motivated by hegemonic aims already existed during the fledgling stage in Canadian studies. Indeed, this belief has never disappeared. As mentioned in Chapter 1, some of the more nationalistic elements in the Canadian studies community that emerged in Canada during the 1960s and 1970s were highly suspicious of Canadian studies south of the border and very much opposed to the idea that the Canadian government should encourage these activities. These nationalists were the dutiful sons and daughters of Innis, who in *The Strategy of Culture* (1952) admonished Canadian academics that, "We must rely on our own efforts....We can only survive by taking persistent action at strategic points against American imperialism in all its attractive guises" (Innis 1952: 2–3).

During this period, the United States government occupied the role of interested observer. Already in the 1930s the increasing importance of Canada to the American economy was acknowledged by officials in the State Department (Stewart 1992: 145–149). They advocated greater continental economic integration—a strategy intended to pull Canada away from the British Empire system of preferential tariffs and bring about a recognition of what a former Harvard professor and Canada expert at the State Department referred to as "Canada's natural economic ties...with the United States" (Stewart 1992: 146). At the same time, and despite the fact that by 1950 Canada was the United States' major trading partner, its main source of imports for a number of strategically important raw materials, and the main location for American direct foreign investment, the relationship with Canada occupied much less time and energy in American government circles than the bilateral relationship might seem to have warranted. The uncomplicated explanation for this was provided in a 1950 State Department memorandum:

> Perceiving no reason to fear or envy the Canadians, we have the friendliest of feelings towards them as neighbors and as partners in various international endeavors, including the Cold War. We have no designs on their territory or their sovereignty. In fact, we are not as a rule deeply interested in

or well-informed about Canadian affairs. As for harmonious relations, we are inclined to take these for granted, having too many compelling troubles elsewhere in the world to search for more beneath the surface of U.S.-Canadian relations. (quoted in Stewart 1992: 195)

While there was what might be described as a generally and sometimes even strongly supportive disposition among State Department officials for greater Canada–US economic integration, it would be too much to describe this as an imperialist strategy for domination of America's northern neighbor. Such a strategy was unnecessary when Canadians themselves proved so willing, for so long, to cooperate in this continentalist enterprise. "At every critical stage of the increasingly integrated relationship," writes Gordon Stewart, "Canadian governments led by freely elected, experienced, and well-educated politicians, advised by competent officials, chose to follow the path of cooperation with the United States" (Stewart 1992: 197).

One of the important ways through which the United States government encourages the study and understanding of other countries is through the Fulbright Program. Launched in 1946, for many years Canada was not among the countries from which scholars and students could apply to do research, teach or study in the United States. Nor did the program support Americans going to Canada to study their northern neighbor. Given what was widely believed in the United States to be the overwhelming and obvious cultural, economic, and lifestyle affinities between the two countries, it seemed pointless to include Canada and Canadians among the countries and peoples that Americans should get to know better. This would not change until 1981.

The Mature Stage: Centers, Programs, and More Private Money

The period from roughly the early 1960s to the beginning of the 1970s was marked by a significant maturation of Canadian studies in the United States. Several university-based centers and programs for the study of Canada were established. There was a proliferation in the number of seminars, conferences and publications on Canada and on Canadian–American relations. A new generation of Canadianists emerged, keen to make the study of Canada an ongoing enterprise at their universities, similar to other regional studies programs. The entrepreneurialism of key

American academics and significant private funding were key drivers during these years. As was also true of the previous stage in the development of Canadian studies in the United States, the focus of this activity was overwhelmingly on Canadian–American relations, including matters of politics, economics and defense.

In calling this the mature stage in Canadian studies, I do not mean to suggest that it was marked by any serious breakthrough in the sense of a wider and better understanding of Canada by Americans and their leaders. Indeed, in 1970, a major conference on Canada–US relations held at Columbia University took as its theme the already very familiar and somewhat thread-worn theme of "Canada: The Unknown Neighbor" (Murray 1971). One might have been forgiven for wondering if much had changed over the course of the preceding 40 years. Some prominent Canadianists in the United States, including Edward Miles, founder of the Canadian Studies Program at the University of Vermont, believed that the answer was, "not nearly enough" (Miles 1972).

The maturity that was arrived at during these years involved the establishment of what might be described as a reasonably stable infrastructure for Canadian studies, funded by several American universities and by private donors, and by the emergence among those studying Canada of a sense of identity as a community of Canadianists. The existence and activities of centers for and programs in Canadian studies was key to the development of this sense of identity. It would be given a major boost when this community of Canadianists acquired the accoutrements and support of a professional association in 1971.

Table 2.2 shows the programs and centers for Canadian studies in the United States in 1971. With a couple of exceptions they were clustered in the Northeast of the United States, within close proximity to Canada. Some of the programs, particularly the Canadian studies program within the Center of Commonwealth Studies at Duke University and the Center of Canadian Studies at Johns Hopkins University, were focused at the graduate level and on research and publications. Others, notably the Canadian Studies Program at the University of Vermont and the New England-Atlantic Provinces-Quebec Center (NEAPQ) at the University of Maine were structured around undergraduate teaching and related activities. History, political science, and economics were the main disciplines represented in these programs. At the same time, there were signs of a more diverse range of interests in Canada, including French Canadian literature and culture and Canadian–American environmental

Table 2.2 Programs and centers for Canadian studies, 1971

	Clarkson College of Technology (Potsdam, NY 1968)	Duke University (Durham, NC 1955)	Harvard University (Cambridge, MA 1967)	John Hopkins University (Washington, DC 1969)	University of Maine (Orono, ME 1968)
Graduate or Undergraduate focus	Undergraduate	Graduate	Both, in a way*	Graduate	Both
Minor or degree in Canadian studies	Minor or part of a double major	No, Canadian studies was part of the *Center for Commonwealth Studies*	No	No	No
Private funding	No	Yes, funding from the Carnegie Corporation in 1955 for the *Center for Commonwealth Studies*	Yes, an endowment contributed by David Rockefeller and other American donors	Yes, major support from the Donner Foundation	Yes, funding from the Donner Foundation
Courses of activities specifically on French Canada	Yes	No	No	No	Yes
Activities other than courses and supervision	Field trips, a Canadian-American seminar	Symposia, invited speakers and extensive research and publications	An endowed Chair in Canadian Studies to invite a distinguished Canadian scholar for a year	Speakers, a 1969 conference on joint military affairs, a visiting researcher	Invited speakers

	Michigan State University (East Lansing, MI 1957)	Western Washington State College (Bellingham, WA 1979)	University of Rochester (Rochester, NY 1954)	University of Vermont (Burlington, VT 1963)	State University of New York (Plattsburgh, NY 1970)
Graduate or Undergraduate focus	Mainly undergraduate through several courses on Canada-US relations, or that had significant Canadian content.	Undergraduate	Two senior undergraduate courses and an occasional graduate seminar	Undergraduate	Undergraduate
Minor or degree in Canadian studies	No	Minor	No	Minor	Minor
Private funding	No	No	Yes, support from the Donner Foundation	No	No
Courses or activities specifically on French Canada	No	No	Yes, this was an important focus of the program	No	Yes
Activities other than courses and supervision	Organized through a Committee of Canadian-American Studies, occasional seminars, symposia and publications	No	Occasional faculty seminars and invited speakers.	Extensive, including speakers, colloquia, field trips and "Summer in Quebec"	Yes, this program involved a requirement of one or two semesters studying in Montreal

*An undergraduate course on Canadian history and culture was taught by the holder of the Chair in Canada in 1970 and by a Harvard professor in 1970–1971. Holders of the Chair also gave a series of lectures that would have been of interest mainly to graduate students and faculty

Source Based mainly on information provided by representatives of these programs and centers, publications Vol 9, No 2 (Autumn 1971), 41–72

concerns. Private money provided by foundations or, in the case of the Mackenzie King Chair in Canadian Studies created at Harvard in 1967, donated by wealthy individuals, was on the balance sheet of six of the ten programs.

Another snapshot of the state of Canadian studies in the United States during this mature phase is provided by the survey of teaching and research on Canada undertaken by Johns Hopkins University in 1969. The survey was sent to 1256 American universities and achieved the remarkably high response rate of 85%. The survey's results were summarized by Dale Thomson and Roger Swanson in the *Journal of Canadian Studies* in 1970 and a year later in the first issue of the *ACSUS Newsletter*. The data had already provided the basis for discussion of the state of Canadian studies at a conference sponsored by Johns Hopkins University and held in May 1970 at Airlie House in Warrenton, Virginia, an hour's drive from Washington, DC.

The picture that emerged from the Johns Hopkins survey suggested that while Canada was not on the radar screen of the vast majority of American schools, a significant number had some interest in Canadian studies. Only 9% of the universities and colleges surveyed offered at least one course on Canada.[5] Nevertheless, this represented 89 responding institutions. Another 8% indicated that they offered courses that included some Canadian content. About two-thirds of institutions offering Canadian content courses were located in states adjoining Canada or bordering the Great Lakes. History, political science, and economics accounted for all but a rather small fraction of the Canadian courses taught in the United States.

The actual amount of Canadian studies activity in the United States was, Thomson and Swanson argued, significantly greater than these numbers suggested. Their survey found that 164 universities and colleges had between them a total of 473 faculty members with a special interest in Canada. Moreover, 38 schools accounted for 213 doctoral and master's theses where Canada was the principal subject. Significant interest existed, they concluded, but organization was lacking. There was, they observed,

...a widespread series of activities of varied nature and scope, with little coordination, or even communication, among them. Each is largely autochthonous, in the sense that it has been developed on an individual campus with little outside support, and with little assistance from others working in the same field. Most are inspired and maintained as somewhat artificial growths by a very limited number of individuals – frequently only one or two – with some personal involvement with Canada... (Thomson and Swanson 1970: 7)

At roughly the same time that the John Hopkins survey was undertaken, the Canadian Embassy in Washington carried out its own survey of courses on Canada at American universities (Cowley 1972). The results were quite similar to those obtained by Thomson and Swanson. Over 9 out of 10 institutions did not have a single course on Canada. In reporting the survey's results, the First Secretary of Cultural Affairs, George Cowley, mixed irony with humor. Compared to the general neglect of Canada, he observed, fewer than 1 out of 10 American universities did not have at least one course on Mexico. "My favorite statistic," wrote Cowley, "was the number of courses on the economy of Canada: three. Given the fact that the United States has $34 billion worth of investments in Canada, this statistic seemed to represent a wonderful sense of trust that nothing could go wrong!" (Cowley: 89).

Thus, by the beginning of the 1970s, the state of Canadian studies in the United States was, to use Thomson and Swanson's adjective, "underdeveloped" (Thomson and Swanson: 7). At the same time, however, it was better than it had ever been, boasting a number of Canadian studies centers and programs, significant interest among faculty across the United States, and continuing interest in Canada among graduate students at American universities. In regard to this last point, a non-exhaustive list of doctoral and master's theses in history and related disciplines[6] found that 104 had been completed between 1964 and 1970. Whereas Columbia, Yale, and Harvard had been the universities of choice for a previous generation of scholars, graduate work on Canada was now spread across many more universities with Maine, Duke, and Johns Hopkins at the forefront. "[O]ne is surprised to learn," observed Peter Yurkiw, responsible for compiling this register of theses, "that almost 15 percent of the doctoral dissertations being done on Canadian topics are registered with American universities" (Yurkiw 1972: 142). Of course 40 years earlier, most theses on Canadian topics, at least at the doctoral level, were supervised at American universities. The dramatic growth in the Canadian university system during the 1960s ensured that there were more possibilities for graduate supervision in Canada, at the same time as it created a new dilemma in the eyes of English

Canadian nationalists. Many of those doing the supervising in Canada were Americans, hired during this period of rapid expansion of Canadian universities (Preston 1975; Cormier 2004).

THE INSTITUTIONALIZED STAGE: RAPID GROWTH, GOVERNMENT FUNDING, AND PROFESSIONALIZATION

The launching pad, so to speak, for the institutionalized stage in Canadian studies in the United States was the Airlie House conference organized by Johns Hopkins University in the spring of 1970. Attended by academics from both sides of the border, American and Canadian government officials, and representatives of the Ford and William H. Donner Foundations—the Canadian and American branches of the Donner Foundation provided financial support for this conference—this was not the first such gathering over the years. It was, however, the best attended and it took place at a moment in time when a number of factors, not all of them having to do with existing interest and programs in Canadian studies, aligned so as to make the next step possible.

Among these factors was the entrepreneurship of several of the scholars who organized the Airlie House conference and its agenda, particularly those from Johns Hopkins and Duke. But timing was also a factor. Issues involving pollution, energy, natural resources, and communications had always assumed a trans-boundary aspect in Canadian–American relations. This sense of inevitable interdependence and the need for cooperation across the shared border was increasingly obvious to all except the Canadian nationalists who rallied behind Ian Lumsden's polemical slogan, "Close the 49th Parallel!" (Lumsden 1970). Moreover, the anti-Americanism that characterized Pierre Trudeau's first years in office, described by Thomson and Swanson as a "confrontation course on which [Trudeau] has embarked in Canada-U.S. relations" (Thomson and Swanson: 8), probably helped raise the profile of Canada in the United States, at least among those who were predisposed to pay attention to their northern neighbor.

The Airlie House conference and the smaller meeting that followed in October 1970 at Michigan State University led to the creation of ACSUS. Six months later, ACSUS held its first biennial conference at Duke University, with the financial support of Alcan Aluminum Corporation, International Nickel, Metropolitan Life, and Standard Oil. The conference took as its theme, "The Influence of the United States on Canadian Development: A Series of Studies." Most of the papers given at that first conference were subsequently included in an admirable book edited by Richard Preston and published by the Commonwealth Studies Center at Duke. The theme of Canada–US relations and the involvement of major American-based corporations with important investments in Canada must have confirmed Canadian nationalists' suspicions that ACSUS would be a Trojan horse for the cultural imperialism that James Eayrs had warned against in his Columbia University talk a year earlier.

At the time of this first ACSUS conference, the organization's membership was 117, eight of whom resided in Canada. Notwithstanding that some of the prestigious Ivy League universities historically had played an important role in the graduate education of scholars interested in Canada, Harvard, and Yale were unrepresented in ACSUS's original membership. There were three members from Columbia. Eight of the original members appeared to be business, foundation, or government officials, six of whom gave Washington, DC as their address.

Only two years later, the Association's membership had exploded to 419. Not only was its growth remarkable, the composition of the membership was also changing in significant ways. American-based academics continued to comprise the majority of members. They were joined, however, by an increasing number of persons with ties to either the American or Canadian government, foundation officials, and a smattering of business representatives. At this early point in its history almost every state was represented in ACSUS's membership. The Association was also proving to be popular with Canadians. Between the fall of 1972 and the spring of 1973 almost one-quarter of the 109 new members of ACSUS were persons residing in Canada. By 1991, ACSUS's membership had grown to about 1300 (Reisman Babby 1991: 22), making it easily the largest of the 20 associations for Canadian studies that existed across the world. ACSUS also had 11 corporate contributors at that point, continuing the tradition of private funding that had been important to the growth of Canadian studies in the United States since the 1930s.

Aside from the financial support that such public universities as Maine, Vermont, and SUNY-Plattsburgh provided for their respective programs, state support for Canadian studies had been conspicuously absent before the 1970s. This was true of both the American and the Canadian government. Indeed, the failure of the Canadian government to make a serious investment in cultural diplomacy had been remarked on and sharply criticized by the Massey Commission's 1951 report. The rather limited support that began in 1966 through a newly created Cultural Affairs Division of the Department of External Affairs was largely focused on francophone countries.

Serious attention to the United States began in 1968 when George Cowley was appointed to the position of First Secretary of Cultural Affairs at the Canadian Embassy in Washington. He had no budget and no programs to administer. Fortunately for the future of Canadian studies in the United States, Cowley had perseverance and vision, not to mention a good sense of humor. "[T]he encouragement of Canadian studies at U.S. universities," was one of the goals set by Cowley and his fledgling division at the embassy in Washington. "We decided early on," he wrote, "that [this would be] the most potentially productive field in which we can concentrate" (Cowley: 89). In the beginning, this encouragement amounted to little more than such assistance as the donation of books on Canada, providing "teacher's kits" and other informational material, free subscriptions to some government periodicals, and very modest financial support to help pay the costs of bringing speakers to American campuses (Cowley 1971). External Affairs also provided some small financial support for the creation of ACSUS.

Cowley's efforts might have come to nought had it not been for the rapid growth of ACSUS in the first couple of years after its creation. ACSUS was the institutional catalyst that helped forge a professional identity among the hundreds of Canadianists at universities across the United States. These scholars were largely unknown to one another until ACSUS's biennial conferences, its newsletter, and its journal helped transform what previously had been a community *in potentia* into one that that had leadership, opportunities for participation, and forums for the exchange of information on teaching, research, and conferences. All of this happened before and without any financial support worthy of the name from the Canadian government.

This changed in 1975 when Canada's Department of External Affairs launched the Canadian Studies Abroad Program. Through individual grants that over the years would typically amount to only a few thousand dollars, the Canadian government began direct support for teaching, research, conferences, and other mainly university-based activities intended to enhance knowledge and understanding of Canada. From the beginning, more grant applications were received from the United States than from any other country. Figure 2.1 shows the number of

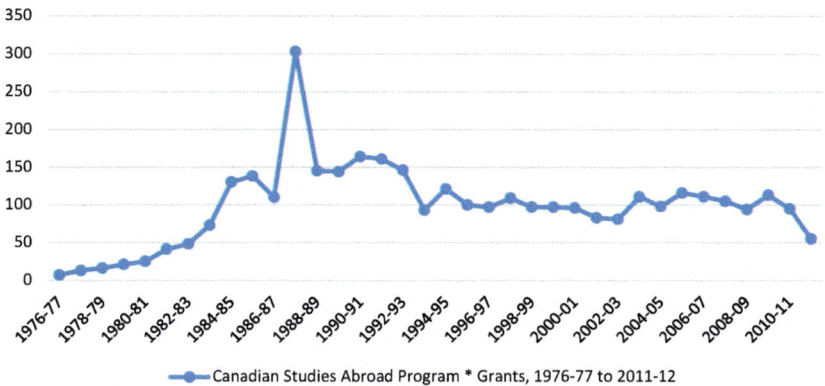

Fig. 2.1 Canadian studies abroad program* grants, 1976–1977 to 2011–2012 (*This program was renamed the Understanding Canada Program in 2006)

grants awarded in the United States between 1976 and the termination of funding for Canadian studies abroad in 2012.

The story of the background to the Canadian government's financial support for Canadian studies abroad was told in Chapter 1. The Canadian Studies Abroad Program made its first grants in 1976. They immediately became a significant part of the Canadian studies scene in many countries, including the United States. Although quite small alongside the support of Canadian studies provided by American universities, governments, foundations, corporate donors, and individual benefactors,[7] these Canadian government grants helped hundreds of American scholars offer new courses on Canada, carry out research, engage in community outreach activities, and send American students to Canada. It is impossible to calculate the leveraging effects these grants had in attracting additional funding from other sources. Their importance in this regard became quite obvious, however, once these grants were gone.

In the first several years of the Canadian Studies Abroad Grant Program, the number of grants per year to scholars and institutions in the United States was relatively small (see Fig. 2.1). By the mid-1980s, however, the average annual number had reached well over 100 and in 1987–1988, it reached 303. The number of grants per year remained close to 100 or higher most years until 2010–2011, the year before the program's abrupt termination. The range of disciplines receiving grants was vast and the variety of projects supported by this program was nothing short of astounding. Hundreds of colleges, universities, and research institutes received these grants. Every state was represented over the 37 years of the program's existence. Slightly more than half of all grants went to states sharing a land or water border with Canada. Three states—Michigan, Washington and New York—accounted for 28% of all grants over the program's history.

It is difficult to demonstrate conclusively that these grants contributed to the impressive growth in Canadian studies in the United States that took place between the mid-1970s and the first decade of the twenty first century. Perhaps the membership of ACSUS would have grown from roughly 500 in 1975 to almost three times that number 20 years later without the incentives and the leveraging effects that some have attributed to the grant program. Perhaps the number of programs and centers for Canadian studies would have increased from about a dozen when the grant program began to over 50 when it ended. And perhaps most of the thousands of articles and books produced by Americans about their northern neighbor would have been written without the support, direct and indirect, that this Canadian government funding provided.

In fact no one who has been active in the Canadian studies community in the United States believes that this funding did not make an important difference in all of these ways. Most of the Canadian studies grants were tied to very specific purposes such that it was a simple matter to know whether the proposed new course on Canada was created, the conference took place, or the internship program sent students to Ottawa. As we will see in the next section of this chapter, the elimination of these grants very clearly contributed to an immediate and significant decline in Canadian studies activities across the United States. Those relatively few programs that had always depended on endowment money, including Harvard and Johns Hopkins, or that had National Resource Center status under the Higher Education Act, were much less affected by the end of the Canadian government's grant program. But in ways large and small, most programs were.

The institutionalized stage in Canadian studies in the United States also saw financial support from the American federal government and some state governments. The most important form this support took and continues to take began in 1990 when Canada was included among the countries included under the umbrella of the Fulbright

Program. Between 1991 and 1992, when the first grants were made, and 2016–2017, 371 American scholars and 397 American students studied, did research or taught in Canada under the rubric of the Fulbright Program. Included among them were individuals who any Canadianist in the United States will immediately recognize as important builders of Canadian studies during its institutionalized phase, including Joseph Jockel, André Senécal, Earl Fry, and Diddy Hitchins.[8] One of those who went to Canada as a Fulbright Student, Christopher Sands, is now the Director of the Canadian Studies Program in SAIS at Johns Hopkins. Heading in the other direction, 411 Canadian scholars and 316 Canadian students received Fulbright grants to study, do research, or teach in the United States during this period. As is also true of the American Fulbright Scholars who traveled to Canada, this is a very distinguished group that includes such prominent scholars as John Helliwell, Stephen Clarkson, Michael Hawes, Charles Taylor, Louis Balthazar, and Donald Savoie. While it is not the case that all of the Canadian scholars who spent time in the United States on Fulbrights taught courses or gave seminars on aspects of Canada, a great number did. Indeed, for many years Fulbright Canada has emphasized the importance of Canadian–American relations in its applicant selection process.

Another channel of American government support emerged in the 1970s when Canada was added to the list of Title VI Programs under the Higher Education Act administered by the United States Department of Health, Education, and Welfare. Title VI includes grants for area studies, funding that has been important over the years for a handful of Canadian studies programs across the United States. In 1983, three National Resource Centers on Canada received Title VI funding: the partnership of SUNY-Plattsburgh, the University of Maine at Orono and the University of Vermont; Michigan State University; and Duke University. Michigan State and Duke both eventually lost this funding, but in 1988 the University of Washington and Western Washington University received a Title VI grant in support of their National Resource Center on Canada. The National Resource Centers at SUNY-Plattsburgh and Maine and at the University of Washington and Western Washington have received Title VI funding on a continuous basis since their initial grants. The value of this funding is quite significant. In 2014, the Center for the Study of Canada at SUNY-Plattsburgh in partnership with the Canadian-American Center at the University of Maine received a four-year grant of US$1.5 million.

The National Resource Center on Canada at the University of Washington in collaboration with Western Washington University received US$1.65 million for this same period.

State governments also have provided assistance to some Canadian studies programs over the years. A notable case in point involved the financial support that the Canadian Studies Center at Bowling Green State University received from the Ohio legislature between 1989 and 2009. BGSU's Canadian Studies Center had its own line in the state budget for all of this period, receiving an annual appropriation of as much as US$164,000 for many of these years. State government funding on this scale and over such a continuous period of time was, however, quite untypical. More commonly it assumed the form of support for a particular event, such as a regional conference, or for a specific aspect of a university's Canadian studies program. An example of the latter was a contribution from the Commonwealth of Massachusetts Endowment Incentive Program to help fund an endowed Chair in Canadian Studies at Bridgewater State College, created in 2007.

The period from the 1980s into the early years of the twenty first century was one of remarkable growth and activity in Canadian studies in the United States. Having a national organization with a full-time secretariat helped facilitate this growth. A grant from the Exxon Education Foundation in 1982 enabled ACSUS to establish an office in Washington, DC. Another grant from the William H. Donner Foundation in 1984 enabled ACSUS to move its secretariat to the National Center for Higher Education where it would remain until 2014. Financial assistance from the Canadian and American governments, some American state governments, and from American foundations, corporations, and private benefactors complemented that provided by universities to produce a network of Canadian studies that at its peak probably involved 60 or more programs and centers. In 2010, Christopher Kirkey, the Director of SUNY-Plattsburgh's Center for the Study of Canada, compiled a list of 61 such programs and centers (Center for the Study of Canada 2010). This impressive number did not even include what might be described as quasi-programs that, in some cases, were more active than certain formal programs. Examples of these would include James Baker's Canadian Parliamentary Internship Program, created at Western Kentucky University in 1997, and the trio of Canadian studies activities—an undergraduate course on Canadian Politics, a five-week Ottawa parliamentary internship program, and a joint Master in Public

Policy with the University of Windsor—that existed at the University of Michigan-Dearborn from 2005 to 2015.

The robust health of Canadian studies during this period could also be seen in the proliferation of regional and state Canadian studies associations, including the Midwest Association for Canadian Studies, the Mid-Atlantic-New England Council for Canadian Studies, the Western Canadian Studies Group, the Pacific Northwest Canadian Studies Consortium (which, unlike the other regional associations, has included several Canadian institutions), and the Southern Association for Canadian Studies. With the encouragement of Canadian consulates in the United States, annual or biennial roundtables became a regular part of the Canadian studies calendar in Michigan, Ohio, Kentucky, and several other states. A perusal of any ACSUS newsletter from the late 1980s until 2012 conveys a picture of a large, robust, and enthusiastic community of American scholars mining virtually every corner of Canadian studies. This may also be seen in the publishing activity of American scholars. According to ICCS, they produced well over 900 books, articles, reports, and other publications between 1980 and 2000 (ICCS).

One of the markers of a fully institutionalized area studies community is the existence of a flagship journal that is seen by specialists as a desirable venue for the publication of their research. Two years after the creation of ACSUS, the *American Review of Canadian Studies* (*ARCS*) was launched, initially as a twice-yearly publication and eventually becoming a quarterly by the mid-1980s. As befits the multidisciplinary and interdisciplinary character of Canadian studies in the United States, *ARCS* has represented the wide range of interests of the ACSUS membership, as may be seen in Table 2.3. *ARCS* publishes articles in both English and French. Many of the articles on topics dealing with Quebec and French Canada, particularly those falling into the literature category of Table 2.3, were written in French.

Biennial conferences of ACSUS provide another measure of the scale and scope of activities among the community of Canadianists in the United States. When ACSUS held its nineteenth conference in Toronto in 2007, the first biennial conference to be held outside the United States, attendance peaked. There were about 460 formal participants, a number that does not include those who attended but did not give a paper, sit on a panel, or play some other formal role at the conference. The Toronto conference involved 110 panels and roundtables, covering 15 disciplines. Interest continued to be high two years later in

Table 2.3 Percentage and number of ARCS articles in each subject category*

	1971-1980	1981-1990	1991-2000	2001-2010	2011-2017
Politics and Policy	40% (47)	39% (80)	52% (112)	49% (121)	55% (98)
History	21% (25)	23% (48)	16% (34)	24% (58)	19% (34)
Literature	18% (21)	25% (52)	17% (35)	10% (24)	13% (23)
Quebec/ and French Canada	14% (17)	17% (36)	16% (35)	8% (19)	17% (31)
Culture and Communications	15% (18)	12% (25)	7% (16)	17% (41)	21% (37)
Economics	4% (5)	4% (9)	13% (27)	5% (13)	6% (11)
Indigenous Peoples	2% (2)	9% (18)	1% (1)	11% (26)	6% (11)
Sociology	5% (6)	3% (7)	4% (9)	6% (14)	8% (15)
Environment	2% (2)	2% (4)	8% (17)	3% (7)	7% (12)
Women	2% (2)	7% (14)	1% (1)	1% (3)	3% (6)
Canadian Studies in U.S	5% (6)	1% (2)	2% (4)	--	3% (5)
	N=119	N=207	N=216	N=247	N=178

*An article may be included in more than one subject category. For example, an article on acid rain pollution in the 1980s and government responses to this issue would have been counted under both the "Environment" and "Politics and Policy" categories. I have tried to identify the predominant focus of each article, but in some cases an article was placed under two or even three categories. Consequently the percentages in each column add up to more than 100%

This table includes all articles published in the ARCS and a very small number of editorials and pieces included under "Miscellany" that were, in my judgement, quite similar to original articles. It does not include comments on articles or rejoinders to such comments, book review essays, or other pieces that are not articles

ACSUS published a semi-annual Newsletter in 1971 and 1972. Its journal, ARCS, began as a semi-annual publication in 1973, switching to three issues per year in 1982 and then four issues per year in 1985

San Diego, with about 400 formal participants. Since then, however, the ACSUS conferences have undergone a steady decline in participation from 350 at the Ottawa biennial in 2011 to 250 at Tampa in 2013 and 210 at Las Vegas in 2017. Another change has also occurred. The Canadian share of biennial conference participants, which has always been significant, appears to have increased. At the 2017 Vegas conference, roughly half of all participant roles were filled by Canadians. It appears that a disproportionate part of the decline in conference participation has been among Americans.

When the Canadian government announced in 2012 the end of almost four decades of financial support for Canadian studies abroad, one of the many articles criticizing this decision carried the title, "Canada's image abroad: fade to black" (Martin 2012). This rather apocalyptic prognosis overlooked important sources of resilience that, at least in the case of Canadian studies in the United States, predated the involvement of the Canadian government and that continued to exist after Ottawa retreated from the field. Among these sources of resilience, three stand out.

One is the passion and dedication of hundreds of scholars in the United States who, for diverse reasons, became interested in the study of Canada and who have continued this interest through their research, writing, and teaching. A second involves the money donated by American foundations and private benefactors over the years, money that continues to nurture Canadian studies through endowments at such institutions as Johns Hopkins University[9] and Harvard, and that contributed to the development of dozens of programs and centers across the United States. A third source of resilience is the support of the American government through the Fulbright Program and through Title VI grants that support the two National Resource Centers on Canada at SUNY-Plattsburgh/University of Maine and at the University of Washington/Western Washington University.

Several years after the termination of Canadian government support for studies abroad, Canadian studies in the United States continues to have the characteristics of an institutionalized community of scholars. The national association, ACSUS, and its quarterly journal continue to exist. The biennial conferences continue to take place and to attract scholars, albeit fewer than in the past, from across the United States and Canada. The National Resource Centers on Canada continue to be exceptionally active, not least of all because of the exceptional leadership of the Canadian studies programs at the universities where they are based. Dozens of Canadian studies programs continue to offer courses, organize events, and provide hubs for research.

There is no getting around the fact, however, that Canadian studies takes place on a diminished scale and that much has been lost in recent years. What has been lost and by whom is the subject of the final section of this chapter.

THE DAY THE FLAG PINS DISAPPEARED: LIFE WITHOUT THE UNDERSTANDING CANADA GRANT PROGRAM

As discussed in Chapter 1, the 2011 survey carried out for ICCS found that a significant percentage of Canadianists in countries across the world indicated that the Understanding Canada grant program (previously called the Canadian Studies Abroad Program) provided them with the incentive to do research or teach courses on Canada and that a reduction in funding opportunities through this program would likely result in a decline in Canadian studies at their institution. This was as true in the

United States, where the infrastructure for Canadian studies was quite extensive, as it was for most other countries. We cannot know how many potential Canadianists have not taught or carried out research because of the absence since 2012 of the modest but important funding incentives provided by this grant program. We can, however, ascertain with some confidence the consequences for those who were already part of the community of Canadianists in the United States.

Some of these consequences will seem quite trivial. I don't recall exactly when it happened, probably in the early spring of 2013, but I vividly recall that my request to a Canadian consulate for the Canada–US flag lapel pins that I would annually distribute to my American students in a Canadian Politics course was met with the unexpected reply, "We don't have a budget for such things any longer." For many years those of us involved in Canadian studies in the United States had grown used to the cultural and academic affairs officer at the regional consulate providing what we jokingly referred to as "Canadian swag." Alas, the lapel pins, the pens, and the rest of the swag had disappeared, along with the Canadian studies grants.

Other consequences were much more significant. To get a more precise sense of the impact of the termination of Canadian government support for Canadian studies in the United States, I sent a questionnaire in March 2013 to those individuals who had received an Understanding Canada grant during the three years before the program ended. The response rate was 80%.[10] Those who responded were not only grant recipients, they also tended to be scholars who were well established in the Canadian studies community. Almost two-thirds of them had received at least two grants from the Canadian government. Three-quarters had published at least one or two journal articles on Canada and almost half had published several articles and/or one or more books. Over half the respondents were 45 years of age or older.

It has often been argued by those who advocate cultural diplomacy that one of the potentially valuable functions performed by foreign scholars and researchers may be to explain the country that they study to lawmakers, opinion leaders, and the attentive public in other countries. Over half of the respondents to this survey reported having been contacted by the media at least once or twice to comment on a matter having to do with Canada. Although only 4% said that they had been contacted frequently, 25% said that they had been contacted once or twice and another 24% stated that they had been contacted occasionally.

Almost 1 in 5 respondents reported that they had appeared before a government body, such as a legislative committee or a commission, where their Canadian expertise was the reason for their presence. Just over 60% said that they had been invited to speak to a community organization on a topic related to Canada, almost 30% saying that they had been invited to give such talks several times.

Only one year after the termination of the Understanding Canada program, the impact of its loss was being felt in the United States. Over 4 out of 5 respondents (82%) affiliated with a Canadian studies program or center said that the decision would affect their program's or center's activities quite a lot. Another 16% said that the effects would be marginal and only 2% said that no impact would be felt. As Fig. 2.2 shows, many respondents reported an immediate impact on their teaching and research on Canada and most expected negative consequences in the future.

The respondents' rather gloomy prognostications are confirmed by the obvious signs of decline in Canadian studies activities in the years since 2012. Many programs or centers continue to exist in little more than name only, including some that were once important hubs of Canadian studies activities such as those at Michigan State University

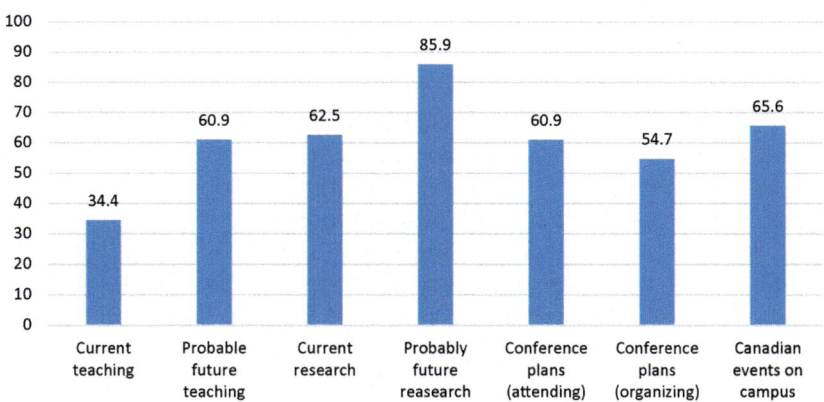

Fig. 2.2 Perceptions in the United States of the impact of the termination of the understanding Canada program. Question asked in the survey: Has the Canadian Government's decision to end funding through the Understanding Canada program affected you in any of the following ways? The numbers indicate the percentage of respondents reporting a negative impact

and Bowling Green State University. The closure of the ACSUS secretariat in Washington, DC, an indirect casualty of the Canadian government's withdrawal of support for Canadian studies abroad, has deprived the community of Canadianists in the United States of professional, full-time management of their national association's affairs.[11] One by one the state Canadian studies roundtables and the regional associations for Canadian studies have become moribund and disappeared. ACSUS membership, which had been declining even before the termination of the Understanding Canada program, had fallen to about 250 in 2017, smaller than at any time since the first couple years of its existence.

Nevertheless, Canadian studies in the United States continues to engage the energies of hundreds of academics (perhaps even thousands if we loosen the definition of a Canadianist to include the professor who assigns one of Alice Munro's works in his course on the modern short story or the professor who includes Nunavut as a case study in her book on models of indigenous self-government across the world). Every year, thousands of American university students, not to mention a significant number of K-12 students (Kirkey 2013), are exposed to information and ideas about Canada, although the number is almost certainly smaller than it was several years ago.[12] We may conclude that the termination of the Canadian government's financial support for Canadian studies abroad has contributed to a significant decline in Canadian studies activity in the United States. We may go further to say that the impact has been serious. It has not, however, been devastating.

The other question involves whether and how the Canadian government's 2012 decision has affected Canada's relations with the United States. There are many moving parts to a relationship as vast and deep as that between these two countries. Cultural diplomacy, its advocates insist, is an important investment in generating understanding and goodwill, and is particularly important when bilateral relations hit rough patches. Are there any reasons to think that Canada's relations with the United States have suffered or may suffer in the future in consequence of a decline in Canadian studies in the United States?

The answer is that we do not know. Just as the returns on investment in cultural diplomacy are seldom immediate and direct, the consequences of disinvestment are unlikely to be felt straight away. The Canadian government's original decision to provide financial support for Canadian studies in the United States was not taken in the expectation that it would produce any specific outcomes for Canada's national interests beyond the rather broad goal of helping to make Canada better known in the country most vital to the protection and promotion of those interests.

Several years after the launch of the Canadian Studies Abroad Program, Don Alper carried out a survey of members of Congress to ascertain their knowledge of and feelings toward Canada. He found that Canada was well liked, but that American lawmakers did not fully appreciate that Canadian security and economic interests were not necessarily identical to those of the United States (Alper 1980: 35). It is unlikely that the picture would have been much different among American journalists or other opinion leaders in the United States. Nor, aside from the classrooms of the Canadianists teaching in universities across the country, would the picture have been different on American campuses.[13] Canada remained, as Bruce Hutchison famously called it, the "unknown country."

Decades of financial support for Canadian studies in the United States may not have changed matters very significantly. Walking into my first Canadian politics class of the semester at a Michigan university, only a 30-minute drive from the border with Canada, it has been rare that more than a couple of students would know that Canada is the United States' second largest trading partner after China and was the largest for decades until 2015, or that Canada has long been the single most important supplier of energy to their country. I know that hundreds of colleagues across the United States can attest to the same experience. But that is the point of Canadian studies: to make the unknown country better known. This is not something that can be achieved with a one-time investment. It is accomplished and maintained through a continual effort to raise Canada's profile and make the country known to its American neighbors.

It is hard to imagine that there is or ever has been a more cost-effective way of doing this than through support for Canadian studies abroad (see Chapter 1). Such an investment will never guarantee that a member of the United States Senate Subcommittee on International Trade, considering reforms to the North American Free Trade Agreement, will better understand the reasons for supply management in Canada's agricultural sector or feel more positively about Canadian softwood lumber imports. And it may not be obvious how Americans knowing about and reading Alice Munro, Margaret Atwood, and Yann Martel advances Canadian interests beyond increased sales of their books in the American market.[14]

In the 2017 Thomas O. Enders Memorial Lecture on US–Canada Relations, given at Johns Hopkins University's Center for Canadian

Studies, Canada's Parliamentary Secretary to the Minister for Foreign Affairs, Andrew Leslie, explained why Canadian studies in the United States deserve the support of the Canadian government:

> Canadian Studies programs here, and at other universities across the U.S. and Canada, play an important role in reinforcing the strong bonds that exist between our countries. Given the highly integrated nature of our ties, we all benefit from any research and study—conducted here and elsewhere—that examines the many aspects of our relationship. (Leslie 2017)

Although most of Leslie's remarks focused on economics, trade, and border security, he acknowledged that "mutual awareness and understanding of life" across national boundaries involves more than these. The title of his talk was "Advancing Canada's Interests and Defending Canadian Values in Washington." Canadian values involve more than economic prosperity. Part of what the Canadian studies community in the United States has done for decades is to interpret these Canadian values to Americans. These intrepid Canadianists will never reach all Americans—nor is this necessary—and it is a good bet that Canada will continue to be associated mainly with ice hockey and cold weather by many of its southern neighbors (Blackwell 2013). Making the "unknown country" known in the United States has always been a Sisyphissian task. But how much heavier the boulder without the efforts of the Canadian studies community in the United States?

NOTES

1. China surpassed Canada in 2015 as the United States' leading trading partner. Canada continues to be a close second.
2. The 2015 election of the telegenic Justin Trudeau as Prime Minister has changed this somewhat, as when Trudeau appeared on the August 2017 cover of *Rolling Stone* magazine alongside the story title, "Why Can't He Be Our President?" Presumably, however, Canada can't count on always having a head of government who is frequently described in the American media as "hot."
3. Harold Innis, himself trained in economics at the University of Chicago before returning to Canada at the University of Toronto, commented that in his field "the most important work has been done by Canadian students doing graduate work in the United States" (Innis 1956: 5).
4. Of course they were not the first to believe this. Half a century earlier, Goldwin Smith (1891) had argued that the economic and political union of Canada and the United States was both inevitable and desirable.

5. A Canadian course was defined as one in which Canadian material accounted for over half the course.
6. These other disciplines included literature, economic history, political science, communications, geography, and sociology.
7. There were many such benefactors. For example, the Reddin family of Bowling Green, Ohio financed the annual Reddin Symposium on Canada–US relations held at BGSU between 1988 and 2012. Those who have been involved in Canadian studies across the United States can tell many similar stories of the generosity of private benefactors.
8. I ask readers' forgiveness for my failure to mention other prominent Canadianists who spent time in Canada as Fulbright Scholars and who subsequently have made major contributions to Canadian Studies in the United States. I could have written an entire paragraph consisting of nothing but the names of such persons. I am indebted to Dr. Michael Hawes, CEO of Fulbright Canada, and Mr. Brad Hector, Program Officer for Fulbright Scholars, for providing the data that I needed for this section of the chapter.
9. In the case of the Center for Canadian Studies within the School for Advanced International Studies at Johns Hopkins, it was founded in 1970 with half million dollar contributions from both the William H. Donner Foundation and the Arthur Vining Davis Foundation. This endowment is now worth about $6 million. I am grateful to Christopher Sands, the Center's director, for this information.
10. The data from this survey were used in Jennifer McGreevy's major research paper for the degree of MA in Political Science at the University of Windsor. Copies of the questionnaire and figures are available on request from brooks3@uwindsor.ca.
11. Responsibility for the management of ACSUS affairs was assumed in 2015 for a three-year term by the Canadian Studies Program at the University of Buffalo, under the direction of Munroe Eagles. His efforts have been heroic.
12. Many of these efforts fly below the radar. One example is the Canadian studies course and annual week-long field trip to Canada organized by Patrick McLean, the Director of the Gerald R. Ford Institute for Public Policy and Service at Albion College, Michigan. How to quantify the value of a trip that every year exposes a dozen or more American students, some of whom will one day be opinion leaders and decision-makers, to the Hockey Hall of Fame in Toronto, the Art Gallery of Ontario, the Canadian Canoe Museum in Peterborough, Parliament in Ottawa, and much more?
13. In one of his more entertaining segments of "The Mercer Report," a popular CBC comedy, Canadian comedian Rick Mercer visits the campus

of Columbia University in New York. He proceeds to interview students and even professors, presenting them with rather preposterous "fake news" about Canada, which these highly educated Americans at one of the country's most prestigious universities respond to as if it were true. The message for Canadians seemed to be that even smart Americans don't pay any attention to us!

14. All three of these Canadian authors are published by Penguin Random House, based in New York, so even increased sales in the United States wouldn't count as a financial gain for Canada.

REFERENCES

Alper, Donald. 1980. Congressional Attitudes Toward Canada and Canada–United States Relations. *American Review of Canadian Studies* X (2): 26–36.

Berger, Carl. 1972. Comments on the Carnegie Series. In *The Influence of the United States on Canadian Development: Eleven Case Studies*, ed. Richard A. Preston. Durham, NC: Duke University Press.

Blackwell, Richard. 2013. Canada's America-Sized Perception Problem. *Globe and Mail*, December 1.

Brebner, John Bartlett. 1945. *North Atlantic Triangle: The Interplay of Canada, the United States and Great Britain*. New Haven: Yale University Press.

Brison, Jeffrey. 2005. *Rockefeller, Carnegie, and Canada: American Philanthropy and the Arts and Letters in Canada*. Montreal: McGill-Queen's University Press.

Center for the Study of Canada. 2010. Canadian Studies Programs in the United States, SUNY-Plattsburgh. http://web.plattsburgh.edu/offices/academic/cesca/connect/canadianstudiesprogram.php.

Cole, R. Taylor. 1949. *The Canadian Bureaucracy: A Study of Canadian Civil Servants and Other Public Employees, 1939–1947*. Durham, NC: Duke University Press.

Cormier, Jeffrey. 2004. *The Canadianization Movement: Emergence, Survival, Success*. Toronto: University of Toronto Press.

Cowley, George A. 1971. What the Canadian Embassy Can Do for You. *ACSUS Newsletter* I (1): 19–22.

Cowley, George A. 1972. How to Have Cultural Affairs Without Really Trying. *ACSUS Newsletter* II (1): 88–90.

Creighton, Donald. 1937. *The Commercial Empire of the St. Lawrence, 1760–1850*. Toronto: Ryerson Press.

Doran, Charles. 1985. *The Forgotten Partnership: U.S.-Canada Relations Today*. Baltimore: Johns Hopkins University Press.

Doyle, James. 2006. Foreign Writers on Canada in English. *The Canadian Encyclopedia*. http://www.thecanadianencyclopedia.ca/en/article/foreign-writers-on-canada-in-english/.

Harvard University. 1890. *Canadian Club of Harvard University*. Cambridge, MA: Wentworth Press.

Howells, William Dean. 1902. Will the Novel Disappear?, an interview with Stephen Crane in *North American Review* 175 (September).

Hughes, Everett C. 1943. *French Canada in Transition*. Chicago: University of Chicago Press.

Hutchison, Bruce. 1942, republished in 2010. *The Unknown Country: Canada and Her People*. Don Mills, ON: Oxford University Press.

Innis, Harold. 1940. *The Cod Fisheries: The History of an International Economy*. New Haven, CT: Yale University Press.

Innis, Harold. 1952. *The Strategy of Culture*. Toronto: University of Toronto Press.

Innis, Harold (ed.). 1956. The Teaching of Economic History in Canada. In *Essays in Canadian Economic History*. Toronto: University of Toronto Press.

International Council for Canadian Studies (ICCS). n.d. Bibliographical Database. http://iccs-ciec.ca/asppages/results_ftp.asp.

Kirkey, Christopher. 2013. Canada and the American Curriculum: A Replicable Investigation of Areas Studies Content State by State. National Research Center Conference, February 27, in Columbus, Ohio. https://umaine.edu/teachingcanada/wp-content/uploads/sites/176/2014/04/Canada-and-the-American-Curriculum-UMaine-SUNY-Plattsburgh.pdf.

Leslie, Andrew. 2017. Advancing Canada's Interests and Defending Canadian Values in Washington. The 2016–2017 Thomas O. Enders Memorial Lecture on U.S.-Canada Relations (May 2), Center for Canadian Studies, School for Advanced International Studies, Johns Hopkins University.

Lipset, Seymour Martin. 1950. *Agrarian Socialism: The Cooperative Commonwealth Federation in Saskatchewan: A Study in Political Sociology*. Berkeley: University of California Press.

Little, Becky. 2016. Most Young Americans Can't Pass a Test on Global Affairs—Can You? *National Geographic*. http://news.nationalgeographic.com/2016/09/survey-geography-foreign-relations-americans-students/. Accessed 4 Aug 2017.

Lumsden, Ian (ed.). 1970. *Close the 49th Parallel Etc: The Americanization of Canada*. Toronto: University of Toronto Press.

Martin, Paul. 2012. Canada's Image Abroad: Fade to Black. *University Affairs*, June 6.

Miles, Edward. 1972. Canadian Studies in the United States. *International Journal* 27 (2): 250–264.

Murray, John Alex (ed.). 1971. *Canada: The Unknown Neighbour: Proceedings of the 12th Annual University of Windsor Seminar on Canadian-American Relations*. Windsor: University of Windsor Press.

Parkman, Francis. 1983, originally published between 1865 and 1892. *France and England in North America*. New York: Library of America.

Preston, Richard. 1975. The New Nationalism Viewed from Across the Border. *American Review of Canadian Studies* V (2): 48–65.

Pross, A. Paul. 1992. *Group Politics and Public Policy*. Don Mills, ON: Oxford University Press.

Reisman Babby, Ellen. 1991. The Association for Canadian Studies in the United States: A Twentieth Anniversary Retrospective. *ACSUS Newsletter* 13 (1).

Smith, Goldwin. 1891. *Canada and the Canadian Question*. Toronto: Macmillan.

Stewart, Gordon. 1992. *The American Response to Canada Since 1776*. East Lansing: Michigan State University Press.

Thomson, Dale C., and Roger F. Swanson. 1970. Scholars, Missionaries or Counter-Imperialists? *Journal of Canadian Studies* 5 (August): 3–11.

Thoreau, Henry David. 1850. The Walls of Quebec, chapter 4. In *A Yankee in Canada*. Boston: Ticknor and Fields. http://thoreau.eserver.org/Canada. html.

Tippett, Maria. 1990. *Making Culture: English-Canadian Institutions and the Arts Before the Massey Commission*. Toronto: University of Toronto Press.

Yurkiw, Peter. 1972. The Register of Dissertations. *ACSUS Newsletter* II (2): 141–151.

CHAPTER 3

Down but Not Out: British Academics Resolutely Determined to Explore Canada

Alan Hallsworth and Susan Hodgett

It has been asserted that Canada's longest-serving Prime Minister—the Liberal William Lyon Mackenzie King—regarded the location of Canada House in Trafalgar Square, London, as the finest in the world. It was therefore particularly fitting that, on 1 July 2017, Her Excellency Janice Charette, Canadian High Commissioner to London, welcomed guests both British and Canadian to Canada House on the day of the country's 150th anniversary. She reminded all that the British North America Act (BNA)—which in effect created the Dominion of Canada—was signed in London on 1 July 1867, quoting Prime Minister Sir John A. Macdonald words—"A British subject I was born – A British subject I will die" (Martin 2013). That month, MacDonald was created the very first "colonial" Knight by Queen Victoria.

In memory of our friend and colleague Professor Tim Rooth (9th October 1939–2nd January 2017) (President of BACS 2002–2004).

A. Hallsworth (✉)
Portsmouth Business School, University of Portsmouth, Portsmouth, UK

S. Hodgett
Area Studies, University of East Anglia, Norwich, UK

© The Author(s) 2019   73
S. Brooks (ed.), *Promoting Canadian Studies Abroad*,
Palgrave Macmillan Series in Global Public Diplomacy,
https://doi.org/10.1007/978-3-319-74027-0_3

For reasons historic, constitutional and familial, academics in Britain had been studying Canada long before the country itself was formally created (Buckner 2005, 2008). Yet, it was not until the mid-1970s that an umbrella group for Canadianists was created—roughly 50 years after Canada House was opened. As will be noted elsewhere, the Tom Symons (Symons 1975)/Pierre Trudeau nexus in the 1970s was a notable pull factor supporting and enhancing such *pre-existing* interest in the study of Canada in the UK. For reasons of geography, history, and politics, it was always likely that the United States, Britain, and France would most quickly form Canadian Studies Associations to support teaching and research on Canada: and so it proved. As we shall see for Britain, the fact that the Government of Canada's *Understanding Canada Programme* was effectively closed in 2012 did not mean that this was the only factor driving decline after a welcome period of growth.

Canadian Studies in the Context of Changes to Higher Education in the UK

Since the 1970s, evolution in higher education in the UK had driven change through "massification" (Giannakis and Bullivant 2016). Government figures indicated an expected participation rate in higher education among those under thirty of some 49%—the highest ever.[1] Significant university fees in England since 2010, of around £9000 per annum (Anderson 2016), have ensured that students are viewed as customers affecting the growth of higher education, changes in institutional status and internal organizational re-structuring. While some of these changes have created potential for an increase in Canadian Studies recruits, others have made recruitment and retention more difficult. In Symons' base year of 1975 there were about 700,000 students in higher education in the UK—a substantial rise on the 1960s—but by 2005 this number had exploded to 2,200,000. Numbers peaked in 2011 following a bulge in the eligible population and in 2015[2] the total was around 2,250,000. Downward adjustments are likely from 2017 with a smaller cohort facing not just increased fees but reduced graduate job prospects and post-sub-prime interest rates on loan repayments higher than anticipated. The question then became—in such a context, why study Canada rather than, for example, medicine or law? The study of Canada is a discretionary choice for students at a time when many attend university not for the joy of intellectual inquiry, but because gatekeepers of their future professions demand credentials. Recent statistics illustrate that credential inflation is becoming the norm, with the UK Higher Education Statistics Agency (HESA) telling us that increased numbers of students are turning to full-time postgraduate qualifications. Postgraduate student numbers increased from 140,000 in 2006–2007 to 180,000 in 2015–2016 (Universities UK 2017: 8). In today's British university system, Canadian or Area Studies is typically increasingly seen as a postgraduate qualification.

Performance Pressures

Teaching and research quality measurement is today the norm in British universities. A consequence of the rise of the "New Public Management" agenda (Hood 1991) and the drive for more evidence-based policy, working conditions for professors in British universities have undergone major changes. Increasingly challenging conditions for academics—including the measurement of performance on several fronts—have been accompanied by unimpressive pay by the standards of the global north and by declining pensions. This has taken place alongside seemingly ever-enhanced rewards for those at the top of higher education institutions, regularly reported in national headlines (*Daily Telegraph* 2017; BBC 2017). In a polarized and increasingly stressful university context, British Canadian Studies has not fared well. Typically, as a research interest, Canadian Studies may be included at UK universities within Area Studies as the base unit of analysis in formal national research assessment (the Research Excellence Framework).[3] The greatest impact of the REF lies in how such activity is valued. Assessment is driven by the need to generate world leading and internationally excellent research outputs, research revenue, a successful academic environment, and acknowledged impact. Achieving this proves easier for hard scientists working within a UK or European context than for those in Area Studies, including Canadian Studies.

A further notable change to the field of intellectual inquiry (and there have been many) centers on the arrival of open access publication methods (Department of Business, Innovation and Skills 2012). For disciplines where "performance" is based mainly on journal publications, one effect, possibly unintended, can be the creation of obstacles to publication for those without research funds. Despite these formidable challenges, researchers and teachers whose interests include or are mainly focused on Canada can still be found in many UK higher education institutions. Canadian Studies covers a wide range of subjects, including geography, history, politics, English, French, language/linguistics sociology, social policy, business studies, criminology, law, and more. The very vastness of the field and its interdisciplinary character contribute to a situation where Canadian Studies remains largely invisible within wider university administrative structures.

In the UK, the usual context for area studies remains arts and humanities faculties and modern language departments. Despite what many believe to be the importance of acquiring other languages, a 2014 decision regarding the school curriculum allowed students to opt out of studying modern languages at 14. Consequently, modern language learning at English schools (age 14–16), fell from 78% in 2001 to 43% in 2011 (British Academy 2013: 7). This was followed by a decline in single honors student numbers enrolling in French, Spanish, German and other modern language degrees in the UK. Undergraduate registration for modern languages at British universities declined from 136,460 in 2006–2007 to 108,355 in 2015–2016; a reduction of 20.6% in a decade (Universities UK 2017: 25). Consequently, several university modern languages departments closed or contracted quite sharply. These departments were important locations for teaching and research on English and French Canadian literature. No longer finding a secure home in modern languages departments, Canadian Studies in many universities have merged into American Studies units or into disciplinary units like history, English, political science, or international relations.

This is the rather unpromising reality in British higher education that Canadianists confront. It is a reality that is experienced by virtually all area studies in the UK, not simply Canadian studies. The factors that have contributed to the current conditions are internal, having to do with choices and policies made by political leaders in the UK. As we will see, the decision of the Canadian government to significantly downgrade the importance of cultural diplomacy, including the total abolition of its longstanding support for Canadian studies abroad, was an external factor that compounded the negative consequences of the changes that had already been underway in British higher education.

Chronologically, the history of Canadian Studies in the UK may be divided into four phases, beginning with the creation of the British Association for Canadian Studies (BACS) in 1975–1985 when BACS's first administrative coordinator was appointed. The second phase was between 1986 and 1993, when a full-scale national office was established based at the University of Edinburgh. The third phase took place during the years from 1994 to the first stirrings of the Canadian government's retreat from Canadian studies abroad in 2007. The fourth phase runs from 2008 to the present day.

Phase 1: The Early Years, 1975–1985

Canadian Studies developed in Britain during the early 1970s (Academic Relations 2000) when Jake Warren, the Canadian High Commissioner in London, established a *Foundation for Canadian Studies in the UK*. The decision created a vehicle and a framework for the financing of Canadian studies:

> British businesses with an interest in Canada, and, vice versa, Canadians with concerns in Britain, together with the Canadian Government all contributed to launch funds. The Foundation is a UK registered Charity and is recognized by Revenue Canada for tax deductible contributions.

Shortly thereafter, in 1975, a group of academics with Canadian interests founded BACS. Historians of Empire and the Commonwealth, geographers, political scientists, and others who had long focused their special interests on Canadian case studies now had the opportunity—accepted by many but not all—to come together under the umbrella of BACS. Finally, as we have seen elsewhere in this volume, the Government of Canada also began to support Canadian Studies abroad.

The benefit to Canada of the launch of BACS and of Canadian Studies programs in the UK was a strengthening of the bilateral relationship between the two nations. As to who engaged with that process and why, many factors were in train. During the almost 40 years of Canadian government funding, until the spring of 2012, it was estimated that the seed funding provided by the Government of Canada and the Foundation for Canadian Studies leveraged up to nine times that amount in terms of university overheads, salaries, and time committed by more than three hundred British academics (Rooth 2007). Academics were teaching and researching on Canada, organizing conferences or field trips to Canada, student and staff exchanges and collaborating with

Canadian counterparts. Students of the French language also began to add Quebec and its literature to their research locations.

Pioneers in this field included the University of Edinburgh's Centre of Canadian Studies, followed by Queen's University (Belfast), Birkbeck College (London), and the Universities of Birmingham, Leeds, Cambridge, Hull, and Nottingham. Most of these still have some Canadian studies interests, but their individual statuses have ebbed and flowed as, for example, activities in Birkbeck exemplify. Along with colleagues at Birkbeck, Professor Michel Blanc promoted both Canadian (Quebec) Studies and the *London Journal of Canadian Studies (LJCS)*. Ably supported by geographer John Davis (a Londoner) and historian Jim Sturgis (from Atlantic Canada) Canadian and Quebec Studies had a high profile in the capital. The February Birkbeck conference was legendary for its friendliness—assisted by a celebratory dinner in Charlotte Street at the same welcoming Italian restaurant.

But the over-reliance of Canadian Studies on the interests of certain enthusiastic academic individuals may be seen in the consequences of the retirement of professors Bland and Davis and sadly in the latter's early death. Their joint mantle was passed onto one person, Professor Itesh Sachdev. Birkbeck was central to the London Conference for Canadian Studies (LCCS) sub-group and Itesh continued to edit the *LJCS*, taking it online. Professor Sachdev became a popular BACS President and moved to a chair at London University's School of Oriental and African Studies (SOAS). At this point, Birkbeck ceased to be a major player; its key personalities had departed. The Birkbeck administrative hierarchy was approached by BACS but could not be persuaded to fund a 50% post in order to continue its tradition of teaching on Canada. The London-based journal, *LJCS*, was taken up by Dr. Tony McCulloch at The Institute for the Americas, University College London, assisted by Professor Richard Dennis. Birkbeck's once-commanding profile was lost. That said, a "green shoot" reappeared in 2017 with the election to BACS Council of Birkbeck's Dr. Rachelle Vessey. The tale of Birbeck's ebbs and flows in regard to study and research on Canada indicate the fragility of these matters within British universities despite our long, and shared, Commonwealth history.

Nonetheless, we should note that the wider influence of the Commonwealth remains significant to BACS. In fact, some members argue that the association was effectively founded at the University of Leeds on 11 September 1975 (Simpson 1992) as part of an "Empire" (later, "Commonwealth") thematic approach there. The existence of the Institute of Commonwealth Studies (ICS), the Chair of Commonwealth Literature in Leeds, and the cluster of interests in other places provided useful support to the study of Canada in the UK; and two of the first five BACS Presidents were based at Commonwealth-focused organizations. Over these years, then, and by reflecting diverse academic backgrounds, Canadian Studies in the UK effectively became a multidisciplinary subject. It is important, however, to remember that more than half of BACS's Canadianists were working outside of the above-mentioned university centers, in different locations and institutions across the UK. They also provided several BACS presidents as the organization developed.

Who Studied Canada?

The original cohort of UK Canadianists included—in addition to the "Commonwealth" experts—two groups who returned to Britain after previous waves of emigration. Some had returned to study and work in Britain after their families had settled in Canada during the immediate post-war decades. Others were beneficiaries of the rapid expansion of Canadian higher education in the 1960s, having gone to study and/ or teach in Canada before returning to Britain. Indeed, in a vast reversal of the present situation, most UK university walls were, in the 1960s, festooned with financial inducements to attract "Brits" to postgraduate study in Canada! Yet, overall, numbers remained small: in over 40 years BACS membership never exceeded 400. If the estimable Tom Symons did not invent the concept, his report certainly established the term Canadian Studies as part of the scholarly vocabulary. This included the establishment of the Foundation for Canadian Studies in the UK and the annual Visiting Chair of Canadian Studies at the University of Edinburgh where James Wreford Watson was Professor of Geography, and George Shepperson was Professor of Commonwealth and American History. The formation of BACS was a natural corollary to these developments. Yet, no centers of Canadian studies were created by the UK government itself. The upshot was that by 1975, if anything was to be done to promote Canada within British higher education, it had to be done by a combination of the personal commitment of enthusiasts and by Canada itself.

The original Canadian Studies community was, as now, small. By 1983, BACS had 195 individual members. Despite an ambitious declaration of aims that stressed the need for public education regarding

Canada, most members came from the higher education sector. Still, formally established posts in Canadian Studies did not exist beyond a single departmental appointment. The Chair in Canadian Studies at the University of Edinburgh, established in 1976, was only a *visiting* post to be filled annually by a distinguished figure from Canada. Nevertheless, the founders of BACS included scholars with considerable academic reputations. At a time when chairs were still relatively few in British universities, five of the six members of the BACS original committee were full professors. They included the first presidents of BACS, Wreford Watson (Edinburgh) and Harry Ferns (Birmingham). Polymath James Wreford Watson had been Chief Geographer of Canada and founder of the departments of Geography at Carleton and McMaster Universities. Other professorial members of the original committee were David Dilks (Leeds), Alistair Hennessey (Warwick), and W. H. Morris-Jones (London). David Dilks, later became Vice-Chancellor of Hull University. His role was taken over by Dr. Peter Lyon, the Secretary of the ICS who became the third president of BACS contributing to international collaboration.

BACs and Commonwealth Links

Peter Lyon promoted the study of another "Old Commonwealth" country, Australia. The result has been a very high-profile center for the study of Australia, the Menzies Center (now at King's College London), named for former Prime Minister of Australia Sir Robert Menzies. The move to establish an Australian Studies Centre in London began under Prime Minister Malcom Fraser but was realized by Prime Minister Bob Hawke. The process offers fascinating parallels with the study of Canada. The Menzies initiative probably originated with Peter Lyon because the ICS already had a strong tradition in the study of Australia. Possibly inspired by the mid-1970s successes in promoting Canada, Dr. Lyon and a colleague approached the Australian Government. This led to the establishment not only of an academic position in Australian history at the ICS but a Center for Australian Studies, funded by annual grants from the Australian Department of Foreign Affairs and Trade (DFAT). Support from the University of London, the Sir Robert Menzies Memorial Trust, and the Britain–Australia Society ensured success. While the center began in 1982, it was officially opened by Prime Minister Hawke in the presence of Her Majesty Queen Elizabeth the Queen

Mother on Tuesday 7 June 1983. Reflecting on his arrival at Oxford in 1953, Prime Minister Hawke recalled:

> I found that the perception of Australia as an independent nation with its own aspirations, with its own identity, its separate patterns of historical and political development, its own social and cultural values, and its need for a specifically Australian foreign and defence policy, not much further advanced' [than] when another Australian arrived in Oxbridge, William Wentworth, well over a century before.

One key difference, of course, was that the Rhodes Scholarships that brought Hawke and a regular stream of future leaders, including US President Bill Clinton, to Oxford University originated in 1902. Rhodes Scholarships remain a remarkable contributor to the notion of *soft power*; the "the ability of a country to persuade others to do what it wants without force or coercion" (Nye 2004). Hawke predicted that the Australian Studies Centre,

> ...will help provide a new understanding of Australia in Britain, particularly among young people, and help to make the people of Britain better aware of the tremendous changes which have occurred in Australia, especially under the impact of the post-War immigration program, and the recognition of Australians that they belong forever to the South-East Asian region.

Within BACS, the Commonwealth link continued as George Shepperson joined the association's council. Shepperson held the William Robertson Chair of Commonwealth and American History at Edinburgh. It had been on his initiative that, in 1971, the Edinburgh History Department created the only lectureship devoted to Canada. The appointee, Philip Wigley, died tragically young as the sole non-professorial member of the original BACS committee. During this time, BACS operated within a rapidly changing academic and administrative context. The launching of the association coincided with the establishment of the Centre of Canadian Studies at the University of Edinburgh. The first annual international seminar on Canada was held in 1974, and just two years later the center was officially launched by the Canadian Minister for External Affairs, the Hon. Allan MacEachen.[4] Another landmark was the establishment in 1977 of the post of Academic Relations Officer (ARO) at the Canadian High Commission.[5]

London was conspicuously under-represented during these fledging years of Canadian studies in the UK. The LCCS was established in 1982 to act as a focus for Canadian interests across the colleges of the federal University of London and the capital's polytechnics. LCCS later extended its activities to include Canadianists in places as far afield as Bournemouth, Portsmouth, Southampton, and East Anglia, and a similar group was established in Wales in 1983.

The Foundation for Canadian Studies (FCS)

Donald Simpson has explained the roots and aims of the FCS (1992):

> The Foundation for Canadian Studies was constituted by Trust Deed in 1974, with the object to educate the British public about Canada and to raise private sector funding to promote the study of Canada at British Universities. The initial capital was raised from British companies with Canadian interests, Canadian companies with British interests, and the Government of Canada; donations were subsequently received from the governments of Alberta, Ontario, and Nova Scotia. A second appeal took place in 1985/86 and attracted donations from companies and individuals on both sides of the Atlantic. At the time of this second appeal, the Foundation defined its aims:
>
> i. To maintain and develop existing commitments to Canadian study centers.
> ii. To support the development of new centers, regional groupings, and programs.
> iii. To encourage teaching about Canada in additional subjects such as Business and Economic Studies; Communications and Media; International Relations; and Law.
> iv. To foster academic links between British and Canadian higher education institutions as a means of promoting cooperative ventures such as joint publications and collaborative research.
> v. To provide awards to extend the study of Canada at the secondary, undergraduate and postgraduate levels.

The Foundation was constituted as a UK-registered Charity. There being both British and Canadian citizens as Trustees, their role was to uphold or amend in any agreed manner the above aims of the Foundation. In the early years, there seemed to be no hard and fast rules about how assets would be deployed in pursuit of these aims, but neither was there much deviation from the 1974 agenda. Michael J. Hellyer has noted that initially there was no particular timetable and so projects would develop for which funding was required and universities could seek funds from the High Commission and/or the Foundation. Applications were simply considered as they arose.

As the number of Canadian Studies Centres, Programs, and Regional groupings increased, especially between 1979 and the late 1980s, the demand for funding began to exceed the funds available from both the Foundation and the Canadian High Commission. This required that there be procedures and criteria in place in order to compare applications and decide which should be funded and to what extent. Fixed application deadline dates were adopted and the High Commission's Academic Relations section worked more closely with the Foundation for Canadian Studies. Applications were peer reviewed by representatives from both bodies, as well as independent academics. Copies of the applications were sent to Ottawa along with the peer-reviewed recommendations for funding by the Department of External Affairs in parallel to the recommendations to the Foundation. After some back and forth between the Foundation and Department of External Affairs a "package" of support would emerge, intended to maximize the use of available funds and spread support for Canadian Studies across the UK as broadly as possible.

After FCS's 1985/1986 funding drive, the Foundation took a more ad hoc approach to fundraising and achieved a notable success in funding from Canadian lawyer Duncan Jessiman (later appointed to the senate of Canada) for the Edinburgh Centre for Canadian Studies, brokered by Foundation member Roger Murray. BACS also gained support from the Eccles Centre which promotes the British Library's North American collections and the study of North America in schools and universities. Once again, stressing the importance of key donors, the Eccles Centre was founded by David and Mary Eccles in 1991. Taking support and sustenance from whence it could be found, BACS continued to flourish.

Phase 2: The Years of Growth 1986–1993

This second phase saw a general expansion of Canadian studies activities, reflected in both membership growth and the development of specialist groups, regional conferences, and programs. The annual BACS conference now drew a larger attendance with a more business-like atmosphere. Vitally, BACS established a national office which provided opportunities for increased efficiency and greater continuity in its operations. This enabled the organization to increase its involvement in international networks. The expansion of programs added considerably to the administrative responsibilities of Michael Hellyer such that, in 1987, a second Academic Relations post was created, that of Canadian Studies Projects Officer, held by Vivien Hughes. The Sustained Studies Project funded by Ottawa also brought in another supporter, Lorna Hawthorne, who would join the Foundation for Canadian Studies. The extent to which scholars in different subject areas were focusing their research and teaching interests was documented in *Canadian Studies in the UK: A Directory of Canadianists, Courses, and Research*, compiled by Annis May Timpson and Julian Baggini (1996). Canadian government funds permitted the rise of Canadian Studies Specialist Groups, starting with the Library and Resources Group, and expanding to a dozen or more, including an active Aboriginal Studies 'Circle' that hosted numerous indigenous speakers. In another significant move, Mark Williams, Head of Modern Languages at Bryanston School, joined BACS Council, taking the initiative in establishing links with the French Department at Leeds and with the *Le groupe de recherches et d'études sur le Canada francophone* (GRECF) group. The creation of GRECF in 1986 reflected the fact that the study of Quebec was from the beginning a strong theme within BACs. Financial support for this initiative came from the Government of Quebec. The award over many years of the *Prix du Québec* testifies to the mutual to the importance of this relationship between BACS and the Quebec government.

During this second phase of significant expansion and institutionalization of Canadian studies in the UK, BACS conferences began to attract notable Canadian speakers. Both the governments of Canada and Quebec were helpful in sponsoring distinguished visits that included Mordecai Richler in 1992 on the topic "Lament for a Divided Nation," Margaret Atwood (who was a returnee for CANADA 150 in 2017) in 1993 and Claude Ryan in 2000. The national office project began with an Administrative Coordinator, Judy Collingwood, based in Alberta House in London. While Quebec is the Canadian province that has always maintained the highest profile in London, at various times Ontario, Alberta, and British Columbia all have been more active than today. Along with Peter Freshwater and other colleagues, Collingwood produced a *Guide to Resources* (Collingwood 1998) that stressed the strong links between the British and Irish Canadian Studies Associations. BACS continued to grow and to thrive.

The British Journal of Canadian Studies

BACS's journal, the *British Journal of Canadian Studies*, first edited by Professor Ged Martin (Edinburgh), appeared in 1986. BACS members and other Canadianists from various countries have contributed articles and reviews. BJCS reached volume 30 in 2017 under the editorship of Dr. Susan Billingham (Nottingham). The *BJCS* reflects the Association's commitment to multidisciplinarity: publishing articles from a range of subjects in each issue from Liverpool University Press. Its editorial board includes many of the UK's most distinguished Canadianists, as well as members from Canada and the United States.

Phase 3—L'age d'or: the Jodie Robson Era 1994–2007

BACS was exceptionally fortunate in the appointment in 1994 of Jodie Robson as our administrator. Over these years, Jodie "became BACS," running the national office, initially at Edinburgh later at other locations. Others soon found that they did not need to know about conference organization, fundraising, membership records, and other such matters because Jodie effectively ran all aspects of the annual meeting and much else besides.[6]

This third BACS phase—from 1994 until the demise set in after the election of the first Harper government—was, nevertheless, marked by some disruptions. These included the British Government's decision in 1991 to create a new slew of universities by renaming English polytechnics, Scottish central institutions, and other higher education colleges. Although the decision was taken before the commencement of this "age d'or" in UK Canadian studies, its effects were not truly felt until this third phase in the history of BACS and the community that it supported. The introduction of the periodic Research Assessment Exercises (RAEs, now REFs) also initiated change that was disruptive from the standpoint of Canadian studies. Existing university organizational structures underwent radical restructuring; the better to meet the constant demands of the central government, its funding councils and research councils and boards, and external funding requirements. Such changes are a reminder that Britain has long been ruled from Westminster, lacking the countervailing power that Canada's federal government finds in that country's provinces.

If the domestic scene became somewhat less congenial, Canadian Studies still had a staunch external supporter. This was, of course, the government of Canada. Annual funding from the Canada's Department of Foreign Affairs and International Trade (DFAIT), together with the legacy managed by the Foundation for Canadian Studies, sustained the concept of Canadian Studies as an independent academic discipline within the UK. It was clear that under administrations of Conservatives or Liberals, Prime Ministers Mulroney or Chretien, UK academics studying or researching Canada were welcomed and valued. They were invited to the front row of the (first) re-opening of Canada House by her Britannic Majesty Queen Elizabeth the Second, Head of State for both countries. They had been lobbyists for the retention of Canada House when short-sighted plans had been mooted to sell off the historic Trafalgar Square building. DFAIT funding continued to underpin BACS's annual three-day residential conference. Each year, universities such as Oxford, Cambridge, and Durham opened their doors and their "dorms" to academics re-living the chicken-coop environments of their youth. Great papers were delivered, great speakers were attracted, and annual dinners held. Canadian High Commissioners would travel to the chosen venue to deliver a message of stout support. British Canadianists did not just feel valued. They could *see* that they were valued and in distinguished company; many High Commissioners holding the Order of Canada. They enjoyed encountering Fred Eaton or Roy MacLaren, the dapper and immensely popular Royce Frith, or the patrician Mel Cappe (to name just four). Such events depended upon funding from the Understanding Canada Programme. When this ended so too did these longer events. How does one place a value on the goodwill generated by such activities? As difficult as it may be, virtually everyone who has been part of such interactions knows that it is real and significant.

In 1995, a survey of Canadianist academic interests in the UK revealed the extent to which studies of Canada and its different aspects featured widely across the British academic world (Timpson and Biggini). More than 6000 students were taking courses in 38 different Canadian subjects, plus 63 postgraduate students. The survey, *Canadian Studies in the UK: A Directory of Canadianists, Courses and Research*, ran to 279 pages. In spite of threats from a series of British governments and university restructuring exercises, and reductions in domestic sources of funding, Canadian Studies retained its identity as a buoyant discipline. With its emphasis on multidisciplinarity and interdisciplinarity, BACS provided a portal to Canada itself and a network within and beyond the formal academic world, to communicate and potentially collaborate. Making international connections for British Canadianists was becoming more important. BACS was helped in this mission by its connections with the International Council for Canadian Studies (ICCS), an NGO based in Ottawa that had been established in 1981. The mandate of the ICCS was "to promote worldwide scholarly study, research, teaching and publication about Canada in all disciplines and all countries" (ICCS 2018). It networked some 23 national and multinational Canadian Studies associations with 5 associate members in thirty-nine countries.

Curiously, however, BACS initially found it hard to be active or visible in ICCS activities. One reason was that the BACS presidency was, normally, held for a single two-year term (see Table 3.1), whereas other Associations often appointed Presidents for longer. That said, former BACS President and Directeur du Centre d'études québécoises de l'Université de Leicester, Chris Rolfe, was elected President of ICCS in 2004, as was, much later, Dr. Susan Hodgett from Ulster University (2015). Moreover, the scale and import of British scholarship on Canada was notable. The first four Pierre Savard Awards for the outstanding academic book on Canada in French or English were won by BACS members Annis May Timpson in 2003, Faye Hammill in 2004, shared by Ged Martin[7] and Steve Hewitt in 2005, and by Colin Samson in 2006. Also, BACS's contribution internationally was seen when it hosted the European Graduate Student Seminar in Canadian Studies at Edinburgh in 1992, Belfast in 1998, and held jointly by the Universities of York and Leeds in 2005.

The Gathering Storm

In 2007, word came from Canada, via DFAIT, that funding for Canadian Studies overseas was not guaranteed beyond June of that year. BACS hoped that a 150-page study of its achievements, edited by past president Tim Rooth (2007) might provide timely evidence of the value, not least of all for Canada, of its investment in Canadian studies in the UK. In effect, this was the beginning of the Harper offensive to remove funding for Canadian Studies. As it turned out, BACS had no Maginot Line. Perhaps understandably, the association's initial response was the old wartime resistance line, *"Keep Calm and Carry On."*

Prior to the election of Stephen Harper's Conservative government, the received wisdom was that the Canada gained an excellent return on its modest investment in Canadian Studies in the UK, nurturing a growing community of informed academics who had empathy with, and knowledge of, Canada. Interest in Canada was spread by teachers and their students past and present, who had studied Canada in depth and in many cases had the opportunity to experience it firsthand. Canadian Studies had developed a high academic profile in the UK, supported by 12 centers, programs, and regional groups for Canadian Studies in the UK. The 1996 survey, *Canadian Studies in the UK*, showed that more than 220 courses on Canada were being taught at over 90 institutions in the British Higher Education sector, reaching more than 5500 undergraduate and 600 graduate students. In 2000, the Canadian Government did not hesitate to join in the celebration of Canadian Studies at 25. Indeed, Canada's Minister of Foreign Affairs, Lloyd Axworthy, wrote, "Canadian Studies have grown..[to become].. an important element in Canada's cultural diplomacy." The High Commissioner from Canada, Roy MacLaren, wrote that the Foundation for Canadian Studies, "is able to support many important initiatives promoting Canadian Studies in Britain." The occasion was marked by the Canada House's publication, *25 years of Canadian Studies in the United Kingdom* (Academic Relations 2000), which showcased initiatives such as the Faculty Enrichment and Faculty Research awards, various partnerships, Sustained Studies Projects, and support for faculty and students to concentrate on Canadian topics.

BACS annual conferences continued. The 2006 conference, held in Cambridge, was well attended with participants from 14 countries and the presentation of 99 papers. Yet, this was just the tip of the iceberg. Canadian Studies in the UK was blossoming, including a large number of regional and specialist subject-centered events that included a large 2002 conference held jointly with the Association for Canadian Studies in Ireland at Queen's University Belfast, organized by Steve Royle and Susan Hodgett.

These successes marked the end of what we have called the *age d'or* of Canadian Studies. Domestically, warning signs were already on the horizon. The revival of the UK Council of Area Studies Associations (UKCASA) in 2004 was a sign of the need for Area Studies interests, including Canadian studies, to collectively defend against those who questioned their value. Indeed, the collaborative defense of area studies has remained a necessity. In May 2017, for example, the University of Manchester proposed a major downsizing of its staffing in its School of Arts, Languages, and Culture (Mancunion 2017). UKCASA coordinated a response from the wider UK Area Studies community, stressing its importance nationally. That such contraction was initiated at all, however, is an indication of continuing, current, downward, and reductionist pressures in this academic field.

BACS was especially fortunate at this time. Its actions taken to enhance links with the ICCS led to the election of Dr. Susan Hodgett, University of Ulster, and former Joint Director of the Centre for Canadian Studies at Queen's University Belfast, as Secretary, and later President. Hodgett was able to use her previous political experience of running a political party to lobby hard on behalf of the global Canadianist community. ICCS was, and today remains, a bulwark of Canadian Studies internationally. All 28 of ICCS's affiliated Canadian Studies associations rely on the support of the organization and the international cooperation it facilitates for study and research on Canada. ICCS attempts to demonstrate to government and to Canadians more generally the benefits that flow from others studying and researching their country. Many high-profile Canadians have supported ICCS in this effort, including award-winning writer Margaret Atwood and the well-known historian Margaret Macmillan.[8]

Phase 4: The Harper Reversal: 2008 to the Present

The gathering storm eventually broke. It took some concerted effort over several years by the Government of Canada to finally kill the Understanding Canada Programme in 2012. By then, Dr. Steve Hewitt was BACS President and leading the actions needed for survival, many of which where unhappy and uncomfortable. The irony was that the efficient operation described in phase three, the Jodie Robson era, had led BACS to become dependent upon one person. The national office system, based in the Canadian Studies Centre at Edinburgh, had become an Achilles heel. When the Harper Government deliberately killed the Understanding Canada Programme, it precipitated the loss of both someone who had in many ways become the administrative embodiment of BACS, Jodie Robson, and the association's office space. Without BACS's stoic resolution to carry on the Harper Government may not only have killed the Understanding Canada Programme, it might well have killed BACS itself. The final loss of Jodie Robson, after 20 years of extraordinary service was organizationally catastrophic and required emergency measures. The crisis that ensued after the news that Canadian government support would was ended led to a move to discontinue the expensive residential BACS conference format. The practice of an annual conference, however, was initially ensured by a move to the facilities at the British Library in central London, itself a magnificent location. Professor Philip Davies of the Eccles Centre and his team including Drs. Phil Hatfield[9] and Cara Rodway—long-term supporters of BACS—were instrumental in securing this switch and in helping to keep the conference alive. Since then, the BACS annual conference has been held in a non-residential format in London with an average attendance of 100–120 persons.

Once the consequences of the Harper government's reversal of Canada's longstanding commitment to Canadian studies abroad were digested, BACS continued to function well. Its morale was lifted and its annual agenda enhanced when, in 2015, Canada House recruited BACS to assist in the Glasgow-based convention to celebrate the 200 years since the birth of Sir John A. Macdonald. Many other instances could be cited of BACS members working with recent Canadian High Commissioners on projects intended to promote deeper mutual understanding between Canada and the UK. Susan Hodgett, for example, initiated a series of Canada–UK bilateral seminars on matters of mutual interest including women, peace and security, and the Canada–EU Trade Agreement.

The road has not been smooth, however. There was a curious retrograde step resulting from a bizarre[10] series of events and unsought after change in the relationship between the Foundation for Canadian Studies and its academic Canadianist members. Some, but not all, of these academics were members of BACS. It must be stressed that relations between BACS and the Foundation had always been utterly cordial. The Foundation and its academic members would meet regularly at MacDonald House (named after Canada's first prime minister) and, once a year, take a pilgrimage to one of the Centres of Canadian Studies that Ottawa was supporting. Occasionally, universities aspiring to host such a center would arrange a meeting with FCS board members.

The usual modus operandi in the relationship between the FCS and the Canadian government stood largely unchanged from the mid-1970s. But times had changed and the Harper government was not content to see the FCS operate in the independent manner it had over the years. It insisted that the orientation of the FCS be changed from "the advancement of the education of the public in the United Kingdom in matters relating to Canada" to one more directly tied to "issues that are of strategic importance to both Canada and the UK, such as energy, transport, communications, the sustainable use of natural resources, multiculturalism and the welfare of indigenous peoples." Several academic members of the FCS board resigned as a result of the imbroglio that led up to this change. The Foundation for Canadian Studies had became the Canada–UK Foundation, with a change of emphasis in the activities that it supports and only one academic, a professor of animal pathology, remaining among its trustees.

BACS itself has soldiered on. A particular success was the historic CANADA 150 conference held over three days during April 2017. It is a matter of record that Robert Hain, an investment firm executive in the City of London who resigned as Chair of the FCS before it was rechristened the Canada–UK Foundation, provided financial support for this major event. By hosting an event in the 150th Anniversary year of what was originally the BNA,[11] in Canada House, opened by High Commissioner Janice Charette, cooperation with BACS was notable. Six keynote speakers from Canada made appearances, including Colin Coates, Will Kymlicka, Guy LaForest, Jocelyn Letourneau, and Quebec Minister J-M Fournier.[12] The center-piece of the conference was a specially-filmed Eccles Lecture interview between Margaret Atwood and past BACS President Coral Ann Howells. The gathering also included a series of Special Panels, including one that featured three former British High Commissioners to Ottawa: Sir Nicholas Bayne, Sir Brian Fall, and Anthony Cary. Other panels included many prominent Canadianists from the UK, Canada, Germany, Finland, and elsewhere.

Faced with the Harper government's reversal of Canada's longstanding support for Canadian studies abroad, including in the UK, BACS has insisted on preserving two of its pillars: the *British Journal for Canadian Studies* and the association's annual conference. Furthermore, BACS has made a deliberate and full contribution to heighten the profile of global Canadianists in Ottawa. In 2017 then ICCS President, Susan Hodgett and her colleagues profiled the work of BACS and other national and regional Canadian studies associations to Canadian parliamentarians (*Hill Times* 2017), making the case for the restoration of funding. After a gruelling four-month consultation, invited by then Foreign Minister Stéphane Dion, a substantial report was submitted to Global Affairs Canada. Sadly for Canadian Studies in the UK and throughout the world, an unexpected change at the helm of Foreign Affairs took place before the 2017 budget. Whereas Dion had been very sympathetic to the restoration of the Understanding Canada Program, or something like it, this did not appear to be a priority for his successor. Today, six years on from the termination of Understanding Canada, it remains an open question as to whether the spirit, commitment, and enthusiasm of individual Canadianists across the UK will be sufficient to carry forward an association that finds itself in reduced circumstances. At the very least, BACS has agreed it will continue to assist postgraduate Canadianists to attend its annual conference which, in 2018, will commemorate the end of the Great War, with a keynote contribution from eminent historian Margaret MacMillan.

Over more than four decades, BACS has worked hard to maintain the visibility of Canada in the UK. To this end it has been successful, as has been its wider role in emphasizing the importance of studying and researching Canada to other parts of the world. New developments offer potential opportunities in the future. BACS may have much to gain with the incipient revival of Area Studies within the UK university system and from the establishment of a collective Area Studies sub-panel within the UK government's Research Excellence Framework. Indeed, the appointment of one of BACS's members as Sub-Panel Chair for Area Studies for REF 2021 is a recognizable achievement for a small academic association within the wider British Area Studies. Gleanings of hope are tangible too in Canadianist Susan Hodgett's 2018 appointment as founding Professor of Area Studies at the University of East Anglia. The *age d'or* of Canadian studies in the UK has surely passed. But circumstances, in both the UK and in Canada, may yet transpire such that BACS and Canadian studies across the UK regain the élan they once had.

NOTES

1. https://www.gov.uk/government/uploads/system/uploads/attachment_data/file/648165/HEIPR_PUBLICATION_2015-16.pdf.
2. Sources vary but the approximate figures are based on various reports by Universities UK. *Higher education in facts and figures 2016.* http://www.universitiesuk.ac.uk/facts-and-stats/data-and-analysis/Pages/facts-and-figures-2016.aspx.
3. Details about the REF can be found here: http://www.ref.ac.uk/about/whatref/ (accessed 4 Jan 2018).
4. Edinburgh's first Director, Ged Martin—Historian of Sir John A Macdonald—was appointed in 1983. The University of Leeds was designated a Centre of Canadian Studies in 1979, followed by the University of Birmingham in 1981, Belfast in 1986 and Birkbeck College in 1988.
5. Michael J Hellyer, who held the post for 26 years until his retirement in 2003. Successors have included Dr. Bill Lawton and the late Viveca Abrahams.

6. Fittingly, Jodie received the ICCS Certificate of Merit in 2003 in recognition of ten years of outstanding work (see Jaumain 2006).
7. Professor Martin's study, *Past Futures*, had been submitted by the Association for Canadian Studies in Ireland.
8. See http://www.iccs-ciec.ca/index_en.php.
9. Dr. Hatfield assumed the Directorship of the Eccles Centre in 2017.
10. *Globe and Mail* (2015). See https://www.theglobeandmail.com/news/politics/staff-quit-amid-meddling-allegations-at-canada-uk-foundation/article22974366/.
11. Since 1982 it is known officially as the Constitution Act.
12. In keeping with their long and much-valued tradition of generous support in many manifestations, Quebec Agent-General Christos Sirros hosted a notable opening reception at Quebec House on the first evening.

Annex

Table 3.1 Presidents of BACS

1975–1978	Professor James Wreford Watson	University of Edinburgh (Acting 1975–1976)
1978–1980	Professor Harry Ferns	University of Birmingham
1980–1982	Dr. Peter Lyon	Institute of Commonwealth Studies, University of London
1982–1984	Dr. Cedric May	University of Birmingham
1984–1986	Mr. Donald Simpson	Royal Commonwealth Society, London
1986–1988	Dr. James Sturgis	Birkbeck College London
1988–1990	Dr. Alan Williams	University of Birmingham
1990–1992	Dr./Professor Ged Martin	University of Edinburgh
1992–1994	Dr./Professor Coral Ann Howells	University of Reading
1994–1996	Mr. John Othick	Queen's University, Belfast
1996–1998	Mr. Christopher Rolfe	University of Leicester
1998–2000	Professor Alan Hallsworth	University of Staffordshire
2000–2002	Dr. Ken Atkinson	University of Leeds
2002–2004	Professor Tim Rooth	University of Portsmouth
2004–2006	Professor Itesh Sachdev	School of Oriental and African Studies, University of London
2006–2008	Professor Rachel Killick	University of Leeds
2008–2011	Dr. Susan Hodgett	Ulster University
2011–2014	Dr. Steve Hewitt	University of Birmingham
2014–2017	Dr. Tony McCulloch	UCL, London
2017–2018	Professor Alan Hallsworth	University of Portsmouth

REFERENCES

Academic Relations. 2000. *25 Years of Canadian Studies in the United Kingdom*. London: Academic Relations.

Anderson, Robert. 2016. University Fees in Historical Perspective, Policy Papers. *History and Policy*. http://www.historyandpolicy.org/policy-papers/papers/university-fees-in-historical-perspective. Accessed 19 Feb 2018.

British Academy. 2013. Languages: The State of the Nation: Summary Report, London, British Academy. https://www.britac.ac.uk/sites/default/files/State_of_the_Nation_SUMMARY_WEB.pdf. Accessed 4 Jan 2018.

British Broadcasting Corporation (BBC). 2017. University of Bath Vice Chancellor Quits in Pay Row. http://www.bbc.co.uk/news/education-42152743. Accessed 5 Jan 2018.

Buckner, Philip (ed.). 2005. *Canada and the End of Empire*. Vancouver: University of British Columbia Press.

Buckner, Philip. 2008. *Canada and the British Empire*. Oxford: Oxford University Press.

Collingwood, Judy. 1998. *Guide to Resources on Canadian Studies in the UK and Ireland*. London: British Association for Canadian Studies.

Daily Telegraph. 2017. University Vice Chancellor Criticized for Accepting £70,000 Pay Rise, December 1, Victoria Ward.

Department of Business, Innovation and Skills. 2012. Government to Open Up Publically Funded Research. https://www.gov.uk/government/news/government-to-open-up-publicly-funded-research. Accessed 5 Jan 2018.

Hill Times. 2017. Time to Restore Funding to Canadian Studies Abroad. https://www.hilltimes.com/2017/03/01/time-restore-funding-canadian-studies-abroad/97857. Accessed 5 Jan 2018.

Hood, Christopher. 1991. A Public Management for All Seasons. *Public Administration* 69 (1): 3–19.

International Council for Canadian Studies. 2018. Mandate and Strategic Plan. https://www.iccs-ciec.ca/mandate-strategic-plan.php.

Jaumain, Serge. 2006. *The Canadianists*. Ottawa: International Council for Canadian Studies.

Mancuinion. 2017. Students and Staff Shocked at Impending Job Cuts, Sowerby, G. and Shanks, E., May 14. http://mancunion.com/2017/05/14/students-staff-share-shocked-reactions-impending-job-cuts/. Accessed 4 Jan 2018.

Martin, Ged. 2013. *John A. Macdonald: Canada's First Prime Minister*, 215. Toronto: Dundurn Press.

Mihalis, Giannakis, and Nicola Bullivant. 2016. The Massification of Higher Education in the UK: Aspects of Service Quality. *Journal of Further and Higher Education* 40 (5): 630–648.

Nye, Joseph. 2004. *Soft Power: The Means to Success in World Politics*. New York: Perseus Books.

Rooth, Tim (ed.). 2007. *Canadian Studies in Britain: 1970–2010.* London: British Association for Canadian Studies.

Simpson, Donald. 1992. *Canadian Studies in the United Kingdom.* London: British Association for Canadian Studies; Ottawa: International Council for Canadian Studies.

Symons, Tom. 1975. *To Know Ourselves. The Report of the Commission on Canadian Studies.* Ottawa: Association of Universities and Colleges of Canada.

Timpson, Annis May, and Julian Baggini. 1996. *Canadian Studies in the UK: A Directory of Canadianists, Courses and Research.* London: British Association for Canadian Studies.

Universities UK. 2017. Patterns and Trends in UK Higher Education. http://www.universitiesuk.ac.uk/facts-and-stats/data-and-analysis/Documents/patterns-and-trends-2017.pdf. Accessed 4 Jan 2018.

CHAPTER 4

Canadian Studies in France

Jean-Michel Lacroix

The aim of this chapter is not to give an epistemological definition of the concept of Canadian studies. Rather, it is to trace the historical development of studies on Canada in France by focusing on the institutions that have contributed to a better understanding of Canada while taking into consideration the specific situation of France in its relation within the Ottawa–Quebec City–Paris triangle.[1]

Even if foreigners do not know much about Canada, they feel attracted by this country which, in the best countries rankings (*US News and World Report*, 7 March 2017), is immediately placed after Switzerland as the best country in the world. According to a recent poll, 72% of the French people surveyed had a good impression of Canada, 1% a bad impression and 27% were ambivalent. In a survey of French fantasies, the magazine l'*Express* (the text of the article "Le rêve des Français" was published in *La Presse*, 20 mars 1989) reported that the majority of respondents said that their dream house was a "cabane au Canada". The "cabane" was the only bit of Canadiana that surfaced during the investigation. The myth of the "cabane au Canada" was popularized by the famous novel of the French writer Louis Hémon, *Maria Chapdelaine*, published in 1913 and by a film of Julien Duvivier produced in 1934. It was also a very

J.-M. Lacroix (✉)
University of Paris 3 Sorbonne, Paris, France

© The Author(s) 2019
S. Brooks (ed.), *Promoting Canadian Studies Abroad*,
Palgrave Macmillan Series in Global Public Diplomacy,
https://doi.org/10.1007/978-3-319-74027-0_4

famous song of the international French star Line Renaud. Dating back to 1947 and known as "Cabin in Canada," Renaud's song was one of the greatest hits in the 1950s.

The French think how wonderful it must be to be all by oneself in the primeval forest. They do not seem to have heard of the mosquitoes and black flies of Northern Ontario or of the bogs of Northern Quebec. I can imagine that for Canadians living in France the stereotype surfaces all too often to be funny. "Cabanes" aside, the average French citizen's vague impression of Canada is of vast spaces, clean air, and nice people. But Canada is relatively unknown in France and in that sense it has an image problem. If you ask a French person in the street about Canada, apart from well-known clichés such as immense reaches of forest, fishing, hunting, a different accent, Indians, and Québec separatism, what predominates is that Canada is perceived either as being reduced to Quebec or as being like the United States.

What strikes a foreign observer, particularly in France, is that media coverage of Canadian realities is very poor whereas coverage of the United States is a daily and prominent affair. Americans wonder whether the twenty first century will belong to them (Harter/Jaumain, 240 note 15). For Canada, the main question is whether it will continue to exist in this century as it has in the past. For too long it was said that Canada had not succeeded in defining itself other than in a negative manner, that is to say, in relation to its overwhelming neighbor or its former mother countries.

The purpose of Canadian studies, as practiced in France and elsewhere, is to identify the degree of specificity of Canada in comparison with the United States and to dwell more on the distinctions rather than the similarities. At first sight, there is much that inclines the observer toward the similarities: the standard of living, the context of globalization, the development of a mass culture conveyed through the media, and so on. The specificity of Canada, the French fact aside, requires more attention and is not always so obvious to foreign observers. Canadian studies in France has made major contributions toward the understanding of this specificity.

THE CULTURAL CONTEXT OF CANADA
IN THE 1960S AND THE 1970S

What is a Canadian? The question came from Canadians as often as from visitors to the country. "Our identity is a contested identity," wrote Robin Matthews in 1990, "which is not to say it is an uncertain one"

(Mathews 1990: 1). He went on to say that, "Canadian intellectual traditions are not very often taught in Canadian universities. The subject is to be taught more now than it was in the past, especially since Canadian Studies centers, like the one at Simon Fraser University, have been founded" (Mathews 1990: 1–2).

These declarations were made a few decades after the birth of Canadian studies, signifying that the question of identity that was central to that birth was far from being solved. Indeed the starting point which contributed to the very concept of Canadian studies dates back to the period of nationalism and national introspection which characterized Canada in the 1960s and the 1970s. A.B. Hodgetts (1968) published his *What Culture? What Heritage?*, followed by the Symons Report, *To Know Ourselves/Se connaître*, in 1975, the latter being widely considered the "coup d'envoi" of Canadian studies. But as Luca Codignola (1991) indicates in *La Constitution d'une identité canadianiste*, Canadian studies activities had already started before 1975 in Canada, the United States, Great Britain, and in France.

Apart its lament that Canadians did not know their history and their literature and that it was urgent to teach these subjects at school and in university curricula, the Symons Report of the Commission on Canadian Studies also emphasized the importance of Canadians studies abroad:

> Failure to give an adequate encouragement and support to academic activity relating to Canada in the Social Sciences and Humanities will widen the gap between the universities and their society, discourage promising teachers and researchers from developing their scholarly interest in Canada, and deny to Canadian students the opportunity to study their own country in thorough and substantial way.

Coming almost 25 years after the Massey Commission (1951) insisted on the importance of "the projection of Canada abroad", this lament and call to action were familiar, if ignored by policy-makers.

THE EMERGENCE OF CANADIAN STUDIES IN FRANCE

Canadian studies may be traced back to the long tradition of cultural relations between France and Canada that continued even after the end of the colonial period. Nevertheless, if we limit ourselves to the higher education sphere, then the first seminal work of reference on Canada dates from André Siegfried's, *Le Canada, les deux races*, published in 1906.

The book contains Siegfried's reflections after three visits to Canada, the first of which dated back to 1898. Thirty years later, in *Le Canada, puissance internationale* (Paris, A. Colin, 1937), and impressed by the transformation of the country, the "Tocqueville of Canada" commented on the survival of Canada as an independent nation. In the field of geography, we should also mention the pioneering work of Raoul Blanchard and Pierre Deffontaines. So too in the case of Canadian literature, Auguste Viatte's *Histoire de la littérature canadienne française* was an early and important reference book.

There followed the generation of pioneers who were born between the two World Wars. All of them had built their academic reputation by publishing doctoral dissertations on topics that had nothing to do with Canada, but they all acquired an interest in Canada toward the end of their careers. This group included historians such as Claude Fohlen (Paris 1), Pierre Guillaume (Bordeaux), Yves-Henri Nouailhat (Nantes), Jacques-Guy Petit (Angers), and scholars teaching French or English literature, such as Jacques Leclaire (Rouen), Guy Lecomte (Dijon), André Maindron (Poitiers), Jean Marmier (Rennes), Marcienne Rocard (Toulouse), Pierre Spriet (Bordeaux), and Simone Vauthier (Strasbourg).

A younger generation, that of the baby boomers, who had become full professors in the 1970s or early 1980s, also developed a serious interest in Canada. This postwar generation was quite diverse in terms of research interests and included historians, geographers, literature specialists or *civilizationnistes*, and political scientists. They were found at universities across France and included such prominent Canadianists as Jean-Pierre Augustin (Bordeaux), Alain Bideau (Lyon), Patrice Brasseur (Avignon), Jean Chaussade (Nantes), Marta Dvorak (Rennes), Hélène Greven (Grenoble), Michèle Kaltemback (Toulouse), Jean-Michel Lacroix (Bordeaux and Paris 3), Jean-Claude Lasserre (Lyon 2), Marie-Line Piccione (Bordeaux), Danièle Pitavy (Dijon), Jacques Portes (Paris 8), Jean-Pierre Poussou (Paris 4), Yannick Resch (Aix), Henri Rougier (Lyon 3), André-Louis Sanguin (Paris 4), and Hélène Trocmé (Paris 1).

This list is far from being exhaustive. It was, however, among these professors of the second generation that we find the founders of the first Canadian studies centers in France. Between them they also supervised PhD theses on Canadian topics, thus training the next generation of Canadianists. All of them have now retired but they have passed the torch to younger colleagues who have assumed leadership roles in this community of scholars, including Laurence Cros

(Paris 7), Hélène Harter (Paris 1 and Rennes), Françoise Le Jeune (Nantes), Christine Lorre (Paris 3), André Magord (Poitiers), Claire Omhovère (Montpellier), and Bernadette Rigal-Cellard (Bordeaux). Most of these Canadianists have become full professors. Rejuvenation of the Canadian studies community, however, has not been something that could be taken for granted, and today less than ever. During the early years of the twenty first century a new generation defended their doctoral dissertations on Canadian topics.[2] Unfortunately, the present context of financial restrictions and the elimination of university jobs in France are not favorable to ensuring that this next generation will be able to continue the work of their predecessors.

THE CANADIAN STUDIES CENTERS IN FRANCE (1975–2000)

The period from the mid-1970s to the first decade of the twenty first century was one of remarkable growth in both research and teaching activities relating to Canada. The golden age was the last quarter of the twentieth century, which saw the creation of a large number of Canadian studies centers. The starting point was the 1975 initiative of colleagues in Bordeaux (Pierre Guillaume, Pierre Spriet, and Jean-Michel Lacroix) to develop activities centered on Canada. This involved a major international conference followed by the publication of the first issue of *Études canadiennes/Canadian studies* (the editor in chief being Pierre Spriet, assisted by Jean-Michel Lacroix). It should be emphasized, however, that scientific activities preceded any form of institutionalization. The launching of the journal at the Canadian Embassy in December 1975 with the support of Gilles Duguay provided the occasion for a meeting with academics belonging to several universities. We realized that in the same university there were several colleagues who had connections to Canada without even knowing it. The idea to formalize this interest led to the creation of the Association française d'études canadiennes (AFEC) in May 1976. In the mid-1970s not all diplomats believed that they would be promoted for their support of Canadian studies. Nevertheless, French Canadianists were warmly encouraged by outstanding personalities and men of vision, including René de Chantal[3] and Gilles Duguay and, later, directors of the Centre culturel canadien such as Emile Martel and Jean Fredette. The context was favorable because the financial capacity of the Embassy and of the diplomatic services (notably the budget for communication) was much greater than nowadays and the presence of consulates in such major cities as Bordeaux, Lyon, or Marseille was also a decisive element. The dynamism of Henry Alan Lawless, appointed Consul general in Bordeaux in June 1974 after having been the correspondence secretary in the Prime Minister's Office, was a factor contributing to the success of the Bordeaux center. Pierre Spriet had spent several years at Victoria College in Toronto with Northrop Frye and Laure Rièse and Jean-Michel Lacroix had been a "coopérant" (an overseas volunteer) for two years at Laval University. Along with Pierre Guillaume, they easily convinced the president of Bordeaux University, Robert Escarpit (a prominent writer who as an expert in communication had had intellectual exchanges with Marshall McLuhan) to finance the center. At this early stage, University of Ottawa historian Pierre Savard[4] played the role of "passeur culturel" generously welcoming us when we visited Canada and thus facilitating contacts with Canadian colleagues.

The Bordeau center was followed by many more: Grenoble in 1979, followed by Dijon and Poitiers in 1982, Rouen and Strasbourg in 1983, Lyon in 1984, Nantes in 1985, Aix in 1987, and Montpellier and Paris 1 in 1988. Six other centers were founded in the 1990s, including Paris 3 in 1990, Rennes in 1992, Avignon and Toulouse in 1996, Angers in 1998, Valenciennes in 1997, and finally Nice in 2000.

During this period, one might well have had the impression that the Canadian Embassy was eager to plant a Canadian flag almost everywhere in the country in order to show their efficiency and eagerness in supporting Canadian studies. The reality was, however, that the support of the Canadian government, which was provided without conditions that might have limited our intellectual independence, was perceived favorably by French universities which then decided to match the financial effort of Canada. The other factor which stimulated this expansion was that our Canadian partner and financial benefactor was less obsessed than the French with formal administrative procedures, including France's hierarchical system that tended to support initiatives coming from full professors rather than from junior academics. The map of the different locations of these centers shows that they are not concentrated in Paris, as one would expect in a centralized Jacobine country, or even in the same region. On the contrary, they form a network throughout the country (Map 4.1).

The last decade has seen considerable decline in this network of Canadian studies centers. Severe budget cuts in French universities and the decision of the Harper government to put an end to the "Understanding Canada" program have combined to force some centers

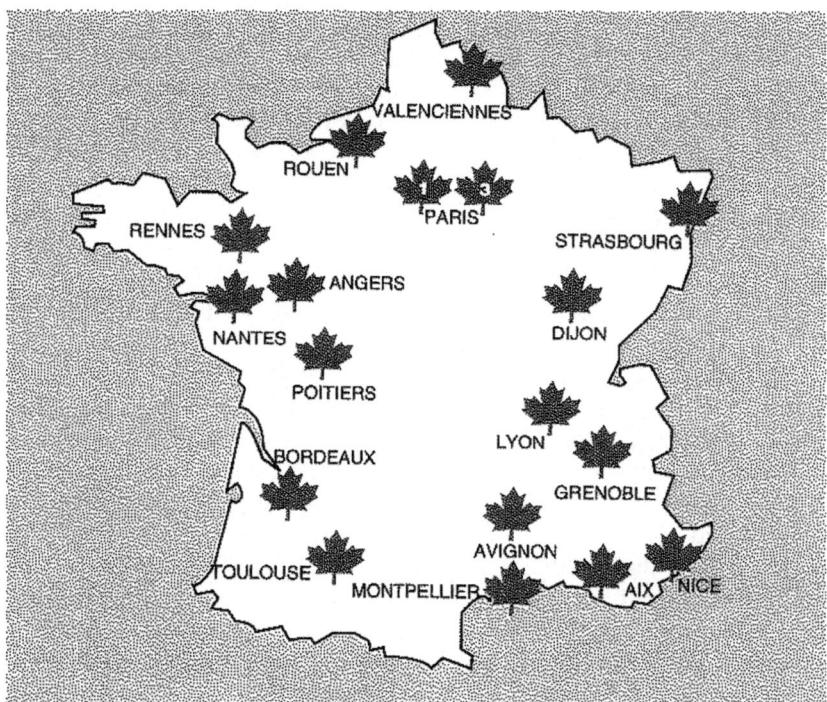

Map 4.1   Canadian studies centers in France

to cease their activities or, if they continue to exist, it is in little more than name. This is the case at Aix, Montpellier, Nice, Paris 3, and Strasbourg. Only two-thirds of the centers have survived (13 out of a total of 18). But there are other causes for this decline. The elimination of university jobs is one of these. Very often the vitality of the centers relied on the dynamism of their directors and when these persons retired they were not replaced. An example of this is the case of Jean-Michel Lacroix, one of the founders of the Bordeaux center. Appointed at Paris 3 in 1989, he created a Canadian studies center in 1990 that he directed until 2011 when he retired. He was not replaced by a Canadianist.

Another element which must be taken into account is the impact of the EU-wide Bologna process of university reform and the necessity to standardize teaching programs. The visibility of Canadian studies was overshadowed by the creation of North American structures or, worse, by programs focused more generally on the English-speaking world. The best illustration is that of the center at Paris 3, initially named "Centre d'études canadiennes," which became the "Centre de recherche sur l'Amérique du Nord" (CRAN) before becoming the Center for Research on the English-Speaking World (CREW). Owing to this evolution the status of Canada was reduced. "Études canadiennes" or "études sur le Canada" was part of the name of all but two of the Canadian studies centers in France. This reflected, in part, their association with the Canadian government. Two centers, however, were more inclined to work with the Délégation générale du Québec. These included the Centre Saint-Laurent in Aix and the Centre Jacques Cartier in Lyon.

The gender and disciplinary affiliations of the centers' directors are noteworthy. Notwithstanding France's reputation for being male-chauvinist, at the beginning the group of 18 directors was constituted of 10 males and 8 females. Today, the balance has changed to 8 females and 4 males. In terms of their disciplinary affiliations, the 12 directors are quite varied. The group includes one linguist, a specialist in French literature, three historians, and seven who hold appointments in English departments. All belong to faculties of arts and social sciences and three of them have or have had connections with Institutes of Political Science (Aix, Bordeaux, and Grenoble). It is perhaps surprising in a French speaking country that is one Canada's "founding peoples" to see that the English part of Canada receives more representation than Québec. The reason for this is not of a political nature and goes beyond the political relations between the province of Québec with "the rest of Canada".

The reality is that most university professors teaching French literature have been trained in France and often did not have the opportunity to go abroad. Moreover the definition of French literature very often includes authors from Belgium or Switzerland and when teachers want to introduce courses on Québécois literature they have to alternate with francophone literature from the West Indies or in Africa. In the case of French historians, the majority work exclusively on France and those whose specialization involves foreign countries seem rather "exotic". The "civilisationnistes" attached to English departments are influenced by the methodologies of history, sociology, anthropology, political science, and are by nature open to multidisciplinarity.

The introduction of Canadian studies has been easier in English departments than in French literature or other fields because the former have diversified their interests over the decades. Beginning with teaching and research programs on the United States after World War II, and with the strong encouragement provided by Fulbright programs since 1946 and the creation in 1948 of the Commission franco-américaine, the study of literatures in the English-speaking countries and in the context of the Commonwealth became more popular.

STUDIES OF COMMONWEALTH COUNTRIES OR NORTH AMERICAN STUDIES?

In the late 1960s and early 1970s some French academics, including Michel Fabre (Paris 3), Victor Dupont (Toulouse), and Robert Mane (Pau), started to develop an interest in the New Literatures in English. In September 1971, they founded the Society for the Study of Commonwealth Countries (SEPC). Their perspectives seemed too ambitious for the Bordeaux Canadianists who chose to focus solely on the study of Canada with the possibility of including research beyond the limited field of literature. SEPC and AFEC were to develop on parallel lines, establishing friendly relations. Indeed some of these English literature specialists are members of both associations, including the president of SEPC, Claire Omhovère (Montpellier) and the editor of the association's journal, Christine Lorre-Johnston (Paris 3). In 1991, SEPC launched a peer-reviewed journal of criticism entitled *Commonwealth: Essays and Studies*, devoted to the study of postcolonial literature. It publishes two issues per year. This journal's contribution to the study of Canadian literature has included issues on Margaret Atwood and Alice Munro.

The orientation and aims of AFEC have been to consider Canada as part of North America and to study its society and culture in a continental context. The fundamental conclusion of *Canada et Canadiens* (Lacroix 1994) was that Canada is "une Amérique différente". For all their similarities, Canada and the United States are different in a number of important ways—a perspective that continues to inform the work of AFEC's membership.

THE FRENCH ASSOCIATION OF CANADIAN STUDIES/ASSOCIATION FRANÇAISE D'ÉTUDES CANADIENNES

The French Association of Canadian Studies was created in May 1976, after the creation of ACSUS in 1971 and BACS in 1975. Its founder was Pierre George, a prominent geographer at the Sorbonne (Paris 1), member of the "Académie des sciences morales et politiques," and president of AFEC from 1976 to 1986. His successor, Claude Fohlen, was a historian specializing in the United States who likewise was attached to the Sorbonne (Paris 1) and served as president of AFEC for eight years (1986–1994). He was followed by Jean-Michel Lacroix, who had been from the start the secretary treasurer of AFEC. Lacroix held a chair in Canadian studies from 1979 and was appointed in 1989 at the Sorbonne in the English department (Paris 3). His term as president ran from 1994 to 2002. At this point, the Association had a long debate on whether AFEC presidents should be prestigious "Sorbonnards" and the decision was taken to decentralize this function. Jacques-Guy Petit, a historian who had created the Maison des sciences de l'homme in Angers became president (2002–2008). A premonition of danger led the governing body of AFEC to fear budgetary cuts. Jean-Michel Lacroix was asked to return to the presidency during this critical period (2008–2010). In 2010, AFEC's vice president Hélène Harter (a historian attached to Paris 1 and now to Rennes) became president, the first woman to lead the association. More than 40 years after its creation, the greatest achievement of the Association is the regularity of its annual conferences and of its twice-yearly journal. Since 1992 the best master's thesis on Canada and, beginning in 2011, the best doctoral dissertation are recognized with a special prize. These activities and achievements were placed in jeopardy by the 2012 decision of the Canadian government to end its support for Canadian studies abroad. In order to reduce costs, the administrator of AFEC was dismissed in October 2012. AFEC's secretariat at the Maison des Sciences de l'Homme d'Aquitaine in Talence (Bordeaux) had to be transferred to the Institut des Amériques in Paris in 2013. Membership has also fallen from about 415 when this Canadian government ended the "Understanding Canada" program, to about 200 in 2017. Increasingly, AFEC has become a federation of centers in order to support those which need assistance. For several years, an annual meeting of the directors of France's Canadian studies centers is held at the Centre culturel canadien in Paris to better coordinate their strategies and activities.[5]

ISSUES OF ÉTUDES CANADIENNES/CANADIAN STUDIES

AFEC's journal, *Études canadiennes*, has managed to maintain an exemplary regularity with 2 issues per year. This accomplishment has been made possible, in no small part, by the efforts of several dedicated editors-in-chief, including Pierre Spriet with the assistance of Jean-Michel Lacroix (1975–1993), Jacques Portes (1993–1996), Pierre Guillaume (1996–2000), André-Louis Sanguin (2000–2006), Patrice Brasseur (2006–2012), and Françoise Le Jeune (2012–). The range of subjects covered by the journal since its first issue in 1975 has been vast, including important attention to history, literature, politics, and sociological–cultural topics. Recent thematic issues have examined such topics as "Canada and the Commonwealth" (2013), "Revisiting Canada Through Doctoral Research: New Themes, Sources and Methodologies" (2014), "Alice Munro's *Dance of the Happy Shades*" (2014), "The Harper Years" (2015), "Canada and the Great War" (2016), and "The Renewal of Historiography on New France" (2017). In common with many journals that have abandoned print issues, in 2016 AFEC made the decision to publish *Études canadiennes* through OpenEdition, a comprehensive platform for electronic publishing in the humanities and social sciences. It brings together four platforms including one dedicated to journals (Revues.org). OpenEdition is developed by the Center for Open Electronic Publishing (Cleo), a non-profit public initiative promoting Open Access. In December 2017, Revues.org became OpenEdition Journals. (Open Access for issue 72 to issue 80.)

The Evolution of Research and the Focus of Canadian Studies in France

Before defining what was, only half a century ago, the new field of research called Canadian studies, I would like to start with an anecdote concerning the discussion we had in France to find the ideal name to identify experts on Canada. We know that at the beginning was the word and that naming gives existence. Even if we had not been influenced by Michel Brunet's book *Canadians and Canadiens* (Ottawa: Fides, 1955), we hesitated between "canadiènistes" and "canadianistes" and finally opted for the latter, which was more adequate in the English version. I also remember that when being interviewed by Radio Canada during one of my visits to Canada, I was presented as a canadologue. Needless to say, I immediately wanted to reassure listeners by telling them that I was not a someone akin to a vulcanologue, studying a potentially explosive country!

The first innovation of studies on Canada is their multidisciplinary nature, an approach that is perhaps unavoidable. Scholars who concentrate on one discipline with a resulting narrowing of focus are often uneasy about multidisciplinary activity that offers a larger perspective. In this respect, Jack Granatstein's polemical *Who Killed Canadian History?* summarizes the rejection of multidisciplinary:

> Canadian studies was not a single discipline with a methodological basis; instead, it was whatever those who taught something, anything, about Canada wanted it to be- an amalgam of literature, art, current events, politics and public issues, and the environment. (Granatstein 1998: 241)

The point at issue is to know whether Canadian studies is a discipline or not. We would be tempted to answer in the negative. The novelty is that the contribution of several disciplines converging to study Canada led to the discovery that we could reach similar conclusions as regards the same objects of study in spite of different methodologies. Many conferences have dealt with the definition of interdisciplinarity and multidisciplinarity without always reaching a consensus. But we would think that the very fact of having colleagues from different intellectual backgrounds attending the same conference on a theme likely to inspire reflections and to generate debates and exchanges of views was in itself a new challenge.

Then the problem is to ask if researchers are recognized by academia and what place they have within their universities. The principle adopted by AFEC has always been to find a topic which does not exclude anyone. Different disciplines can address similar issues but the most difficult discussions have always been between the literature specialists and social scientists.

Notwithstanding these challenges, Canadian studies in France have managed to avoid descending into a sort of disparate universe with only the focus on Canada holding it together. Playing a key role in this cohesion has been AFEC's biannual *Études canadiennes*. It would publish the proceedings of the annual conference in one issue while the other, which for a long time contained *Varia*, has been a thematic issue for the past several years, with a call for papers being widely addressed to all Canadianists. This has been important in creating the sense of belonging to a community in which the norms are tolerance and openness to other disciplines, perspectives, and methodologies.

We have moved through successive stages as regards the "content" of Canadian studies. At the very beginning the interest in Canada was there, but we still had to broaden the study and understanding of this country. Our approach was rather romantic, more affective than cognitive, influenced by the myth of an ideal America. After a few years, thanks to grants and exchange programs, we learnt more about this "exotic" country. The expertise we developed led us to privilege what we could call "area studies" on the model of American studies, Irish studies, and Australian studies.

Canadian studies in France has not totally abandoned this approach even if we have been careful to redefine and modernize the concept of area studies, taking into account the well-known dangers of falling into orientalism. The Institute of the Americas has devoted much debate to this epistemological evolution, abandoning the notion of "aires cultur-elles" and replacing it by that of "études aréales". The tendency was to move gradually from area studies to cultural history.

The community of Canadianists then moved to comparative studies. The approach has proved to be most stimulating and fruitful in reaching a wider audience, even if it can also lead to dangerous extrapolations or generalizations. We were conscious that the comparative approach was also a strategy to increase our membership, bringing in academics who introduced some Canadian content into their research. In the end, how-ever, the focus on Canada was reduced.

Finally, a fundamental point is that we had to ask ourselves whether Canadian studies was a political concept or a research field. Our research and teaching conclusions have never been influenced by political and economic diktats and as a community of scholars we have preserved our academic independence. Nevertheless, it must be acknowledged that the evolution of the Canadian government programs that invited us to diver-sify our fields of study, privileging societal and economic realities instead of literary studies, had an impact. Canadian governments were, perhaps understandably, interested in seeing the Canadian identity defined in ways that contributed to national unity. In that respect, Pierre Trudeau's vision of one Canada, a Canada that was not a mere extension of the United States and which rejected the notion of Canada as two nations, had a decisive influence.

Before long, the familiar premises about the nature of Canada that we had at the beginning of Canadian studies in France began to be quali-fied. One of these premises was Seymour Martin Lipset's view of Canada as a "conservative" alternative to the United States or as a counter-rev-olutionary society. For a long time, Northrop Frye was respected for his definition of Canada's national character based on the opposition between the bush as the dominant literary myth of the Canadian imagination compared with the garden myth of British literature. Convincing too was the contribution of Margaret Atwood and her idea that the central metaphor of Canadian literature, and thus of the culture, was that of survival in a harsh natural environment and Canadians presented as victims because of their (usually unacknowledged) will to lose. For a long time, the tendency was to define Canada negatively by saying what Canada is not. All these theories probably did not adequately take into account the nature and positive consequences of Canadian diversity. The idea that Canada "holds together" in spite of its different components is no longer perceived as a source of fear and anxiety but instead as a strength. The idea that Canada could be defined on its own terms, as a unique object of study and not a place with a history that can only be understood in terms of differences and in juxtaposition to what it is not, achieved widespread acceptance.

The Canadian Cultural Center (CCC) in Paris

Inaugurated in April 1970 by Minister of External Affairs Mitchell Sharp, and originally directed by Guy Viau, the CCC is an original and unique institution in Europe that aims to foster the dissemination of Canadian culture. As a "symbol of Canadian unity" (Duguay 2010: 492), it has always been supported by both Canadian and Québécois governments of all parties. Already in 1964 the project had been conceived by Ambassador Jules Léger, who was committed to deepening cultural relations between Canada and France. On 7 November 1965, Canada and France signed a first cultural agreement to develop exchanges between the two countries in culture, science, technology, and the arts, and to promote the establishment of closer ties between Canadian and French institutions such as cultural institutes or centers. The idea of the CCC's creation was also discussed at the time of General de Gaulle's controversial visit to Canada in 1967.

The establishment of the CCC in Paris (the first such center, followed by the opening of others in London, Rome, Brussels, and New York) was consistent with the Canadian government's apparent conversion to the idea that it was important to project Canadian culture abroad. The center's role needs to be understood in the broader context of the relations between Ottawa, Québec City, and Paris during this era. At the time of its creation and during the CCC's early years, these relations were uneasy, to say the least. Cooperation between the Canadian Embassy in Paris and the Délégation du Québec depended on the political context back in Canada, the temperature of the debate over Quebec independence, and also on the personal relationship between the Délégué and the Ambassador.

In the early 1990s, the Canadian government was confronted with a difficult financial situation which involved budgetary cuts and organizational restructuring. Closure of the CCC was considered by the Conservative government in 1993, but after the election of the Liberal Party the decision was made in 1994 to preserve this jewel of Canadian cultural diplomacy in France. Director of the CCC, Jacques Crête, found arguments that convinced Minister of External Affairs, André Ouellet. In the spring of 1994, Ouellet's department reaffirmed the importance of culture as an essential pillar of Canadian foreign policy (the other two pillars being security and prosperity). In 1995–1996, the CCC was renovated and, under the direction of Raymonde Litalien, the archives were turned over to the National Archives of Canada with the joint financial support of the Department of External Affairs and the Department of Canadian Heritage. In addition to organizing cultural and artistic activities of high quality (the CCC gave Canadian music an especially high profile), the center has generously welcomed many of AFEC conferences and meetings of the directors of Canadian studies centers from across France. For decades, the French students of Canadianists had access to the rich documentary resources of its library. As a result of budgetary cuts, however, the librarian positions at the center were eliminated and, in June 2012, the library and the documentation center were officially closed, their 18,000 books removed and dispersed between the universities of Poitiers, La Rochelle, and Limoges. The CCC's chief archivist, Raymonde Litalien, was unflagging in her encouragement of researchers, notably historians working on New France. Another invaluable resource person for Canadianists was Orietta Doucet-Mugnier, head of Academic Relations at the Center until she retired in March 2011. What is true of other countries is also true in the case of France: the growth and vitality of Canadian studies depended to a considerable degree on the efforts and commitment of individuals who believed that the Canadian story was worth telling and worth knowing.

The important role performed by the CCC is summed up by Emile Martel,[6] who served as minister-advisor for Culture and Communication at the Canadian embassy in Paris and director of the CCC from 1994 to 1998. "[T]he CCC has served in Paris, and for all of France, as a showcase for Canadian culture, a place for exchange and dialogue in the context of the cultural policies of the federal government". This is a role that France's Alliance française, Germany's Goethe Institutes, the Sweden House in Paris, and other national organizations for the dissemination of a country's culture have played and continue to play.

The General Delegation of Quebec and France–Quebec Cooperation Since the 1960s

Ottawa's support for Canadian studies in France, tentatively in the 1960s and then as part of a larger policy of cultural diplomacy in the 1970s, cannot be analyzed without reference to the political domestic context of relations between the province of Quebec and the "rest of Canada" (Lacroix 2016). In Canada, the 1960s were dominated by the Quebec question. Beginning with the Quebec Liberal government of Jean Lesage, the province was more assertive in projecting its identity on the international scene. Domestically, the nationalist claims of Quebec to have a special status within the Confederation took several forms ranging from independence to sovereignty-association. The general movement of decolonization in Latin America and Africa was propitious for those Quebeckers who, in Pierre Vallière's words, considered themselves to be the "negrès blancs" of America. Even if the great majority of English Canadians did not really care to answer the question of "what does Quebec want?", a significant part of the francophone population in Quebec wanted to be recognized at home and abroad as a nation having a distinct identity. The upsurge in Quebec nationalism compelled Ottawa to launch the Royal Commission on Bilingualism and Biculturalism in 1963, with a mandate to report on the existing state of relations between the two founding peoples. Quebec nationalism was not always moderate during these years. Bombs set off by the Front de libération du Québec (FLQ), and two kidnappings and an assassination during the October 1970 crisis were followed by the victory of the Parti québécois in 1976 and the organization of the first referendum on sovereignty-association in 1980. During this same era, cultural relations between Quebec and France were deepening and even and before the much publicized official visit to Canada of General de Gaulle in 1967, Quebec had strengthened its ties with its former mother country.

This deepening of the Quebec–Paris relationship began with the creation in March 1961 of the "Office de la langue française" and of the ministry of Cultural Affairs of Quebec, alongside with the 1961 opening of "la Maison du Québec" in Paris. In 1964 the Maison du Québec became the Délégation générale du Québec, acquiring quasi-diplomatic status despite and contributing to occasional turmoil in the Ottawa–Québec City–Paris triangle (Duguay 2010). In the context of Quebec's Quiet Revolution, a fervent movement of social reform combined with a strong desire to open up to the world, the Maison du Québec had been inaugurated in the presence of André Malraux by Quebec Premier Jean Lesage, who was received by French President de Gaulle with the honors due to a head of state. The Lesage government expanded Quebec–France cultural and academic exchanges by signing a cooperation agreement in the field of education in February 1965 (signed by the two ministers of Education, Christian Fouchet and Paul Gérin-Lajoie) and creating the Commission permanente de coopération franco-québécoise. Even if Quebec could not claimto have a ministry of foreign affairs as such, given that it was not a sovereign state, it nevertheless developed international relations and France became a privileged partner. Among other things, this involved inviting a Québécois delegation to the francophone summit of the ministers of education in Libreville (Gabon) in February 1968. Ottawa immediately reacted by increasing its spending on cultural relations with francophone countries. It feared that Quebec would be seen as the only genuine voice abroad for French-speaking Canada.

Needless to say, the attention of the French to the question of Quebec was increased with the visit of de Gaulle in 1967 and his "vive le Québec libre" declaration in Montreal. His insistence on starting his visit in Quebec City and not in Ottawa did not please Lester Pearson's government, in which Pierre Trudeau, an ardent anti-separatist, was already a member. Pearson and Trudeau rejected de Gaulle's obvious suggestion that Quebeckers needed to be liberated. The 1965 agreement signed by Quebec's premier Jean Lesage was followed by the Peyrefitte-Johnson agreement in 1967, through which the governments of France and Quebec increased the number of grants available to enable their citizens to study in the other country. This was soon followed by the creation in 1968 of the Office franco-québécois pour la jeunesse (OFQJ) and the Associations France-Québec and Québec-France which were to play a crucial role in developing exchanges. Over a period of 50 years, the OFQJ brought more than 150,000 young people (aged 18–35 years old) across the Atlantic. The 2000 French "coopérants" (volunteers who served abroad instead of doing their military service) sent to Quebec from 1965 to 1974 have decisively determined the development of Quebec/Canadian studies (Mesli 2014: 250–259). It was a fascinating experience for such future Canadianists and Americanists as Jacques Portes and Jean-Michel Lacroix, one that determined the orientation of their careers.

The Canadian government's 1970 White Paper on foreign policy and momentum to increase Canada's cultural relations with Western Europe (and especially with France) was a clear response to the political stance of Quebec and that province's projection of its identity abroad. Henceforth, Canadian studies was to be an important tool of foreign policy. Not only was this a reaction to Quebec's more assertive actions on the international stage, it was also an attempt to develop a counterweight to American cultural influence that, internationally, so often took the form of Canada being seen as a mere extension of its southern neighbor.

The early 1960s until the end of the 1970s was the most intense period of cooperation between Quebec and France. During those two decades, more than 5000 French researchers and professors were invited to spend some time in Quebec to develop links with the network of the Université du Québec (Mesli 2014: 15, 101, 237). During the 1970s roughly 200 teachers from Quebec and France participated each year in an exchange program between their respective elementary schools. The economic crisis of the mid-1970s put this exchange program under great stress, despite the two governments' best intentions. Another bilateral France–Quebec initiative involved the creation of five chairs in Quebec studies at Strasbourg, Caen, Poitiers, Aix, and Bordeaux. Unfortunately, a lack of good candidates soon put an end to that initiative (Mesli 2014: 270–273) and the project to create a Quebec studies center in France floundered (Mesli 2014: 279–282).

Since 1979, France and Quebec encourage student mobility to promote the study of the partner country and academic exchange programs as a means of strengthening mutual cooperation. These exchanges have always been rather unbalanced. For every five French students who go to Canada, only one from Quebec comes to France. French universities have also signed numerous collaboration agreements or memoranda of understanding with partner universities in Quebec to develop joint research projects.

The Centre de coopération interuniversitaire franco-québécoise (CCIFQ) created in May 1984 (with Jacques Gelas as Director General and Yolande Cohen as Executive Director) closed in March 2007 for budgetary reasons. The leading role in France–Quebec academic cooperation has been left to the Conférence des présidents d'université (CPU) and the Conférence des recteurs et des principaux des universités du Québec (CREPUQ). An important initiative arising from their cooperation is the framework convention creating the co-tutelle (joint enrollment) programs and double doctoral degrees, signed by France's Institut national de la recherche scientifique (INRS) in November 1996 and approved in May 1997 by the Board of Governors of the Université du Québec.

Maison des étudiants canadiens (MEC)

Non-academic organizations have also played a role in projecting Canada's image in France, the best example being the "Maison des étudiants canadiens" (MEC). The MEC is highly symbolic of a perception that many French people have of Canadians. Some will say that it is an outdated vision. Be that as it may, many remember the heroic participation of Canadians in the World War I and in World War II. The centenary of the battle of Vimy, where Canada lost 3600 soldiers in 1917, was celebrated in the presence of the Canadian Prime Minister and the President of the France. One of the consequences of World War I was the will to preserve peace and to create, in the same spirit that led to the creation of the League of Nations, a "Cité internationale universitaire" where students from all over the world could meet.

Alfred Croiset, the former dean of the Faculty of Arts at the Sorbonne, was the inspiration behind the project. Following an initiative by the founders of the Cité internationale, Philippe Roy, the Canadian Commissioner General in Paris, supported the idea of building a Canadian House which opened in 1926. The House was built thanks to Canadian senator Joseph-Marcelin Wilson, who raised most of the private money that paid for its construction.

Many notable Canadians have resided at the MEC since it opened its doors over 90 years ago. The list is a very long one, and includes artists, politicians, professors, and journalists, among others. Pierre Trudeau, governor general Jules Léger, Adrienne Clarkson, Louise Beaudoin, Jean-Luc Pépin, Camille Laurin, and Jean-Marc Léger but also Alfred Pellan, Paul-Emile Borduas, Marcel Barbeau, Hubert Aquin, Gaston Miron, and Roch Carrier and Canada's current Prime Minister, Justin

Trudeau, are among those who have been guests at this well known Canadian landmark in the 14th arrondissement. "The [MEC]," writes Robert Panet-Raymond, its vice president, "has played a major role in France–Canada relations. Those who have stayed there, however long their stay, have established solid connections with others from around the world." The contribution made to Canada's image abroad Panet-Raymond argues, goes even beyond what the Canadian House has meant for relations between Canada and France (Panet-Raymond 2017).

The Institute of the Americas/Institut des Amériques (IDA)

The project to create the Institute of the Americas started in the 1990s. Jean-Michel Blanquer and Jean-Michel Lacroix were the founders of the Institute, launched officially by France's Minister of National Education in the presence of all ambassadors of the Americas in March 2007. It is a Scientific Interest Group (GIS/Groupement d'intérêt scientifique) supported by the National Center for Scientific Research (CNRS), the French Ministry of Higher Education and the French Ministry of Foreign and European Affairs.

The primary mission of the IDA is to be a leading European institution dedicated to the study of the American continent. The Institute contributes to the dynamics of research on the Americas through the organization and support of scientific events (e.g. the annual symposium) and by granting thesis awards and support for doctoral research. It coordinates studies in the humanities and social sciences by developing a trans-American and cross-disciplinary approach, and ensures the promotion of international chairs for the study of the Americas in France. Comprising a network of 62 French higher education institutions (universities and "grandes écoles"), it brings together more than 1000 researchers. It also contributes to the spread of French research through the publishing partnerships with Armand Colin and Rennes University Press, as well as through the publication of the four-language online journal, IdeAs.

Although IDA is a French institution, it contributes in significant ways to Canada–France relations and to Canadian studies in France. The Institute has signed a cooperation agreement with the University of Montreal enabling a French doctoral student to study in Montreal for a period of three years. Since 2012, when Ottawa's support for Canadian studies abroad was terminated, the IDA has provided administrative support for regional Canadian studies centers, financial support for some of their projects, and generously hosts the AFEC secretariat in a small office in Paris.

French Participation in International Networks of Canadian Studies: The European Network for Canadian Studies (ENCS)

Created in 1990, the ENCS is the umbrella group for all national and regional Canadian Studies associations in Europe. AFEC was a founding member of this European network of Canadianists. The roots of ENCS may be traced to a 1990 conference in The Hague at which members from Canadian studies associations across Europe participated. The overarching aim of these European Canadianists was to offer an original vision of Canada. Seen through foreign eyes, European scholars have long believed that their perspectives on Canada are not identical to those of scholars who study Canada from the inside. Although there was no plan to create a new organization, it emerged organically out of this first gathering of European Canadianists. Subsequent to the Hague conference, the ENCS would organize one or two meetings a year, often held in France. The 39th and last of the meetings was held in Brussels in November 2014.

The concrete results of ENCS's activities was that Canadianists from various European countries established relations, organized joint research projects, and had the opportunity to meet and share ideas with European colleagues at ENCS conferences and seminars. In 1992, the Network launched an annual European graduate students' seminar on Canada to encourage younger scholars to report on their research by subsidizing some of their costs, including travel. Avignon hosted the 10th seminar in 2001 and the 20th seminar (the last one) was held in Groningen in 2011.

Between 2010 and 2012 ENCS organized an annual EU–Canada Study Tour and Internship Programme called "Thinking Canada", financially supported by the European Commission. Alas, like so many institutions for the study and projection of Canada in Europe, ENCS fell victim to a lack of funding and ended its activities in 2014.

ICCS/CIEC (International Council for Canadian Studies)

After the publication of the Symons' Report in 1975, Canadianist James E. Page made convincing recommendations to the Canadian Secretary of State that led to the creation of ICCS. From the beginning, notably in Halifax (1981) and in Vancouver (1983), AFEC was one of the founding members of ICCS and has regularly participated to the annual meetings of the Council's board of directors. AFEC contributed to the Strategic Plan discussed at the 2007 meeting in Edmonton. Over the years, French Canadianists have received many of ICCS's awards, including for Best Doctoral Thesis in Canadian Studies, the Pierre Savard Award, which recognizes each year outstanding scholarly monographs on a Canadian topic, and the Governor General's Prize for a scholar who has made an outstanding contribution to Canadian studies internationally. But perhaps most importantly, AFEC members have regularly been the beneficiaries of the Faculty Enrichment Program (FEP), assisting academics in developing and teaching courses about Canada in their own discipline, as well as the Faculty Research Program (FRP), the Doctoral Student Research Program, the Graduate Student Scholarship, the Library Support Program, and Conference Travel Assistance. All of these were administered by ICCS until the termination of Canadian government funding in 2012.

Jean-Michel Lacroix served as President Elect of ICCS from 1987 to 1989, as President from 1989 to 1991 and as Past President from 1991 to 1993. Another French Canadianist, Hilligje van't Land, served as Treasurer of the Council from 1999 to 2003. During his mandate, Lacroix launched the *International Journal of Canadian Studies*, published twice a year and multidisciplinary in scope, with thematic issues containing articles, research notes, and review essays. This bilingual journal was intended to interest a readership from a variety of disciplines and became an important venue for the publication of the work of French Canadianists. Despite the straightened circumstances that have characterized Canadian studies in recent years, the journal continues to be published.

THE IMPACT OF POLITICAL DECISIONS ON THE CANADIAN CULTURAL POLICY

At the beginning of May 2012, without receiving any official notice, AFEC and the community of Canadianists in France heard the decision that Canada's Conservative government had terminated funding for Canadian studies abroad. The decision came as a shock given Ottawa's longstanding support, under Liberals and Conservatives, for Canadian studies and what had appeared to be their belief in the importance of cultural diplomacy. Grant applications from foreign Canadian studies centers would no longer be accepted. Canadian studies grant programs were cancelled, as well as individual research grants for students and professors. The "Understanding Canada" program that cost $5 million a year, or approximately 14 cents per Canadian, was entirely cancelled. Although the budget savings were paltry, it is doubtless true, as some commented, that the average Canadian citizen did not or would not see the importance of financing such activities abroad (Coates, February 2015). As was also true of the other major national Canadian studies associations, including ACSUS (US) and BACS (UK), AFEC was compelled to function without a paid full-time administrator and the support of its own secretariat.

In France, as elsewhere, there can be little doubt that the elimination of Canadian government funding contributed directly to a significant decline of Canadian studies activities. The Chair in Canadian Studies at the Sorbonne (Paris 3), which had been partly financed by Ottawa, ended after 11 years of existence. Some of the most prominent academics from Quebec and from English Canada had held this position, teaching French graduate students about Canada and contributing in other ways to Canada's profile in France.[7] Fortunately for Canadian studies in France, teaching about Canada has never been entirely dependent on the generosity of Ottawa. There has long been a corps of dedicated scholars whose salaries are paid by the French Ministry of Higher Education and whose teaching and research activities are focused to some degree, and in some cases mainly, on Canada.

The Canadian government's decision was all the more surprising because it was in total contradiction to the spirit of the prior decades. The enthusiasm generated by the official launching of the Centre d'études canadiennes at l'Université de Paris 3 in 1990 and the creation of a Chair in Canadian studies in 2000 had been high points in Canada–France cultural relations and proof of Canada's commitment to the value of cultural diplomacy. The Chair at Paris 3 had been the branchild of Jean-Michel Lacroix. Ottawa agreed to provide $50,000 a year for three years, matching the financial contribution of the university. Even though the financial support of the Canadian government was to diminish somewhat over the subsequent years, the contract was renewed until 2011 and 11 topnotch Canadian academics were invited to teach 5 hours a week during 26 weeks at master's and doctoral levels, and to organize an annual conference.[8]

The inauguration at the Sorbonne of this prestigious chair of Canadian studies by Prime Minister Jean Chrétien on 22 June 2000 was a great moment. One can only react with nostalgia tinged by regret when recalling the words of the Canadian Prime Minister at an official dinner hosted by Lionel Jospin, the Prime Minister of France:

> We must continue our efforts to promote a greater understanding of the benefits to be gained from the international institutions that we have created. We are committed to expanding the exchanges between our countries' young people, students, educators, researchers and artists. Our objective is clear: to expand the dialogue between our two nations to include all spheres of activity- not just political and economic- but cultural and intellectual as well. That is why the establishment of a Canadian Studies Chair at l'Université de Paris 3 Sorbonne nouvelle is so important, as is the creation of similar chairs in many French universities. To my mind, these programs bespeak a bright future in France-Canada relations.

WHAT DOES THE FUTURE HOLD?

When Duke University made the decision to end its decades-long support for Canadian studies, its provost posed an important rhetorical question: "If [Prime Minister] Harper does not support Canadian Studies why should we?" (Coates, June 4, 2015). One understands the sentiment, but in France those who are part of the community of Canadianists are too invested in Canadian studies and have too many friendly and professional relations with our Canadian colleagues to abandon hope. The community is resilient even if we must acknowledge the difficulties in continuing, let alone restoring, Canadian Studies programs in France. Culturally prominent voices in both France and Canada have called for a reinvestment in Canadian studies abroad. Apparently, however, their cultural prominence is not matched by political influence.

As someone who has been involved in Canadian studies in France from its earliest days, I hope that some personal reflections will not be out of place. We in France try to maintain our teaching and research activities with the help of our universities and of local and regional authorities. We sorely miss, however, the "multiplier effect" of the Canadian government subsidies. We hope that the benefits of the energy that we put into training younger colleagues will not be lost. Canadianists in France had the feeling that the Conservative government under Prime Minister Stephen Harper had a profound mistrust of the academic community because of the community's predominantly liberal ideological leanings. We were hopeful that the election of the Liberal Party of Justin Trudeau would see a reinvestment in cultural diplomacy. Now into the second half of its mandate, however, the signs are much less promising than we had hoped.

In a parliamentary address from Foreign Minister Chrystia Freeland in June 2017, she laid out the priorities and tools of Canadian foreign policy going forward. The Minister largely agreed with the previous government that the priorities of this policy must be economic prosperity, international terrorism, religious extremism, and political violence. There was silence on the question of reinvesting in Canadian cultural diplomacy. Indeed, the cultural policy of the Trudeau government is summed up in the declaration made by the Heritage Minister Mélanie Joly on 28 September 2017 regarding a deal reached with Netflix on Canadian content. The minister expressed confidence that the commitment from Netflix will lead to the creation of more Canadian content and increased activity for Canada's creative industries. The very notion of cultural "industries" is in itself significant and something that many Canadians have criticized over the years as a very American approach to culture. The promotion of culture appears to be first and foremost an economic activity for the current federal government, as it was under the previous Conservative government. In the case of Québec, however, a heavier emphasis is still placed on the preservation of culture, including literary production and artistic creation for reasons of national survival.

As a sovereign country, Canada must conduct relations with states throughout the world in order to secure its national interests, if for no other reason than the timeless one of creating counterweights to American influence. It is difficult to believe that the Canadian government believes that this can be done without promoting its values, characteristics, and stories abroad. More than 70 years after the publication of Bruce Hutchison's book, Canada remains a largely unknown country and there is still work to do in getting its stories, successes, and opportunities known. But despite the current adverse circumstances, French academics continue their work and still believe in the value of Canadian studies. They are convinced that their commitment has been useful, not least in changing the French perception of a Canada as a former colony to one of an equal partner in the community of nations. Moreover, academics as informal ambassadors for Canada do not cost much!

Notes

1. I would like to thank Hélène Harter, president of AFEC, for her careful re-reading of this chapter and for her constructive comments.
2. They have included Sandrine Ferré (1999), Laurent Batut (2000), Nadia Azzimani (2001), Hélène Quanquin (2001), Sirma Bilge (2002), Thierry Nootens (2003), Charlotte Sturgess (2003), Ariane Cyr (2003), David Niget (2005), Sandrine Tolazzi (2005), Gwendolyne Cressman (2006), André Dodeman (2008), Florence Cartigny (2009), Raphaël Eppreh-Butet (2009), Anthony Grolleau-Fricard (2009), Geneviève Chevalier (2011), Catherine Hinault (2011), Charlotte Leforestier (2012), Astrid Lohöfer (2013), Sandrine Garon (2014), Sheena Trimble (2015), Anne-Sophie Letessier (2016), Aurelia Ayala (2017), Caroline Durand-Rous (2017), Alice Lemer (2017), and Ludovic Marin (2017).
3. René de Chantal (1923–1998), writer, professor of Quebec literature at l'Université de Montréal, had defended a thesis on Proust at the Sorbonne in 1960, was the dean of the Faculty of Arts and vice Rector of UdeM and served as cultural minister in Paris until 1983.
4. Pierre Savard (1936–1998), well-known historian, director of the Center for Research on French Canadian Culture (CRCCF) at the University of Ottawa from 1973 to 1985, and president of ICCS/CIEC between 1983 and 1985.
5. We would like to pay tribute to the dedication and exceptional commitment of the senior Foreign Affairs officials who have constantly encouraged our initiatives and fought hard to maintain the Understanding Canada programs: Dick Seaborn, Deputy Director at the International Academic Relations Division until 1997, Brian Long who has been for 20 years responsible of the International Education and Youth Division, Jean Labrie from 1989 to 1994 and then as Deputy Director at the International Academic Relations Division from 1997 until 2012, without forgetting our almost day-to-day contacts in charge of France, Marie-Laure de Chantal and Nöella de Maina.
6. Emile Martel, one of Canada's leading poets, won a 1995 Governor General's literary award for poetry in French, and was a prominent member of the Canadian foreign service. He was active in the cultural field, particularly during postings in Paris, where, from 1994 to 1998, he was instrumental in revitalizing the Centre culturel canadien.
7. An unfunded chair dedicated to Canada, the "Chaire Deffontaines", co-directed by André Magord, was created in November 2012 with the financial support of the universities of La Rochelle, Poitiers and Limoges and of the regional authority.

8. The list of Canadian professors who spent a year in Paris: 2000–2001: Denis Monière (science politique, université de Montréal); 2001–2002: Danielle Juteau (sociologie, université de Montréal); 2002–2003: Philip Resnick (political science, UBC, Vancouver); 2003–2004: Peter Leslie (political science, Queen's University); 2004–2005: Henry Milner (political science, université Laval); 2005–2006: Gérard Boismenu (science politique, université de Montréal); 2006–2007: Linda Cardinal (science politique, université d'Ottawa); 2007–2008: Stephen Brooks (political science, University of Windsor and University of Michigan); 2008–2009: John Dickinson (histoire, université de Montréal); 2009–2010: David Haglund (political science, Queen's University); 2010–2011: Pierre Hamel (sociologie, Université de Montréal).

APPENDIX 1: LIST OF CANADIAN STUDIES CENTERS IN FRANCE

- AIX-EN-PROVENCE (1987): CENTRE SAINT-LAURENT (CSL)
  Université Paul Cézanne—Institut d'Études Politiques
  Founded by Yannick RESCH, has ceased its activities
- ANGERS (1998): CENTRE D'ETUDES ET DE RECHERCHE PLURIDISCIPLINAIRE D'ETUDES CANADIENNES DE L'UNIVERSITÉ D'ANGERS (CERPECA)
  Maison des sciences de l'Homme Confluences
  Directeur: Éric PIERRE
  Founded by Jacques-Guy Petit
- AVIGNON (1996): CENTRE D'ETUDES CANADIENNES D'AVIGNON ET DES PAYS DE VAUCLUSE (CECAV)
  Université d'Avignon et des Pays de Vaucluse
  Directrice: Anika FALKERT
  Founded by Patrice Brasseur
- BORDEAUX (1975): CENTRE D'ETUDES CANADIENNES INTER UNIVERSITAIRE DE BORDEAUX (CECIB)
  Maison des Sciences de l'Homme d'Aquitaine,
  Directrice: Bernadette RIGAL-CELLARD
  Founded by Pierre Guillaume and then successively directed by Jean-Michel Lacroix and Jean-Pierre Augustin

- DIJON (1982): CENTRE D'ETUDES CANADIENNES DE DIJON (CEC)

  Université de Bourgogne

  Directrice: Fiona McMAHON

  Founded by Guy Lecomte and then directed by Danièle Pitavy
- GRENOBLE (1979): CENTRE D'ETUDES CANADIENNES DES UNIVERSITÉS DE GRENOBLE (CEC)

  PACTE-Institut d'études politiques de Grenoble

  Directrice: Pauline BOUCHET

  Founded by Alain Faure and then run by André Bernard, Jean Tournon and Sandrine Tolazzi
- LYON (1984): CENTRE JACQUES CARTIER (CJC)

  Founded by Alain BIDEAU
- MONTPELLIER (1988): CENTRE D'ETUDES CANADIENNES DE MONTPELLIER (CECAM)

  Faculté de Droit

  Founded by Jean-Philippe COLSON and then directed by Régis Marchiaro

  Has ceased its activities
- NANTES (1985): CENTRE D'ETUDES SUR LE CANADA (CEC)

  Université de Nantes: Centre International des Langues

  Directrice: Françoise LE JEUNE

  Founded by Yves-Henri Nouailhat
- NICE (2000): CENTRE D'ETUDES ET DE COOPÉRATION CANADIENNES (CECC)

  Université de Nice-Sophia Antipolis (UNSA)

  Founded by Dennis FOX, has ceased its activities
- PARIS I (1988): CENTRE DE RECHERCHES D'ÉTUDES CANADIENNES (CREC)/Centre d'histoire nord-américaine (CHNA)

  Université de Paris I Panthéon-Sorbonne

  Directrice: Annick FOUCRIER

  Founded by Claude Fohlen and then directed by André Kaspi, Hélène Trocmé and Hélène Harter
- PARIS III (1990): CENTRE D'ÉTUDES CANADIENNES (CEC)

  Université Paris Sorbonne nouvelle

Institut du Monde anglophone
Founded by Jean-Michel Lacroix, has ceased its activities
- POITIERS (1982): INSTITUT D'ÉTUDES ACADIENNES ET QUÉBÉCOISES (IEAQ)
    Maison des Sciences de l'Homme et de la Société (MSHS) de Poitier
    Directeur: André MAGORD
    Founded by André Maindron
- RENNES (1992): CENTRE D'ETUDES CANADIENNES (CEC)
    Université de Rennes 2 - UFR Sciences sociales Département histoir
    Directeur: Jean-François TANGUY
    Founded by Jean Marmier and Andrée Stephan and then directed by Bernard Hue and Marta Dvorak
- ROUEN (1983): INSTITUT PLURIDISCIPLINAIRE D'ETUDES CANADIENNES (IPEC)
    Université de Haute-Normandie Faculté des Lettres
    Directrice: Cécile FOUACHE
    Founded by Jacques Leclaire
- STRASBOURG (1983): CENTRE INTERDISCIPLINAIRE DE RECHERCHES ET D'ETUDES CANADIENNES (CIREC)
    Université des Sciences Humaines de Strasbourg,
    Département d'Études Anglaises et Nord-Américaines
    Founded by Simone Vauthier and Helene Ventura and then directed by Charlotte Sturgess and Gwendolyne Cressman
    Has ceased its activities
- TOULOUSE (1996): GROUPE DE RECHERCHES EN ÉTUDES CANADIENNES (GREC)
    Université de Toulouse II/Le Mirail
    Département d'Anglais
    Directrice: Françoise BESSON
    Founded by Pierre Vellas, Marcienne Rocard and Michèle Kaltemback
- VALENCIENNES (1997): CENTRE MULTIDISCIPLINAIRE D'ETUDES CANADIENNES (CMEC)
    Université de Valenciennes et du Hainaut-Cambrésis
    Faculté de Lettres, Langues, Arts et Sciences Humaines
    Directeur: Stéphane HIRSCHI
    Founded by Nathalie Lemarchand

APPENDIX 2: ANNUAL CONFERENCES ORGANIZED BY AFEC

The following list clearly indicates the wide range of interests of the AFEC membership, as may be seen in the themes of the conferences:

- March 1976/Bordeaux pluridisciplinary conference (no. 2)
- December 1976/Paris (geography)
- January 1977/Paris (history)
- December 1977/Paris (literature)
- November 1978/Bordeaux (judicial colloquium)
- May 1979/Paris (linguistic rights)
- October 1979/Paris (literature)
- October 1979/Paris (historical demography)
- 1980/Brest, "Conference on Louis Hamon," no. 10
- 1981/Bordeaux "Sociology of Information," no. 12
- 1982/Nantes "Atlantic Canada," no. 13
- 1983/Bordeaux "Sociology of Canadian Drama"
- 1984/Rennes/Saint-Malo "Jacques Cartier," no. 17
- 1985/Créteil/Rouen "The Representations of the City in Canadian Literature," no. 19
- 1986/Bordeaux "Ethno-cultural Minorities and the State," no. 21 and meeting of ICCS
- 1987/Dijon "Man and the Forest," no. 22
- 1988/Grenoble "Ethnic Belonging and National Identity"
- 1988/Rouen "Man and the Water"
- 1989/Paris Créteil "Métropoles en mutation," no. 29
- 1990/Grenoble-L'Alpe d'Huez "Man and the Mountain," no. 31
- 1991/Montpellier "The Environment and Waste"
- 1992/Nantes "The International Role of Canada," no. 33
- 1993/Bordeaux "Wines and Spirits in Canada: Production, Distribution and Culture," no. 35
- 1994/Poitiers "Acadians: Myths and Realities," no. 37
- 1995/Andorre "Canada, Its Borders and Frontiers," no. 39
- 1996/Paris "Translating Culture," no. 41
- 1997/Nantes "The Influence of the United States on Canada," no. 43
- 1998/Avignon "Language Rights and Strategies in Canada," no. 45
- 1999/Toulouse Pluridisciplinary Conference, no. 47
- 2000/Angers "Rivers and Identities in France and in Canada," no. 50
- 2001/Paris "25 Years of Existence," no. 52

- 2002/Strasbourg "Canada Otherwise," no. 54
- 2003/Rouen "Canada's Peoples," no. 56
- 2004/Poitiers "Adaptation and Innovation: Acadian Experiences," no. 58
- 2005/Valenciennes "Suburbs in Canada and in Europe," no. 60
- 2006/Saumur "National and Regional Parks, Open Spaces and Wilderness in Canada and in France," no. 62
- 2007/Aix "Fragmented Cities," no. 64
- 2008/Bordeaux "Quebec as a Political and Cultural Lab: What Changes since the Quiet Revolution?," no. 66
- 2009/Grenoble "Living in Canada: accords et dissonances," no. 68
- 2010/Avignon "Cultural Minorities in Canada: Expressions and Territories," no. 70
- 2011/Montpellier "Beyond Frontiers: Until Where does Canada Go?," no. 72
- 2012/Nice "Mutations and Ruptures in Canada," no. 73
- 2013/Rennes "Memory/Memories: Construction, Interpretation, Challenges," no. 74
- 2014/Poitiers: one day symposium
- 2015/Nantes "Cross-Views on Canada/Europe," no. 79
- 2016/Grenoble "Canadian Identity/Identities and Global Change," no. 81
- 2017/Paris "The 150th Anniversary of the Confederation: Defining Canada, 1867-2017"
- 2018/Avignon "Migrations to and from Canada"

APPENDIX 3: UNDERSTANDING CANADA GRANTS AWARDED IN FRANCE BETWEEN 1987 AND 2012

- FEP*: 10 (87), 8 (88), 8 (89), 9 (90), 6 (91), 8 (92), 9 (93), 9 (94), 8 (95), 3 (96), 8 (97), 9 (98), 5 (99), 8 (2000), 8 (2001), 3 (2002), 7 (2003), 3 (2004), 7 (2005), 6 (2006), 8 (2007), 6 (2008), 5 (2009), 1 (2010), 7 (2011), 10 (2012)
- FRP**: 5 (88), 9 (89), 10 (90), 1 (91), 5 (92), 4 (93), 7 (94), 9 (95), 11 (96), 9 (97), 11 (98), 12 (99), 7 (2000), 11 (2001), 11 (2002), 7 (2003), 12 (2004), 9 (2005), 8 (2006), 5 (2007), 6 (2008), 8 (2009), 5 (2010), 3 (2011), 4 (2012)

*Faculty Enrichment Program
**Faculty Research Program

References

Brunet, Michel. 1955. *Canadians et Canadiens*. Ottawa: Fides.

Coates, Colin. 2015a. Who Killed Canadian Studies? February 19. Website activehistory.ca/2015/02.

Coates, Colin. 2015b. If Stephen Harper Does Not Support Canadian Studies, Why Should We? June 4. Website activehustory.ca/2015/06.

Codignola, Luca. 1991. *La Constitution d'une identité canadianiste. Les premières années (1981–1991)*. Ottawa: CIEC.

Duguay, Gilles. 2010. *Le Triangle Québec-Ottawa-Paris*. Septentrion: Québec.

Granatstein, Jack. 1998. *Who Killed Canadian History?* New York: HarperCollins.

Harter, Hélène, and Serge Jaumain (eds.). 2016. *Le Canada, un pays divers. La Diversité culturelle au Canada vue par Jean-Michel Lacroix*. Bruxelles: P.E.I. Peter Lang.

Hodgetts, A.B. 1968. *What Culture? What Heritage?* Toronto: OISE.

Lacroix, Jean-Michel (eds). 1994. *Canada et Canadiens* (3rd ed.). Bordeaux: Presses universitaires de Bordeaux.

Lacroix, Jean-Michel. 2016. *Histoire du Canada des origines à nos jours*. Paris: Tallandier.

Mathews, Robin. 1990. *The Canadian Intellectual Tradition: A Modern People and Its Community, A Study Guide*. Burnaby: Centre for Canadian Studies, Simon Fraser University.

Mesli, Samy. 2014. *La Coopération franco-québécoise dans le domaine de l'éducation de 1965 à nos jours*. Montréal: Septentrion.

Page, James. 1980. *Réflexions sur le rapport Symons. L'état des études canadiennes en 1980*. Ottawa: Ministère des Approvisionnements et Services.

Panet-Raymond, Robert. 2017. La Maison des étudiants canadiens à Paris est une fête depuis. *Nouvelles*, June 1, 2017.

Symons, T.H.B. 1978. *To Know Ourselves/Se Connaître: The Report of the Commission on Canadian Studies*, 2 vol. Ottawa: Association of Universities and Colleges.

CHAPTER 5

Canadian Studies in China: Dividends from a Near-Forgotten Age of Hope and Opening

Jeremy Paltiel

Canadian studies in China have origins in a state-directed program that helped steer China's spectacular globalization. Very soon after China embarked on its program of reform and opening, Canada began a foreign aid program managed by the Canadian International Development Agency (CIDA) that was agreed in 1980, began operating in 1981 and which lasted two and a half decades. Very early on, CIDA determined that Canadian aid efforts were best directed not towards the furnishing of hardware to boost China's economic development, but rather the furnishing of software and the transfer of human capital to aid in China's opening to the world. Canadian programs focused on a broad range of programs to train government officials, and to help reform China's legal system in ways conducive to market economics and trade.

One area that both sides determined was extremely important in the development of human capital in China was the reform of tertiary education, particularly the university system. Chinese universities had been

J. Paltiel (✉)
Department of Political Science, Carleton University, Ottawa, ON, Canada

© The Author(s) 2019
S. Brooks (ed.), *Promoting Canadian Studies Abroad*,
Palgrave Macmillan Series in Global Public Diplomacy,
https://doi.org/10.1007/978-3-319-74027-0_5

directly targeted and damaged by the decade long Cultural Revolution (1966–1976). They also had suffered enormously from decades of isolation as well as efforts to reorient the university system along the rigid lines of the Soviet model, efforts that included successive waves of revolutionary efforts to extirpate Western and bourgeois influence. Chinese higher education was like Rip van Winkle waking up after decades of somnolent isolation and worse, during which science and technology had made spectacular leaps. The Chinese government had identified the country's universities as a focal point of China's modernization efforts. CIDA agreed to cooperate by instituting a wide-ranging university linkage project managed by the Association of Universities and Colleges of Canada (AUCC) (Hayhoe et al. 2016).[1] This university linkage program lasted nearly two decades and survived the aftermath of the events of June 1989 in Tiananmen Square.

This program expanded and extended an already existing scholarly exchange program that had been in place since Prime Minister Pierre Elliot Trudeau's visit to China in 1973. Between these two programs, literally hundreds and thousands of Canadian and Chinese academics traveled between academic institutions in Canada and China, systematically modernizing education in medicine, management, engineering, and a broad range of academic programs in the social sciences and humanities. Therefore what distinguishes Canadian Studies in China from Canadian studies elsewhere in the world is that rather than being established on the basis of spontaneous interest of scholars in various disciplines, the initial exposure of Chinese academics to Canada came as part of a state-directed program on both sides that provided linkages for scholars working within their own disciplines. Canadian studies and the Canadian studies program administered by the Department of Foreign and International Trade in its various forms and under different names over the years served to maintain academic relations that had already been pioneered through other programs and which allowed Chinese academics to maintain a focus on Canada as they pursued their academic interests.

In parallel, over time, specific academic interest in Canada was fostered through the entrepreneurial efforts of certain academics, particularly Professor Hsieh of the University of Regina. In addition, officially recognized programs of Canadian Studies came to be recognized by the Chinese ministry of Education, often in institutions with already existing American Studies programs. In this way, Canadian studies became an adjunct of American Studies.

In consequence of these developments and efforts, the Canadian Studies Association in China was established in 1984 (Yang 2009: 25). Among the key promoters of Canadian studies in China was Prof. Pei-chih Hsieh of the University of Regina (Evans 2011). Such associations in China cannot be established without explicit official support and sponsorship. With state support, the association then sponsors academic meetings and journals. A whole academic field of inquiry was seeded by initial official nurturing on the Canadian side, and maintained by official government support on the Chinese side. Moreover, the continued existence of the Canada–China Scholars Exchange has enabled academic linkages to survive despite the demise of the Canadian government's Understanding Canada program in 2012.

Among the most influential centers of Canadian Studies in China are the two sponsored by the Chinese Ministry of Education at the Guangdong University of Foreign Languages and Trade and at Beijing Foreign Studies University. However, the most prestigious may be the Center for Canadian Studies at Beijing University which publishes *Jianada Yanjiu* (Canadian Studies/Etudes canadiennes). This interdisciplinary center brings together over a hundred scholars in languages and literature, Canadian history, urban environment, environmental studies, politics, geology and law, as well as housing a Canadian studies library with over 5000 volumes. Among the other significant centers for Canadian studies, mention should be made of the Shanghai Foreign Studies University Institute of International Relations and Public Administration. Professor Hao Qian (Isabella), a scholar of American studies and international relations, has played a leading role in training graduate students, including PhDs on Canadian topics.

From 28 September to 30 September 2017, the Canadian Studies Association of China held its 17th biennial conference in Kunming, Yunnan Province, China, at the Yunnan Agricultural University. It was hosted by Professor Du Fachun, President of the Association of Canadian Studies in China and Dean of the Institute of New Rural Development of Yunnan Agricultural University. Currently, there are 94 dues paying members of the Association, of which 73 are full-time university faculty and 21 are student members. Altogether some 260 people are affiliated with the Association. The 17th Biennial Conference attracted 120 participants, of whom 13 came from Canada. Chinese participants came from 17 different provinces across the country. Currently, the board of directors of the Association includes members from 14 different institutions (Institute of Rural Development Yunnan Agricultural University 2017).

The backbone scholars of Canadian studies in China are still those who emerged out of the University Linkage programs of the 1980s and 1990s. These mature scholars form a strategic core that has acquired status in their home institutions, in part because their longstanding international linkages with Canada helped solidify their home departments' international reputation, now a key metric of academic prestige and power in China. These professors now have graduate students of their own, and it is these scholars who currently enjoy the benefits of ongoing scholarly exchange between Canada and China, maintaining the living linkage of Canadian studies scholarship.

The early "Canadianists" were language teaching specialists, whose facility in English (and French) enabled them to access Canadian academic programs. The relationship of Foreign Language Colleges to the foreign affairs "system" (*xitong* 系统) provided a link with the bureaucratic network that had China's Foreign Ministry at its apex, but at its middle and lower levels was mainly concerned with the management of foreigners attached to Chinese institutions. Because these institutions trained translators and officials who dealt with foreign matters, they evolved programs in "international relations." These programs, however, were not staffed with people rigorously trained in the social sciences and international relations theory. At best they had a journeyman knowledge of diplomatic relations and diplomatic history, and were not trained in rigorous social science methods. For that reason, few if any Chinese Canadianists rank among leading scholars of international relations.

Conversely, however, language facility has in important cases enabled some Chinese scholars, such as Qian Hao of Shanghai Foreign Studies University, to gain deeper academic qualification though prolonged exposure to political scientists and diplomatic historians at Canadian universities. These scholars in turn have been able to train a generation of graduate students in China who now have both deep disciplinary training and a good grasp of Canadian politics and Canadian policy.

In addition to the wide range of self-selected Canadian studies scholars, there are now two full-time Canadian Studies centers that are supported by the Chinese Ministry of Education. One is at Beijing Foreign Studies University (BJFSU) in Beijing, and the other is at the Guangdong University of Foreign Languages and Trade in Guangzhou (Canton). Each of these centers produces annual publications. BJFSU (commonly known in Chinese as Beiwai) hosts the Canadian Policy Development Annual Report (*Jianada zhengce fazhan baogao*) and the GDFLT issues the Canada "Blue Book" that is published by the Chinese Academy of Social Sciences (Blue Book 2016). Since 1992 the Canadian Studies Centre of Peking University (PKU) has published *A Glimpse of Canada* 加拿大掠影 *Jianada lueying*. In 2003, this became *Jianada Yanjiu* or "Canadian Studies" (Center for Canadian Studies, Peking University 2011). This annual publication includes a variety of articles in Canadian studies roughly divided between about 40% cultural and literary subjects, another 30–40% on historical, political, economic, and issues of international relations, and 20% on a variety of topics from education to indigenous issues. Roughly speaking, this parallels the variety of interests reflected in the biennial Canadian Studies conferences. Searching by keyword "加拿大" ("Canada") from 1 January 1979 (the earliest date available in the database) to 31 December 2017 and including all fields and subjects, there are 60,317 publications in total (retrieved on 15 February 2017). Figure 5.1 shows the general trend over time.[2]

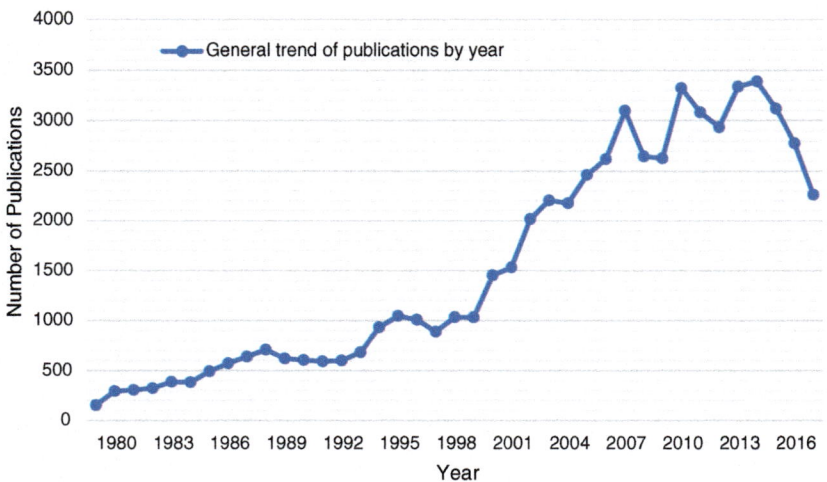

Fig. 5.1 General trend of publications relating to Canada, 1979–2017

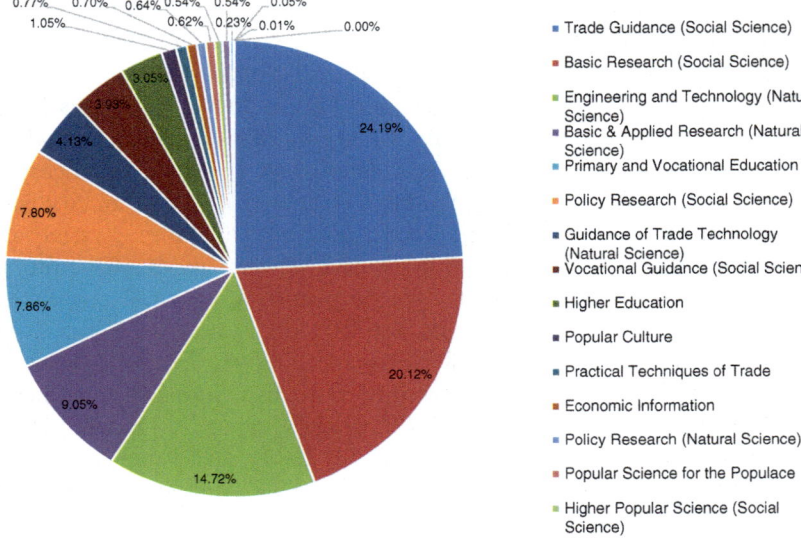

Fig. 5.2 Distribution of publications by research fields

As may be seen in Fig. 5.2, the majority of publications related to Canada are in the fields of social science (24.19% in industry guidance, 20.12% in basic research, 7.86% in basic education and secondary vocational education, and 7.80% in policy studies and some other subjects in social science). Engineering technology accounts for 14.72% of publications relating to Canada, and the rest constitutes studies in all other research fields.

The top 10 sources of publications are East China Normal University (213), Wuhan University (199), Beijing Normal University (176), Peking University (170), Fudan University (179), Zhejiang University (164), Shandong University (164), Nankai University (163), Xiamen University (161), and Renmin University of China (149), as displayed in Fig. 5.3.

The 10 authors who have the most publications related to Canada are from Neijiang Normal University, Nanjing University, Inner Mongolia Agricultural University, Information Center of Ministry of Land and Resources of People's Republic of China, China Education and Research Network, Nankai University, Nanjing Agricultural University, Liaoning Normal University, and again Inner Mongolia Agricultural University

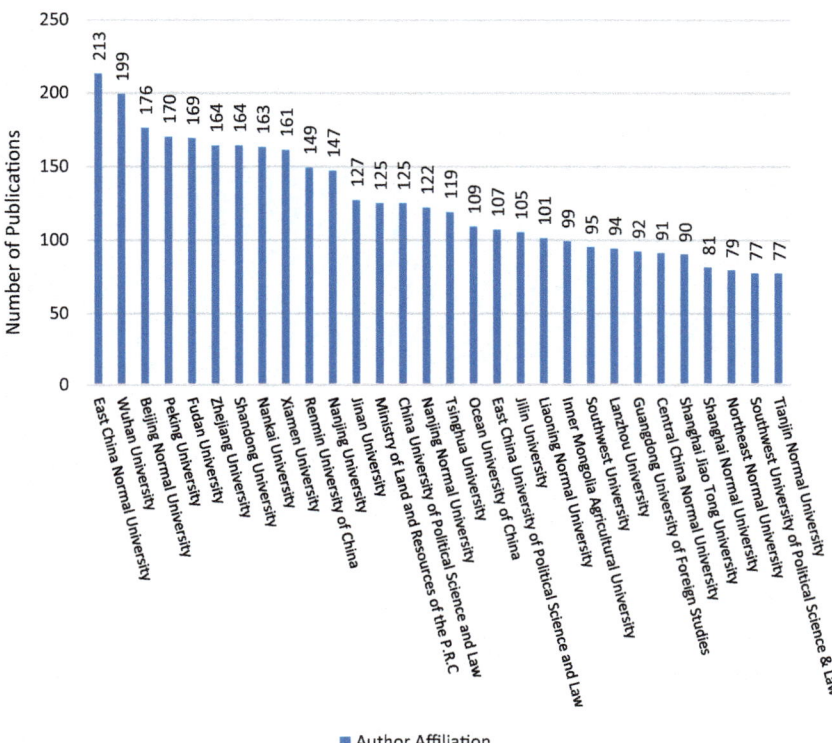

Fig. 5.3 Top 30 institutional sources of publications

and Liaoning Normal University (see Fig. 5.4). Interestingly, although the top 10 or 20 institutional sources of publications include some of the most prestigious universities in China, and funded by the two major research fund programs (i.e., the National Natural Science Fund and the National Social Science Fund of China), only one or two of the most published authors are from these prestigious universities.

As for funding sources, the bulk of scholarly publications are associated with the National Natural Science Fund and the National Social Science Fund of China (464 and 360 publications, respectively). Other funding projects from both the national and local levels of Chinese government also contribute to fruitful research related to Canada, including the National Key Technology R&D Program (85), the China Scholarship Council (73), etc. Figure 5.5 depicts the top 30 funding sources of publications relating

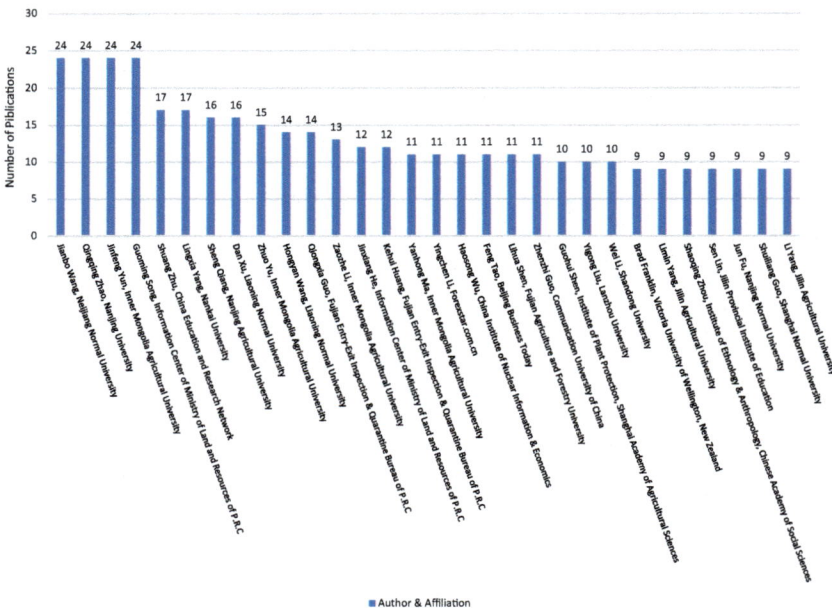

Fig. 5.4 Top 30 authors with the most publications related to Canada in the period 1979–2017

to Canada. In comparison, the publications are more evenly distributed in terms of specific fields and subjects of study, as displayed in Fig. 5.6.

Consistent with the data reported on the research field distribution shown in Fig. 5.2, Fig. 5.6 shows that most of the publications on Canada are in the realm of social science. For instance, about 19% of the publications are on the subject of industrial economy, followed by roughly 9% on Chinese politics and international politics, 8% on trade and economy, about 12% on secondary education and post-secondary education, 5% on agricultural economy, another 5% on macro-economic management and sustainable development, and 4% on economic reform. The attention given by Chinese research to post-secondary education in Canada may be a legacy of the University Linkages program that paired Canadian universities with Chinese counterparts.

Using Canada as key word, scholarly publications count for less than half of the total Chinese publications relating to Canada. The top 20 publication sources consist mostly of newspapers and magazines rather than scholarly journals. As Fig. 5.7 indicates, the primary sources of publications include *Work & Study Abroad* (13.14%), *Foreign Nuclear News*

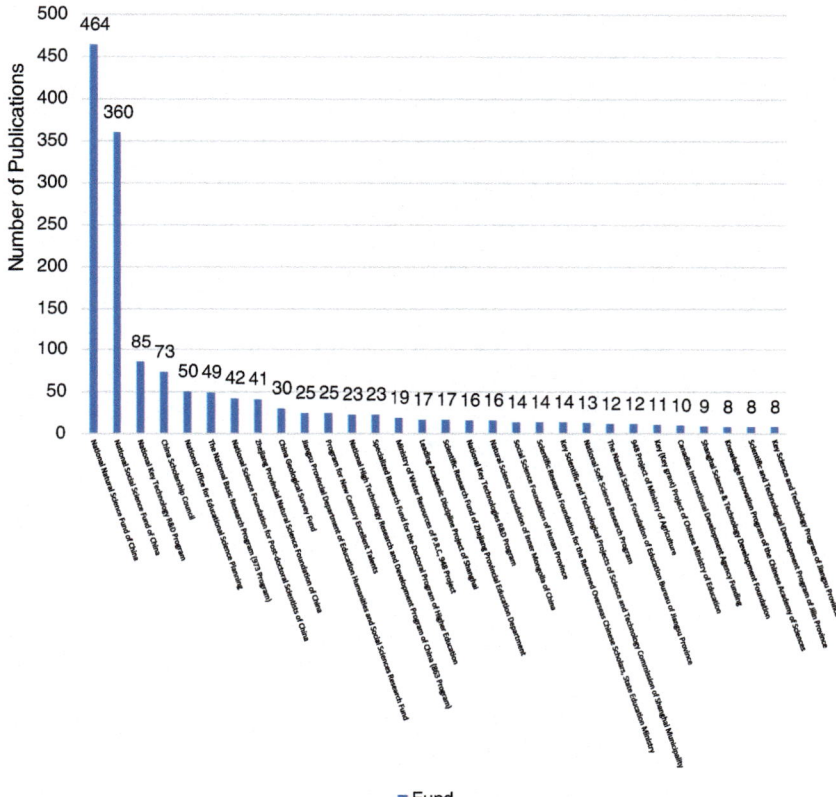

Fig. 5.5 Top 30 funding sources of publications

(9.64%), *International Business Daily* (8.28), *The People's Daily* (7.98%), and *Science and Technology Daily* (6.61%). This might help explain why the authors with most publications are not necessarily from the prestigious institutions that have sources of research funding. We would expect that researchers with such funding generally will publish their results in scholarly and specialized publications rather than in newspaper magazines and other general interest publications.

Finally, a summary of the key words provides further information on what Chinese intellectuals are interested in or allowed to write when it comes to Canada. Other than the most obvious key word, "Canada", which most of the publications contain (2850), "Solidago canadensis" (Canadian Goldenrod) comes next (452), followed by "implications" (409).

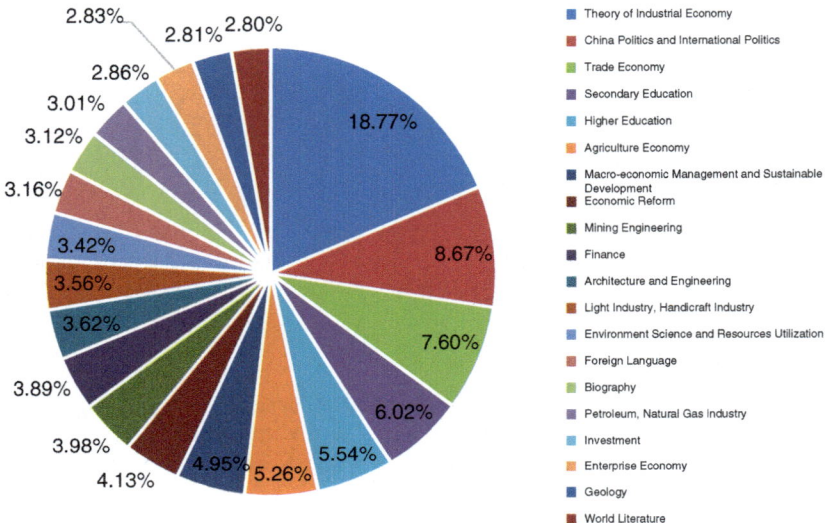

Fig. 5.6 Subject fields of publications on Canada

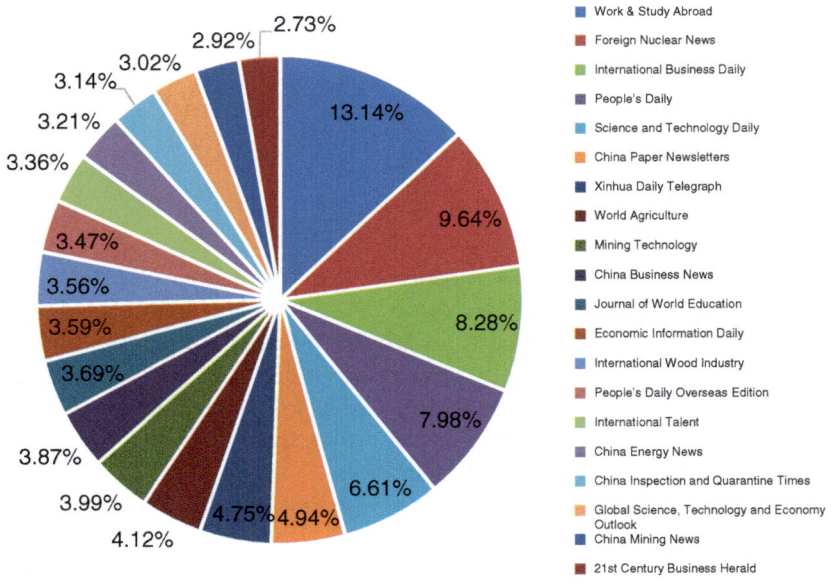

Fig. 5.7 Top 20 publication sources

This latter is rather interesting, appearing to suggest that the most important, if not the only qualification for publication is to provide implications for policy-making in China. Other words that show up often in publications on Canada include "the United States" (288), "China" (277), "post-secondary education" (135), "comparison" (114), "comparative studies" (104), "vocational education" (104), "multiculturalism" (99), and various other themes and key words including "Quebec", "development", "environmental protection", etc.

The data reported in Figs. 5.6 and 5.8 appear to indicate that interest in policy-related subject matter, as compared to cultural subjects, is relatively high in China. Over the entire period, policy studies represent the bulk of publications (about 40%) of articles with Canada as a key word. We can at least tentatively conclude that Canada remains relevant as a policy reference for Chinese students of Canada and for Chinese involved in various policy-related disciplines, notwithstanding that Canada's international influence and power, compared to that of China, has diminished quite dramatically over the past several decades. The fact that China has become such a significant presence on the global stage has not resulted in Chinese researchers being less interested in what can be learned from Canada.

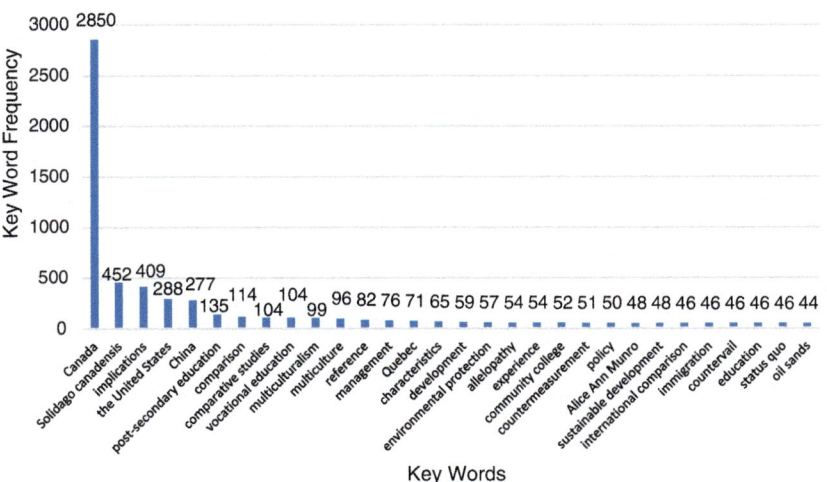

Fig. 5.8 Key words of publications

The correlation between Canada–China diplomatic relations and the number of articles in the fields of politics and international relations that cite Canada as a keyword is quite striking. As may be seen from Fig. 5.9, the peak in terms of articles on politics and international relations using Canada as a keyword was in 2006, the year Stephen Harper's Conservatives replaced the Liberals as Canada's governing party. Articles citing Canada declined sharply over the next three years and did not peak again until Prime Minister Harper made his first official visit to China in 2009 (CKNI). Thereafter, there is a downward drift followed by a small recovery with the election of the Liberal government in 2015.

The combination of Canadian development assistance to China and China's domestically generated effort to modernize and catch-up with the developed West kept Canada salient for Chinese academics over a period of two to three decades after 1980. Canadian studies practitioners helped position Canada as a reference point for China's modernization. This was seen consciously by both sides as a relationship of reciprocity rather than as an invidious relationship of Master and Student. Because Canada was simply one variety of a modern Western state and had no superpower or hegemonic ambitions, it could be seen as one among a number of models of modernity, albeit one with a distinctly liberal and Western character. Moreover, Canada's membership in the club of

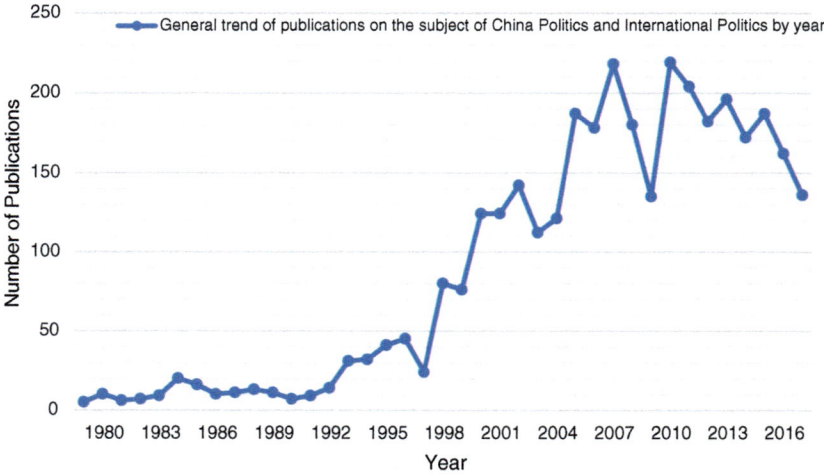

Fig. 5.9 Articles on Canada dealing with politics and international relations

Western capitalist democracies was softened by the country's explicit commitment to multiculturalism. This was an important aspect of Canada that tended to soften the invidious overtones of Western capitalist culture and modernization and that allowed space for a more nuanced reading of culture and modernity. Today, Canada's example looms more modestly than it did in those early years of Canadian studies in China. Nonetheless, the establishment of Canadian studies in China, and the continued relevance of the Canada–China Scholars Exchange, together ensures that Canada maintains a niche in Chinese academia, one that supplements a generally positive international image with opportunities to use Canada as a bridge to establish disciplinary relevance on the international stage.

Inevitably, the institutionalization of Canadian Studies in China exposed Canadian studies to the institutional and bureaucratic politics of China itself. At the same time, when the Canadian government abolished the directorate of Canadian Studies within the Department of Foreign Affairs and International Trade, whatever countervailing leverage was available through Canadian financial and institutional support became relatively weaker. Thus, within the Chinese system, the Canadian Studies Centers officially sponsored by the Chinese Ministry of Education at Guangdong University of Foreign Studies and Trade and at the Beijing Foreign Studies University subject their directors to the political and ideological currents that sweep the Chinese bureaucratic hierarchy. On the one hand, they must maintain a spirit of openness to international partners, particularly their Canadian partners, and maintain these partnerships at a high level with official support of the state authorities. On the other hand, they must maintain their ideological and political standing by conforming to the prevailing ideological perspective coming down from the apex of the Chinese Communist Party.

Public presentations, especially those given in English or French, are rarely if ever censored. However, some may receive a kind of official riposte that delivers the official point of view from someone in an authoritative position. However, the Chinese censorship system works on the basis of mutual responsibility, whereby each article or book is assigned a "responsible editor" who is not connected to the commissioning editor of the publication and whose "responsibility"—a responsibility for which he or she is accountable—is to ensure that nothing appears in print that transgresses official guidelines. This author has had his articles for the annual reviews censored through having whole sections removed regardless of what this may mean for the coherence of the article. In other cases, entire articles are removed from prospective publications due to minor deviations from perceived political orthodoxy. Authors whose work is translated my not even be aware of such changes, and in many cases the commissioning editor is powerless in the face of these censors.

In my experience censorship normally occurs only in relation to comments that directly refer to China and not to Canada. (Certain sensitive diplomatic relationships may occasionally suffer from censorship, as has happened in relation to North Korea or Russian meddling in the Ukraine.) Thus, for example, in a recent article that was excised from a Chinese journal the "responsible editor" objected to this author referring to China's "self-imposed" isolation during the Cultural Revolution of the 1960s. Because Canadian Studies is in most cases associated with centers and units linked to American studies, the prevailing ideological climate is complicated by the ways in which Canadian Studies is squeezed in and in some cases subordinated to American studies and prevailing trends in Sino-American relations. To be fair, most Canadian Studies scholars in China are highly attuned to the distinctions between Canadian policies and their US counterparts. However, the general salience and critical importance of Sino-American relations usually means that bureaucratic directors of official Canadian Studies programs have their eye more squarely on Sino-American relations both in terms of how they view Canada, and in terms of where they wish to move in relation to their professional careers. Canada is not an existential issue for the Chinese.

As China moves into a new era where it offers itself as an "option" to other countries, particularly those in the developing world, knowledge and familiarity with Canada as a variant model of liberal democracy serves to temper binary oppositions between a US-centric representation of "the West" and an exclusive and exceptional reading of "China" (Xi Jinping 2017). Canada is seen as relatively benign, if not exactly benevolent, with policy prescriptions from health care, pensions, fiscal policy and cultural policy that are perceived to be technically relevant and non-threatening. This non-threatening posture is reinforced by an appreciation of multiculturalism as a non-exclusive posture that does not automatically pose "China" and "the West" in invidious and oppositional terms. Chinese academics generally perceive Canadians as more open to their world view and less concerned about competition and superiority than are Americans.

Canadian studies has had an important impact on the development of academic research in China. Gender studies in particular received an important boost from the Canada–China University Linkages program in the 1980s (Hayhoe et al. 2016). This occurred just as academic sociology was making a return in China after the long hiatus created by the Stalinistic Sovietization of higher education in China during the 1950s and the subsequent destruction of academic learning during the chaotic ideological frenzy of the Cultural Revolution.

The irony here is the limited effectiveness of Canadian Studies as a form of public diplomacy. Canadian policy is viewed as a tool to help modernize China and as a means to achieve Chinese goals. There is, however, very little can be done to use Canada as leverage to change Chinese policy in directions that have not already been decided from the top. This is both because of the ways in which ideological control is retained over publication and because interest in Canada is highest precisely in areas that might contribute positively towards achieving stated Chinese goals. Subtly, however, Canadian influence seeps in through the ways in which academic disciplines are approached. Chinese higher education and research institutions have moved on from "exposure to international standards" to direct competition. Here, the benignly welcoming and generally less competitive atmosphere in Canadian academic institutions may help to solidify collaborative endeavors, helped by the ongoing maintenance of the Canada–China Scholars Exchange Program (CSSEP, n.d.). These exchanges have ensured that Canadianists in China have continued access to Canadian institutions of higher learning, despite the termination of official support for Canadian Studies by the Canadian government in 2012 (Meisel and Graham 2012). A sort of quiet collaboration is produced by such exchanges that may, in turn, generate a subtle normative afterglow.

In many ways, the history of Canadian studies in China reflects the trajectory of Canada's engagement with China. First was a period of intensive and heightened engagement from the 1980s through the 1990s, when China was on the receiving end of the learning curve in international society and Canada provided important access to global trends. This has somewhat plateaued as Canadian interest in China wavered because of perceived threats from China's ascendance and less intense interest in Canada from the Chinese side, as it grew to be globally competitive along many dimensions. Today, Canada tends to be seen as a relatively benign example of a modern Western country and a relatively low-cost conduit for internationalization, particularly for Chinese scholars in less prestigious institutions who have established Canadian Studies programs. Canadian studies, possibly more than any other program, carries on the legacy of the substantial assistance that Canada gave to the re-establishment of academic excellence in China during the 1980s and in its modest but significant way, contributes to the projection of Canada's mainly positive image in China in a world that seems to clamor for the attention of a country that has become one of the world's leading powers.

NOTES

1. For more see, Phirom Leng and Julia Pan, "The Issue of Mutuality in Canada-China Educational Collaboration," *Canada and International Education* 42 (2): Art. 6; also Hayhoe, Zha, and Pan, "Lessons from the Legacy of Canada-China University Linkages," *Frontiers of Education in China*, 2013, 8 (1): 80–104.
2. Research for this section was provided by Yili Zhou, a PhD candidate in the Department of Political Science at Carleton University.

REFERENCES

Canada-China Scholars Exchange Program. n.d. http://www.scholar-ships-bourses.gc.ca/scholarships-bourses/can/ccsep-peucc.aspx?lang=eng. Accessed 26 Feb 2018.

Canadian Studies Centre, Beijing Foreign Studies University. Waiyu jiaoxue yu yanjiu chubanshe [Foreign Languages Teaching and Studies Press].

Canadian Studies Centre, Guangdong University of Foreign Languages and Trade. 2016. *Annual Report on the Development of Canada (Blue Book of Canada) [Jianada lanpi shu]*. Beijing: Social Sciences and Academic Press.

Center for Canadian Studies, Peking University. 2011. *Canadian Studies/Etudes Canadiennes* [Jianada Yanjiu]. Beijing: Peking University Press.

Evans, Brian L. 2011. Canadian Studies in China. In *Issues in Canada-China Relations*, ed. Pitman Potter and Thomas Adams, 136–146. Toronto: Canadian International Council.

Hayhoe, Ruth, Qiang Zha, and Julia Pan. 2013. Lessons from the Legacy of Canada-China University Linkages. *Frontiers of Education in China* 8 (1): 80–104.

———. 2016. *Canadian Universities in China's Transformation: An Untold Story*. Montreal and Kingston: McGill-Queens University Press.

Institute of Rural Development, Yunnan Agricultural University. 2017. News: "17th Canadian Studies Association of China Conference Opens at Yunnan Agricultural University", December 31. http://inrd.ynau.edu.cn/index.aspx-?lanmuid=87&sublanmuid=725&id=2004. Accessed 28 Jan 2018.

Leng, Phirom, and Julia Pan. 2013. The Issue of Mutuality in Canada-China Educational Collaboration. *Canada and International Education/Education canadine et international* 42 (2): Article 6.

Meisel, John, and John Graham. 2012. It's Hard to Understand Canadian Studies Cuts. *The Globe and Mail*, June 12. https://www.theglobeandmail.com/opinion/its-hard-to-understand-canadian-studies-cuts/article4408869/. Accessed 26 Feb 2018.

Xi Jinping. 2017. Secure a Decisive Victory in Building a Moderately Prosperous Society in All Respects and Strive for the Great Success of Socialism with Chinese Characteristics for a New Era, Full Text of Xi Jinping's Report at 19th CPC National Congress. http://www.chinadaily.com.cn/china/19thcpcnationalcongress/2017-11/04/content_34115212.htm. Accessed 22 Jan 2018.

Yang, Lingxia. 2009. Gaige kaifang yilaide Zhongguo Jianadashi yanjiu [Of Research on Canadian History in China 1978–2008] *Shixue Yuekan* 4: 24–33.

Zhongguo Zhiwang. n.d. http://www.cnki.net/. Accessed 26 Feb 2018.

CHAPTER 6

Canadian Studies in Japan

Masako Iino

INTRODUCTION

This chapter discusses how Canadian Studies in Japan has developed, focusing on the history of the Japanese Association for Canadian Studies (JACS), which was officially established in 1979. The chapter also includes a comparison of the development of Canadian Studies with that of American Studies in Japan in order to better understand the unique character of Canadian Studies in Japan.

In the immediate postwar years, the Japanese people as well as the Japanese government were so preoccupied with learning about the United States that Canada received very little attention. Some Japanese people even had an image of Canada as being part of the United States. In this context, an episode in the history of Japanese immigration to Canada is illustrative. Mio, a village in the western part of Japan that produced the largest number of immigrants to Canada in the late nineteenth century and early twentieth century, became popularly known in Japan as "America village." In fact, many Japanese immigrants to Canada at the time had intended to go to the United States but stayed when their ship from Japan docked first at a Canadian port. Others made little or no

M. Iino (✉)
Tsuda College, Kodaira, Japan

© The Author(s) 2019
S. Brooks (ed.), *Promoting Canadian Studies Abroad*,
Palgrave Macmillan Series in Global Public Diplomacy,
https://doi.org/10.1007/978-3-319-74027-0_6

distinction between Canada and the United States, calling the two North American nations by the genetic name, "America." Even in the 1890s Canada had an identity problem abroad![1]

Another episode that illustrates similar confusion is related to the order issued by the Canadian government during World War II. The government urged those Japanese Canadians who had been interned in the interior of the province to move "east of the Rockies," instead of returning to the west coast after the war ended. According to the order, if they did not agree to move "east of the Rockies," they were to be "repatriated" (which essentially meant "deported") to Japan. After great confusion in the Japanese Canadian communities, about 4000 Japanese Canadians were shipped to war-devastated Japan in 1946. Even now many of those Japanese Canadians who landed in Japan in 1946 remember their experiences of being called "enemy Americans" by many Japanese people who did not distinguish Canada from the United States. Few Japanese were aware of the fact that, in the years after 1945, Canada played an important role in helping to smooth Japan's entry into the community of nations and, eventually, to become a member of the United Nations.

When Canadian Studies emerged in Japan in the 1970s, this was a direct result of the concerns that many scholars had about the Americanization of Canada. The early conceptualization of Canadian Studies was influenced by Canada's cultural diplomacy, as was also true of other area studies programs in Japan. Interestingly, Canadian Studies, which was expected to emphasize that "Canada is different from the United States," has developed following the path that American Studies took. At the same time, Canadian Studies and American Studies in Japan have shown conspicuous differences, even though they have much in common. Comparing the development of these two area studies in Japan enables us to understand the unique character of Canadian Studies as well as the meaning of Canadian Studies in Japan.

BACKGROUND

It was in a way natural that Japanese people did not know much about Canada before World War II, or even for many years after, as there was little information on Canada. Serious books dealing with Canada and that were available to the Japanese public were few. Available sources of information on Canada were limited to some official surveys and reports prepared by the Japanese Ministry of Foreign Affairs, some stories about Japanese immigrants to Canada, including immigrants' memoirs, and some tourist guidebooks. The books that are considered to be "the first descriptions of Canada to Japanese readers" include Kunpei Matsumoto's *Beifu-Oun-Roku* (American Winds, European Clouds) (1903), based on former Prime Minister Hirobumi Itoh's earlier trip to Britain in 1863 and North America in 1870–1871, Keikoku Kashiwamura's *Hokubei Jicchi Tosa* (North America: A Field Survey) (1913), and Jinshiro Nakayama's *Kanada no Hoko* (A Canadian Encyclopedia) (1922). Volume 9 of Tamiji Naito's 12-volume series of *Sekai Jikkan* (The World Through a Camera) was *Canada and Latin America* (1916). Though there were some highly specialized publications such as *Canada's Steel Industry* by Manabu Sano (1919) and *Establishment of a Central Bank in Canada: Its Process and the Problems Encountered* (1935) by Teruo Nishimura, they did not inspire a more general interest in Canada.[2]

With the improvement of trade relations between Canada and Japan, however, interest in Canada began to grow as early as the 1950s. In his essay entitled *Kanada no Tsuchi, Amerika no Tomo* (Land of Canada and Friends of America), published in 1954, Kotaro Tanaka, the Chief Justice of the Supreme Court of Japan, described Canada's political system and constitution. On a more popular level, a book titled *Kanada to Iu Kuni* (A Country Called Canada), by Japanese professor and adventurer, Ryozo Azuma, was published in 1955 and provided a general, if occasionally impressionistic, view of Canada's geography, history, society, and relations with Japan. This book remained one of the most popular books about Canada for nearly two decades. In 1963, *Kanada no Kenkyu* (The Study of Canada), produced by the Research Institute for World Economic Affairs, was published. It was perhaps the first objective and comprehensive review of Canada's various aspects, particularly its economy, industry, and relations with England and the United States, to be published in Japan. Another book on Canada which appeared at the time was *Kanada* (Canada) (Life and World Library Series, 1963), which was translated by Seijiro Yoshizawa, a former Japanese ambassador to Canada. Even though the trade relations between Canada and Japan ignited greater interest in Canada, until the 1960s serious interest in Canada was limited to a small number of diplomats, researchers, businessmen, and travel writers.[3]

Still, this interest continued to develop in the 1960s, as the new concept of the Pacific Rim gave the two countries a geographical link. This link was reinforced by the steady stream of Japanese tourists who headed to Canada, attracted by Expo '67, the world fair marking Canada's centennial. At the same time, the works of several Canadian scholars were translated into Japanese. Gradually, several Canadian authors were introduced to Japanese intellectuals through translations of their works. Until then practically the only literature that any Japanese could readily identify as Canadian had been *Anne of Green Gables*, which still remains very popular among young people in Japan. Some people explain the reason of its popularity as follows: the book depicts Anne as a very independent girl, whom many Japanese girls adore as this quality is something that, historically, Japanese girls did not experience. (Time has changed and now many girls may be more independent than boys in Japan!) The translated version of *Anne of Green Gables* played an important role in drawing Japanese tourists to Prince Edward Island.

The most notable examples of translated works on Canada in the 1960s and the 1970s included George Woodcock's two-volume *Anarchism*, published in 1968 and Northrop Frye's *The Educated Imagination* (1964), *The Modern Century* (1971), *The Critical Path: Essays on the Social Context of Literary Criticism* (1974), and, later, *Anatomy of Criticism: Four Essays* (1980). Around the same time, some historical and philosophical works about Japan by Canadian E.H. Norman also appeared in translations. Norman was not a scholar in Canadian Studies, but was, and has been, one of the most respected and well-known Japanologists, who contributed to Japanese historiography and represented Canada. Although these books probably had little direct impact on the development of Canadian Studies in Japan per se, they contributed to the growing interest in Canada in Japan and introduced Japanese to Canadians other than *Anne of Green Gables*. Seymour Lipset's *Revolution and Anti-revolution* (1972), which discussed major sociological differences between Canadians and Americans, was one of the most important books dealing with Canada to be translated into Japanese during this period. People started to see Canada as separate from the United States. Lipset's book also alerted students of the United States in Japan to the possibility of comparative studies.

Thus, until the 1960s and early 1970s, Canadian Studies remained in an embryonic stage. It was, however, soon to take a significant step forward. The election of the charismatic Pierre Trudeau, who was determined to pursue a more diversified foreign policy, encouraged Canadian and Japanese policy-makers to think of new ways to promote closer relations between the two countries. Having participated actively as a cabinet minister in the previous government's foreign policy discussions, Trudeau "had firm ideas on the need to recast Canada's place in the world."[4] During his first election campaign in the spring of 1968, he told Canadians: "Because of past preoccupations with Atlantic and European affairs, we have tended to overlook the reality that Canada is a Pacific country too."[5] As a result, in September 1974, Trudeau and Japanese Prime Minister Kakuei Tanaka issued a joint statement in Ottawa, committing both of their governments to contribute one million dollars for the promotion of Japanese Studies in Canada and Canadian Studies in Japan. This cultural agreement paved the way for Canada's foreign ministry to fund Canadian Studies courses at some universities in Japan and to provide subsidies for the translation of books on Canada. It also established a number of scholarships and research grants for Japanese graduate and post-graduate students, and a program that enabled Japanese universities to invite Canadian scholars to offer courses on Canada. As early as 1976, this program enabled H. Vivian Nelles of York University to be the first visiting scholar teaching courses on Canada at the University of Tsukuba. His contribution to Canadian Studies at this fledgling stage caused him to be seen as one of the founders of JACS.

These developments were watched carefully in Canada, where Trent University president Tom Symons was undertaking a major examination of Canadian Studies. Though primarily concerned with Canadian Studies in Canada, the Report of the Commission on Canadian Studies (commonly known as "The Symons Report") also encouraged the government to promote the study of Canada abroad. It noted "with pleasure" the Trudeau–Tanaka initiative and urged Ottawa to provide an annual grant to the Canadian Centre at Sophia University and to find more ways of fostering "a greater interest in and knowledge of Canada at other appropriate universities in Japan."[6]

THE BIRTH OF JACS

Against this background, the turning point in the development of Canadian Studies in Japan came in 1977 when a group of scholars and researchers, who had been individually engaged in Canadian Studies, formed a study group called "Kanada Kenkyu Kai" (Association for Canadian Studies). This would become the JACS in 1979. The same year saw the publication of five scholarly articles about Canada in a monthly magazine, *Kokusai Mondai* (International Issues), published by the Institute of International Affairs. These essays covered Canada's relations with Japan, federalism, politics and government, foreign relations, the economy, and ethnic relations. At around the same time, three books on Canada were translated into Japanese as textbooks for Japanese university students: *The Pelican History of Canada* by Kenneth McNaught, *The Canadian Economy: Structure and Development* by Ian M. Drummond, and *How Are We Governed?* by J. Ricker and John Saywell. Subsidized by the Canadian government, these translated textbooks were distributed to many Japanese who were interested in learning about Canada, "and in many respects, provided the cornerstone for the development of Canadian Studies in Japan."[7] Subsequently, several other texts and works of general interest relating to Canada were translated into Japanese. Among these were *Memoirs of Hugh L. Keenleyside: Hammer the Golden Ray* (1984) by Hugh L. Keenleyside, who served as the first Canadian ambassador to Japan in 1929, *The Maple Leaf Forever* by Ramsay Cook (1984), *Politics, Law, and the Constitution: The Canadian Experience* by John T. Saywell, and *Life with Uncle: The Canadian-American Relationship* by John W. Holmes (1987). Several of the translators, particularly Nobuya Bamba and Yuko Ohara, had an important role in founding JACS.

Thus, the establishment of JACS was part of a broader Canadian national project, and it also had significant meaning for those in Japan who were interested in learning about Canada. It united more than 100 scholars, researchers, and students who had been studying particular aspects of Canada in isolation or in small groups throughout Japan. The birth of JACS provided them with a central organization and allowed many researchers who had considered Canada only as a marginal extension of their primary specialties to see and deal with Canada as a major and distinct theme of their research. Proudly, they came to call themselves "Canadianists."

At around the same time, a number of other important books about Canada were translated into Japanese, including J.M.S. Careless's *Canada: A Study of Challenge* and John Saywell's *Canada: Past and Present*. Several factors explain this growing interest in Canada among the Japanese. One of them was that the 50th anniversary of

Canada–Japan diplomatic relations in 1979 resulted in further publicity about Canada. With the election of the colorful and charismatic Pierre Trudeau as Prime Minister, and his Third Option foreign policy, as well as the establishment of diplomatic relations with the People's Republic of China, Canada began to attract much greater attention among Japanese scholars. It is clear that the Canadian government greatly contributed to this emerging interest, which can be observed in the establishment of JACS and the publication of translated books on Canada.

Many scholars have explained the Canadian government's interest in and promotion of Canadian Studies in Japan as deriving from a "fear of Americanization." This was exactly what Ramsay Cook of York University, who was a mentor for many Japanese Canadianists, said in his essay "Canadian Studies in a Multicultural, Postnationalist World."[8] "[T]hose people who might loosely be characterized as Canadian nationalists in the 1970s," he wrote, "[feared that]the great achievements of Canada's first century, unless effectively reinforced, were in danger of withering away under the impact of external pressure, that is the expanding influence of the United States whose economic potential and cultural aggressiveness threatened to 'Americanize' Canada." Cook concluded that, "The development of Canadian Studies programs in the 1970s was a direct result of these concerns about Americanization."

Adding to "fear of Americanization," other factors contributing to the early conceptualization of Canadian Studies, Cook argues, included, "the growth of a new, Quebec-focused, francophone nationalism" and a perhaps belated recognition of the importance of "cultural diplomacy." The latter is where Canadian Studies abroad entered the equation. It was time, Cook pointed out, that "natural resources, beavers, and Mounties were no longer enough to represent the sophisticated modern culture that Canadians believed they were developing. ... Increased knowledge of Canada in foreign countries, it was hoped, would demonstrate Canada's differences from the United States, promote international understanding and cooperation, and, not least important, promote trade."[9]

THE DEVELOPMENT OF JACS AND CANADIAN STUDIES IN JAPAN

In 2004, when JACS celebrated its 25th anniversary along with the 75th anniversary of the establishment of diplomatic relations between Canada and Japan, JACS conducted a large-scale survey to see how it had grown. The survey results are included in *Twenty-Five Years of Canadian Studies in Japan* (Special Anniversary Edition) compiled by JACS, which depicts the change and development of Canadian Studies in Japan.

With a membership of over 350 in 2004, up from 140 in 1979, JACS had grown to be a comparatively large organization among those of area studies in Japan. According to the survey, the number of universities and colleges that offered courses on Canada also increased, mainly due to Canadian government funding and partly due to the efforts of JACS, from five in the 1970s to almost 50 in 2004. The number of Canada-related courses, programs, and lecture series at universities and colleges had increased to 70, with an estimated number of 6000 enrolled students. Although the figures were still smaller than those for American Studies, Canadian Studies developed quickly in Japan, considering the fact that its history was much shorter than that of American Studies. Not only universities but also many municipal governments and community organizations came to be interested in giving programs on Canada in the form of seminars and lecture series. Members of JACS were invited to participate in those programs. These could be great venues to let the general public know about Canada and promote friendship between the peoples of the two countries.

This conspicuous growth was made possible by programs offered by the Canadian government. In 1981, the International Council for Canadian Studies (ICCS) was established, "dedicated to the promotion and support of research, education, and publication in all fields of Canadian Studies around the world." JACS was one of the nine founding members. ICCS acted as the administrative agent of the Department of Foreign Affairs and International Trade for several of the Department's Canadian Studies Programs. ICCS offered the Faculty Enrichment Program (FEP) and the Faculty Research Program (FRP), which were meant to support Japanese scholars and researchers who would like to study in Canada, and the Canada–Japan Prime Minister's Award, which was meant to support the publication in Japan of books related to Canada. These programs greatly contributed to Canadian Studies in Japan. Between 1987, when Japanese Canadianists first benefitted from those programs, and 2011, a year before the termination of Canadian government support, a total 354 individuals and publishing companies benefitted from the programs.

Another program which contributed to the increased interest in Canada among Japanese students was the Cultural Personalities Exchange Program (CPEP). Starting in 1995, each year three or four professors in the field of Canadian Studies in Canada were invited to teach at various universities in Japan. In addition to teaching at universities, they also participated in the JACS conferences or gave public lectures, and they also engaged with Japanese Canadianists. It was obvious that this support from the Canadian government was effective in helping universities launch courses on Canada, encouraging young students to learn more about Canada and thus developing Canadian Studies in Japan.

JACS grew in the period, not only in size but in the variety and the depth of its academic accomplishments. The evolution of JACS over the 25 years covered by the 2004 survey revealed the maturation of Canadian Studies in Japan. As mentioned above, with the exception of a few pioneering works, Canadian Studies in Japan essentially began with a series of books translated from English or French—mostly English—into Japanese in the 1970s and the early 1980s. Even in the 1990s works of translation abounded and played an important role in introducing Canada to general Japanese audiences. Beginning in the 1990s, however, a great change in the field of Canadian Studies can be observed in Japan. It involved significant growth in the number of original books and papers about Canada by Japanese scholars and researcher. These publications dealt with subjects as varied as history, federalism, multiculturalism, labor law, local government, literature, diplomacy and defense, trade, economics, education, and culture. In addition, collaborative research between Canadian and Japanese scholars increased. Noteworthy results were published, both in Japan and in Canada, particularly in the fields of Canadian politics, Canada–Japan relations, and Japanese Canadians. One good example is Mitsuru Kurosawa and John Kirton, eds., *The Triangle of Pacific States: Contemporary United States, Canada, Japan Relations* (Tokyo: Sairyusha, 1995). The variety of such works was well illustrated by the papers published in the JACS *Annual Reviews*. The 2003 issue, for example, included papers on topics as varied as Stephen Leacock, Chinese and Punjabi speakers in Vancouver, and second-language education in Canada. While the number of these studies increased, some commentators criticized their usefulness and suggested that few of them generate much interest beyond a small circle of experts in the respective fields. Others claimed that, with the exception of those dealing with Canada–Japan relations and Japanese Canadians, these works were not academically sophisticated enough to be published in Canada.[10]

Nevertheless, these developments should be interpreted as signs of the maturing of Canadian Studies in Japan. Many JACS members themselves saw important developments in their own research as well as in

Canadian Studies in Japan more generally during this period. Japanese Canadianists came to believe that they represented a unique addition to Canadian Studies as a whole. Moreover, the enthusiasm of JACS members was greatly appreciated in Japan. This enthusiasm even influenced the Japanese government, which had been, it seemed to the Japanese Canadianists, paying more attention to American Studies programs than to Canadian Studies programs in Japan. In 1996, the Japanese government started a new grant program called the "Canada-Japan Exchange Program for Peace and Friendship," aiming to enhance mutual understanding between Canada and Japan. This program enabled a few Japanese Canadianists each year to spend three months in Canada to conduct research and for a few Canadian Japanologists to spend some time in Japan. JACS was responsible for the annual selection of the Japanese recipients of this grant.

The enthusiasm of JACS members was also seen in the success of the association's first international conference held in 1998. In that year JACS organized, with great support from the Canadian government as well as some private organizations, the Asia-Pacific Conference on Canadian Studies in Tokyo, under the theme, "Asia-Pacific and Canada: Images and Perspectives." Close to twenty Canadianists from Asian countries and Australia and New Zealand, as well as from Canada and the United States, were invited. It was the first conference of that sort to be held in Asia and turned out to be a great success in promoting dialog on Canadian Studies and encouraging the Canadianists who participated to continue their efforts. Its success led to the second international conference held in Australia two years later and the third in South Korea. These conferences sparked hopes that the process of exchange in the international Canadian Studies community would continue and expand, benefitting all Canadianists, wherever they were.

Another notable change in the period can be seen in the composition of the Japanese Canadianist community. Owing to support from the Canadian government, a number of young students studied and received their degrees at universities in Canada. The younger generation of Canadianists with PhDs from universities in Canada in various fields, including political science, economics, history, and sociology, started to be quite active in JACS as well as at universities. They were not like the older generation of scholars who came into the field of Canadian Studies through other programs, such as American Studies. In the 1990s and

2000s, JACS was in its second generation, or even its third, including students of the second generation of scholars and researchers.

One more sign of the increase of interest in Canada and Canadian Studies in the period was that other academic associations with a focus on learning about various aspects of Canada developed at around the same time. These included the Canadian Literary Society of Japan, established in 1982; the Japanese Association for Canadian Education Studies, established in 2003, and the Association Japonaise des Études Québécoises, established in 2008. Often collaborating with JACS, these associations have been quite active in presenting to the public the research results of their members.

Analyzing the survey conducted by JACS in 2004 and the various activities undertaken by JACS, Hiroaki Kato, President of JACS at the time, made the following comments in his paper entitled "25 Years of Canadian Studies in Japan: Problems and Prospects."[11] Noteworthy progress had been "made in the teaching of Canadian Studies at Japanese universities and colleges. JACS members played a critical role in the expansion of Canadian Studies at Japanese educational institutions, and should feel proud of their achievement." In addition to increasing the number of Canadian content courses taught at Japanese universities and colleges, JACS members had also been "actively engaged in the production of academic presentations and papers." In the 25 years since JACS was created, it held 29 major conferences at which there were 307 presentations. JACS also issued 24 volumes of its *Annual Review of Canadian Studies,* in which 144 papers were published. Still, in spite of all this scholarship, Kato concluded that, "it is fair to say that Canada remains misunderstood by the Japanese public. The general image of the country remains that of a land of great natural beauty, of tourists in Banff, Niagara Falls, and Prince Edward Island." Then he proposed: "In order to push beyond the narrow limits of this view, I believe we must reconsider academic strategies of Canadian studies in Japan." He pointed out, based on his critical evaluation of the role of JACS, that its members should have "more interdisciplinary and cross-disciplinary research projects," introduce "a comparative perspective," and "see Canada in an Asia-Pacific perspective," instead of "the North American framework." He concludes his paper saying that "it is necessary to advance and improve our academic perspectives and strategies for the future."[12]

Comparison with American Studies in Japan

While Canadian Studies in Canada and abroad developed and was strengthened by the anxieties arising from a fear of Americanization, as mentioned above, Canadian Studies programs in Japan paradoxically tended to develop along a path similar to that which marked American Studies in Japan. In fact a sizable number of JACS members were previously scholars in the field of American Studies. Some came to be interested in Canada as one way of analyzing the United States through comparison to Canada.

This approach should not be considered unwelcome, as American Studies provides a good model of area studies in Japan. There has been, however, a great difference in the paths followed by American and Canadian studies, respectively, in recent years. In the 1980s and the post-Cold War era, when frictions between Washington and Tokyo were greater than in previous decades, some Japanese scholars in the field of American Studies felt it their mission to help improve the deteriorated relations between the two. Under the pressure of strained US–Japanese relations, they felt that their field should focus more on providing scholarly and public discussions of American affairs and US–Japanese relations against the broader canvas of American history and proper historical perspectives. Although they realized that their influence would remain rather limited in the Japanese media, these Japanese Americanists did their best to restrain the media's "sensationalistic tendency and to present sober views of American affairs and US–Japanese relations." In their opinion, as Japan's relations with the United States had become very close and multidimensional, and as frictions developed in this close relationship, it was necessary for Japanese scholars to reexamine differences and similarities between the cultures of the two nations.[13]

Such was not the case among Japanese scholars in Canadian Studies. No prominent frictions have existed in relations between Canada and Japan over the years and, consequently, Japanese Canadianists have not felt any pressure to help improve relations between the two countries. Indeed, it would seem unlikely that they will feel the need to perform such a role in the future, given that the relationship between Canada and Japan does not include the causes of friction that have occasionally roiled the waters between Tokyo and Washington.

Nevertheless, we can learn a great deal from American Studies in Japan that helps us understand the development of Canadian studies. In particular, a "fear of Americanization" has had an important influence on JACS and its members at all stages of its development. A good example involves the "multiculturalism" of Canada. Many Canadianists in Japan have been interested in learning about Canadian multiculturalism from various perspectives—as a policy in the field of law, and as ethnic relations in the fields of history and sociology, for example. Multiculturalism was for quite some time a popular theme at various conferences, including JACS annual conferences. In the eyes of many Canadianists, the greatest difference between Canada and Japan lies in the ethnic structure of the two countries. Naturally, the ethnic structure is often referred to as the greatest difference between the United States and Japan as well. The Japanese people are not entirely mono-ethnic, and there is a sizable population of non-Japanese permanent residents in Japan. It is undeniable, however, that Japan has a highly homogeneous population and that Japanese democracy and social tranquility depend largely on this high degree of homogeneity. Japanese students of American Studies had been interested in American society with its multiracial, multiethnic, and multicultural population and in how the United States has tried, though not always successfully, to manage diversity and to integrate minorities in a liberal democracy. These scholars found Canada, with its special and official policy of multiculturalism, quite unique and intriguing, and significantly different from the case of the United States. This "discovery" of Canadian multiculturalism coincided with the time when Japan started to receive a large number of immigrants from South America and South-East Asia, generating a heated discussion about immigration policy and whether Japan's door should be open or closed. There has been a great deal for the Japanese people to learn from the experiences of Canada. Thus, a comparison of the Canadian policy of multiculturalism with the American policy has also drawn the interest of Japanese Canadianists.

The Science Council of Japan, the representative organization of the Japanese scientist community ranging over all fields of sciences, now has a committee on area studies, including Canadian Studies and American Studies. The committee has been quite active, making various proposals on the roles of area studies in international cooperation as well as how to strengthen area studies in this globalized era. Those proposals indicate the direction area studies in Japan, including Canadian Studies, move, influencing the themes and methods of research in these fields.

THE CURRENT SITUATION OF JACS AND CANADIAN STUDIES IN JAPAN

The decision made by Canada's Department of Foreign Affairs and International Trade on 1 May 2012, to "phase out the international Canadian Studies program and to reduce the funding and geographic scope of the international Scholarship Program," came as a big blow to JACS. The Association had been heavily supported by those programs and it was immediately clear that JACS' activities would be scaled back. But more than that, many JACS members expressed their disappointment with the Canadian government. Many were afraid that the image of Canada and Canada's international reputation, both in and outside academic circles, would be damaged. With the subsidy from the Canadian government terminated, many universities without alternative resources had to reduce or stop offering their Canadian Studies programs and courses. There were some exceptions, including Kwansei Gakuin University, Ritsumeikan University, and Sophia University. These universities had sufficient independent resources as well as strong leadership that was committed to the continuation of Canadian Studies programs or courses. Across the country, however, the number of courses, and consequently of students in the field of Canadian Studies has declined. As this is written (February 2018), the Canadian embassy in Tokyo and JACS are conducting a survey to grasp the change which has occurred in Canadian Studies in Japan. Although reliable figures are not yet available, JACS is aware that a significant number of universities and colleges have stopped offering the courses on Canada. Even at the University of Tsukuba, where the first Canadian professor was invited to teach courses on Canada over 40 years ago, no courses on Canada are now offered.

In recent years, the membership of JACS has declined to under 300, much smaller than that of the Japanese Association for American Studies whose 2017 membership stood at more than 1200. Nevertheless, and despite the sharp drop in its membership, JACS continues to be active, holding an annual conference and a number of regional study seminars and symposia. Besides the regular publication of its *Annual Review of Canadian Studies*, the Association has published several books on Canada in recent years, including *Documentary Canada*, a collection of documents of important historical events which tell the history of Canada. A certain change can be observed in the themes that have recently interested Japanese Canadianists. Popular themes at recent

JACS conferences have included: security matters, health care systems, non-governmental organizations, education, citizenship, monetary policies, and international contributions such as peacekeeping operations.

JACS's members have produced books and papers aimed at both Canadianists throughout the world and students and the general public in Japan. Some examples include: *Canada's "Status of Women" Policy and Universities* (2017), *Thirty-Seven Chapters to Experience Canada* (2017), *Independency of Canada and North Atlantic World* (2014), *Quebec and Canada: The Pleasure of Area Studies* (2014), *Canadian Kaleidoscope: From Anne of Green Gables to Cirque du Soleil* (2013). Recent issues of the *Annual Review of Canadian Studies* have featured a wide variety of subjects, including articles on "Reflection on Laïcité and the 'Quebec Charter of Values': The Historical Cultural Heritage and Religious Symbols of Quebec," "A Study on the History of Canada in the Age of Globalization," "Shakespeare in Canada: The Function of Canadian Prairies in Romeo and Juliette (1989)," "Social Learning and Political Participation through Public Hearings: A Case Study of the Mackenzie Valley Pipeline Inquiry," and "Controversy over Freight Rates and the Search for National Unity in the First Years of the Mackenzie King Administration."

Today, "globalization" has become one of the key words of Canadian Studies, rivaling "multiculturalism." The recent trajectory of Canadian Studies in Japan reflects the changes that have taken place in the research agenda of Canadian Studies in Canada, as seen in the relatively new fields of Transnational Canadian Studies and Pacific Transnational Canadian Studies. The contributions of Japanese Canadianists to work in these fields are not only possible but also quite important, bringing comparative perspectives to the understanding of Canada.

I was the president of JACS in 1998 when its first international Canadian Studies conference was held. I made it clear that we, the members of JACS, should disseminate and publicize the research and publications being carried out in the field of Canadian Studies in Japan. The period for simply learning from Canadian scholars was long past and it was time to contribute and to share our work. In other words, I tried to convince the JACS members that one of the major roles that the associations should play in promoting Canadian Studies was not limited to home consumption. We should share with Canadianists in other nations the scholarship, perspectives, and insights produced in Japan. This would raise the level of our scholarship, as we would learn more not only from scholars in Canada but from Canadianists in other countries. At the same time, we would contribute to Canadian Studies in Canada and elsewhere by offering our unique vision of the Canadian experience, past and present. JACS began to move in this direction in the twenty first century.

Since that 1998 JACS conference, and prompted by Hiroaki Kato's 2004 criticisms and recommendations, JACS has been working to overcome the relative isolation imposed by the Japanese language. It has encouraged its members to publish more in English (or, to a lesser extent, in French), a step made possible by the increased number of Canadianists who have been educated in Canada. Thus, JACS has been working to incorporate itself more closely in the international network of Canadian Studies associations, organizing a number of international conferences in Canadian Studies. At the same time JACS has made efforts to spread knowledge of Canada in Japan, as that is its mandate.

Although the 2012 termination of Canadian government funding dealt a significant blow to Canadian studies in Japan, as elsewhere, Japan's community of Canadianists continues to be active. The research carried out by JAC's members is specialized, diverse in focus and ramified, reaching beyond Japan. Internet communication allows research to be conducted simultaneously in Japan as well as in Canada or in the United States, influencing research methods as well as the selection of research themes. JACS members are aware that in this globalized network of Canadian studies, it is more important than ever that their research—whatever its focus, approach, and intended audience—should contribute to understanding Canada as a whole. The mature and institutionalized community of Canadianists that exists today in Japan is fully capable of making unique contributions to Canadian studies in the world, contributions that bring Japanese perspectives and sensibilities to bear on the big questions of what is Canada and who are Canadians.

NOTES

1. J. L. Patricia Roy, Granatstein, Masako Iino, and Hiroko Takamura, *Mutual Hostages: Canadians and Japanese During the Second World War* (Toronto: University of Toronto Press, 1990), 5.
2. Kensei Yoshida, "Canadian Studies in Japan," in John Schultz and Kimitada Miwa, eds., *Canada and Japan in the Twentieth Century* (Toronto: Oxford University Press, 1991), 213–223.
3. Ibid., 214.

4. Greg Donaghy, "'Smiling Diplomacy' Redux: Trudeau's Engagement with Japan, 1968–76," in Greg Donaghy and Patricia Roy, eds., *Contradictory Impulses: Canada and Japan in the Twentieth Century* (Vancouver: University of British Columbia Press, 2008) 190.
5. Pierre Trudeau, "Canada and the World," 29 May 1968, Canada, Department of External Affairs, *Statements and Speeches*, No. 68/17.
6. T. H. B. Symons, *To Know Ourselves: The Report of the Commission on Canadian Studies* (Ottawa: Association of Universities and Colleges of Canada, 1975), 2: 55.
7. Yoshida, "Canadian Studies in Japan," 213.
8. Keynote speech at the JACS Annual Conference in 1992.
9. Ramsay Cook, "Canadian Studies in a Multicultural, Post-nationalist World," Japanese Association for Canadian Studies, *The Annual Review of Canadian Studies*, 18 (1998), 49–62.
10. Yoshida, "Canadian Studies in Japan," 215.
11. Hiroaki Kato, "25 Years of Canadian Studies in Japan: Problems and Prospects," Japanese Association for Canadian Studies, *The Annual Review of Canadian Studies*, 25 (2005), 17–31.
12. Ibid., 30.
13. Tadashi Aruga, "Japanese Scholarship and the Meaning of American History," *The Journal of American History*, 79 (1992), 511.

CHAPTER 7

Canadian Studies in the Russian Empire, Soviet Union, and Contemporary Russia

Yuriy G. Akimov and Kristina Minkova

There has long been a common cliché claiming that Canada in many ways resembles Russia. In the 1960s, the song "Above Canada" became widely popular among Soviet intellectuals. According to the song's lyrics, although Canada looks similar to Russia, "it is still not Russia". This song reflects the real state of affairs.

This chapter is devoted to the perception of Canada in the Russian Empire, the Soviet Union, and after its dissolution, in Russia. We will focus on the changes in this perception across different historical periods, including prominent images of Canada, the approaches that dominated in Canadian studies, and the assessment of Canada in scientific and popular publications.

Y. G. Akimov (✉) · K. Minkova
Department of American Studies, School of International Relations,
St. Petersburg State University, St. Petersburg, Russia

© The Author(s) 2019
S. Brooks (ed.), *Promoting Canadian Studies Abroad*,
Palgrave Macmillan Series in Global Public Diplomacy,
https://doi.org/10.1007/978-3-319-74027-0_7

CANADA DURING TSARIST RUSSIA: A WILD COUNTRY
OR THE PEASANT'S KINGDOM

The first more or less reliable information about Canada (as well as about America in general) appeared in Russia in the early to middle eighteenth century. This information originated mainly from the first Russian newspapers, "Gazette" and "The St. Petersburg Gazette" ("Vedomosti", "St. Petersburgskie Vedomosti") and their annexes. In general, the information involved were reprints of news coming from the Western European capitals. Most often information about Canada could be found in the columns entitled "From London" and "From Paris." Attention in such articles was paid mainly to the description of the clashes and conflicts between the English and the French on Canadian soil. Other aspects of Canadian life, as was also true for other European colonies in North America, were given much less attention. One of the few exceptions was an article titled "The News of the Current English and French Villages in America" published in the "St. Petersburg Gazette" at the end of 1750. It contained a rather detailed description of Canada and the main English colonies. The authorship of this article is sometimes attributed to the famous Russian scholar Mikhail Lomonosov [15, p. 608].

The second half of the eighteenth century saw some Russian translations of works on North America written by Western European authors, some of which contained sections on Canada. Unfortunately, the most important works were not always those necessarily chosen for translation. Moreover, for censorship reasons, some of those writings might well have been translated in an incomplete and therefore misleading manner. Nevertheless, the works of Guillaume Raynal [70], William Robertson [72], Friedrich Taube [89], Jean-Bernard Bossu [16], and others became available in Russian.

In 1783, the first work on Canada by a Russian author was published in St. Petersburg. It was a small booklet-like compilation containing a brief description of the English colonies in North America. Its author, Dmitry Mikhailovich Lodygin, a collegiate adviser, was not only known for his writings but also for chemical experiments that he carried out. Describing the history of the Atlantic region of Canada, Lodygin wrote: "And before *Marylandia* [Maryland], there was a population in Acadia or Nova Scotia, and it was weakly bred, and the area passed from hand to hand to the French, then the Englishmen" [52, p. 10]. Later on, one finds this description of these places:

The coast is noticeably cold, and the land is not fruitless, all kinds of grain and vegetables are found, the forests are thick with trees for the ships' masts and animals for hunting, and the rivers are flourishing with a multitude of fish. [52, p. 9]

At the very beginning of the nineteenth century, two articles on Canada were published in the "Bulletin of Europe" by the famous Russian historian Nikolay Karamzin. They were a "Letter of an Englishman from Quebec" [95] and "A Letter from a Young Frenchman from Montreal," [96] reprinted from the German magazine "Minerva." The first of them focused on Upper Canada (Ontario) which was described in the most rapturous tones—as an extremely fertile area with a mild climate, developing rapidly thanks to the hard-working and constantly growing population, as well as "meek rule and general absence of taxes." The second article depicted the adventures of an European who became shipwrecked on the St. Lawrence River and wintered among the Indians. The main part of this letter narrated the history of an Indian who was captured by a hostile tribe (in the text the tribe was called "Magahs" instead of "Mohawk"). The text mentions the Indian custom of admitting a captive to the tribe and the Indians are shown as a mainly generous people capable of the most exalted feelings despite their cruel customs.

A certain surge of interest in Canada arose in Russia in the late 1830s in connection with the anti-British uprisings in Upper and Lower Canada. Russian periodicals of that time reacted to these events with a number of articles written in a reserved and neutral manner. Rumors that appeared in the English and American press of a Russian connection to these rebellions doubtless contributed to the rather neutral tone of this coverage. It obviously stemmed from the rumors of a "Russian trace" in the aforementioned uprisings that appeared in the English and American press.

Nevertheless, until the middle of the nineteenth century, Russians got very little information about Canada and that which reached them was infrequent and fragmentary. One of the notable—though not dominating—trends in the perception of Canada in Russia at that time was its exoticism. British North America was considered a distant and "wild" country which had only recently started being civilized.

The situation changed dramatically with the appearance of Alexander Lakier's book with notes by Dmitry Romanov. A famous Russian historian and specialist in heraldry, Lakier is known, first of all, for his studies on the history of the United States. Indeed, most of his two-volume book "Voyages to the North American States, Canada and Cuba" [50] deals with the description of the author's travels across the USA, accompanied by other different and diverse information. However, the pages devoted to Canada are no less valuable. Lakier began his North American tour in Halifax, a city that he described as "serving as an advanced fortification for British possessions in America" [50, pp. 11–12]. From Halifax, Lakier went to New England and then to New York City, afterwards returning to Canada through the Lake Champlain region in upstate New York. He visited Montreal, Quebec City, and their surroundings. Along with listing the attractions, Lakier drew his readers' attention to differences in French and British policy towards the Indians, the dual ethnic composition of the Canadian population, land usage characteristics, etc. He also noted the effective arrangement of the border between the United States and British North America, which promoted the interests of "two trading nations that understand the price of time and the disadvantages of any stops in trade" [50, p. 306].

Lakier paid a lot of attention to the governance of Canada, stressing the importance of reforms carried out by the British authorities in the 1840s. According to him, their significance lay in the fact that they sharply weakened the influence of the "pro-American party" and contributed to a significant strengthening of the population's loyalty to the United Kingdom [50, pp. 311–313]. This was an astute and accurate observation. Lakier also gave a detailed description of Montreal, describing it as this "purely Catholic city with its numerous churches making it a beautiful sight" [50, p. 319]. He devoted several pages to a detailed description of Montreal, its sights, the ethnic composition of its population, etc. Speaking about Quebec City, Lakier again noted the use of two languages in the proceedings of the colonial legislature, since it was not possible to introduce "exclusive use of English" in Canada [50, p. 332].

On his way back to the United States, Lakier went through the territory of Upper Canada partly by train and partly by steamer. He spent one day in Ottawa, the future capital of the Dominion, which was more often referred to as Bytown. At that time it was still a relatively small settlement with unpaved streets. Nevertheless, the observant traveler noted that although "there was no proper city", Ottawa was located in a very favorable place, "cherished" the claim to become the capital of the entire Canadian territory and was to have "a great future" [50, pp. 342–343]. Through Prescott and Kingston, Lakier reached Toronto which seemed to him a "perfectly English city," bearing, "as the whole of Upper Canada, obvious traces of the influence of the metropolis" [50, p. 359].

Unlike Lakier's book which described Canada in a neutral or positive way, travel notes by the engineer and publicist Dmitry Romanov [73] contain more critical judgments. In particular, when describing Montreal he repeats several times that the city seemed to him "remarkably dirty" (although he does qualify this judgment by noting that it was in the middle of autumn) [73, p. 15]. This gave Romanov a reason to draw parallels with the Russian periphery. He wrote:

> Visit, for example, Ste Catherine street: low one-story houses are molded on the banks of a narrow and impassable dirty street; stretching along them are wooden boardwalks, three boards wide; the general view will remind you of muddy places at home: places such as Syzran, Malmyzh or Rylsk, and this is even more accurate when you walk on these boardwalks and feel that they are as unsteady and as able to break under you, as they are in Khvalynsk, Simbirsk or Irkutsk. [73, p. 15]

Romanov also discussed, more insightfully than Lakier, the relationship between the representatives of the two main ethno-linguistic groups in Canada. On the one hand, he noted that the Franco-Canadian "rural population and the bourgeoisie cherish enmity to the British"; on the other hand, that "the Yankees are unloved here almost as much as the English". From the latter, he concluded that "it was hardly possible to agree with the opinion that Canada would sooner or later join the United States" [73, pp. 15–16]. The prospects for the political future of Canada seemed to him as follows:

> That she [Canada] can be freed from the English dependence, is certain, but not to adhere to the neighbors, but rather to form an independent whole, which is generously endowed with all sorts of favorable conditions. [73, p. 16]

As an engineer, Romanov drew attention to the main technical achievements of Canada at that time: the Victoria Bridge, the Grand Trunk Railway, and a network of telegraph lines. He repeatedly stressed that Russia should model its development along the lines of what he observed in North America, not on Western European experience [73, pp. 16, 21].

To a certain extent, Dmitry Romanov can be considered the pioneer of the "applied school" of Russian Canadian Studies, which started to develop in the last decades of the nineteenth and early twentieth centuries. It was at that time that Canada began to interest Russians as a source of practical experience applicable in their own country.

This involved, above all, agriculture, especially the development of virgin lands, the organization of colonization processes, and railway construction. In the late nineteenth century Canada was often visited by officials from Russian state ministries, engineers, agronomists, journalists, and other public figures. Many of them did not limit their impressions to official reports, but also published travel notes.

In this connection, the experience of constructing the Canadian Pacific Railway (CPR), in conditions not so dissimilar to those of Siberia, was studied by such engineers as Nikolay Kruglikov, Adam Imshenik-Kondratovich, Dmitry Pokotilov, and Nikolay Epanchin. In 1897, the Department of Agriculture of the Ministry of Agriculture and State Property sent to Canada the agronomist Nikolay Kryukov who had previously worked in the Amur region of Russia. Upon returning to Russia, all of them published works describing the Canadian experience and, at the same time, pointing out the need for changes in Russia [28, 46, 47, 66].

In particular, regarding the launching of the CPR, Nikolay Kryukov noted that it was "... to be regarded as a great economic and cultural enterprise, moreover, one of the most progressive across the globe ... The railway became a powerful lever of Canadian colonization. It went ahead of the population, and behind it crowds of farmers were already moving" [46, pp. 224–225].

The main purpose of Kryukov's visit to Canada was to get some insight into Canadian agricultural production. It was for this purpose that he systematically visited farms, elevators, slaughter houses, dairies, creameries, agricultural schools, etc. [53, p. 167]. Kryukov had great praise for the policy of the Dominion government that aimed at supporting farming, and that constantly stressed the importance of private ownership of land for the progress of agriculture and for the country as a whole.

The specificities of legislative regulation of agricultural production in Canada also were studied in Russia during the Tsarist era. On the eve of World War I, the above-mentioned railway engineer Nikolay Epanchin published a Russian translation of the Canadian Grain Act (1912) along with reference materials on the elevator business in Canada [29].

The most significant contributions to pre-revolutionary Canadian Studies in Russia were made Pavel Mizhuev and Sergey Korf. A teacher and historian, Pavel Mizhuev was the author of the first specific work on Canadian history and politics in Russian, entitled "The Peasants' Kingdom" [58]. In the introduction, Mizhuev immediately emphasizes the extremely rapid and significant "economic and cultural progress" of Canada. He associates this progress mainly with the wise policy of England, which drew necessary conclusions from the American Revolution and changed the policy towards its North American possessions. Following the Anglo-Saxon historians of the nineteenth century, Mizhuev dwells on the favorable consequences of the English conquest of Canada, which he regarded as "the happiest event in the history of this country" [58, p. 22]. At the same time, he recognizes that all the benefits received from English rule in Canada (the abolition of medieval institutions, local self-government, free trade, etc.) "did not come immediately, but gradually" [58, p. 23].

Mizhuev's work contained a detailed description of political and socio-economic development of Canada in the second half of the nineteenth century. In addition to a brief analysis of the British North America Act of 1867 and a concise description of the Canadian political system, Mizhuev focuses on the organization of immigration to Canada (including such details as the cost of moving for low-income immigrants, the conditions of their transportation on steamboats, etc.), the system of land distribution, and the organization of school education. He depicts farmers as "peasant proprietors" who played an active role in the life of the country and its politics. Mizhuev also describes their daily life, the machines and mechanisms that they used, their clothing style, diet and habits. Referring to the data on wages and demand for labor, drawn from official English reports, Mizhuev states: "If this information is correct, tens of thousands of small officials in Russia, and not in Russia alone, can envy rural workers in Canada" [58, p. 101].

While Mizhuev's work represented a more general and popular study, the work of Baron Sergei Korf, a well-known lawyer and professor of Helsingfors University, was a fundamental study of the state structure and the party political system of Canada [44]. In the preface, the author presumes that this topic will "in many respects interest the Russian reader" and serve as "an instructive example" [44, p. 5]. After a brief historical essay, Korf describes in detail the twists and turns of the Canadian colonial history of the 1840s and the 1850s. Further on, he analyzes in detail the British North America Act and examines the relationship between the powers of various institutions and branches of the government. He shows how, after the formation of the Dominion, "the administrative functions passed one by one from the metropolis to the hands of the colony, all increasing the self-sufficiency of the latter." It should be noted that Korf stressed the importance of Canada's achievements in the creation of its own navy, as well as its first independent foreign policy steps (the role of the High Commissioner in London, the establishment of representation in Paris, etc.), steps that Korf maintained were for the most part unnoticed. Korf concludes his work with the claim that "Canada is now a state; it has all the requisites and elements of statehood" [44, p. 73].

Korf also pays significant attention to the position of the Franco-Canadians (although he calls them French) and their attitude to the most important issues of domestic and foreign policy. In his opinion, "the French have achieved complete equality in Canada, and all their forces are now aimed at strengthening their position. From this point of view one should consider their view of the British Empire and the connection with the metropolis. They are generally conservative in nature, and particularly conservative on the imperial question" [44, p. 87].

Korf notes that "the French" are "the main opponents of the idea of annexation; for there cannot be any benefits for them" [44, p. 86]. He also draws attention to the "dominance" of the Catholic Church among the French Canadians, which fears "a contagion of modernism" and shields them from the outside world, including Anglo-Canadians, Americans, and the European French. At the same time, it ensures the loyalty and "fidelity" of the French Canadians to England [44, p. 91], although objectively inhibiting their development, in particular by controlling the education system that is "dead," "scholastic," and of "medieval character" [44, pp. 92–94].

Of great interest are Korf's concluding remarks regarding Canada's place in the British Empire and its interaction with imperial structures. He emphasizes that if "Canada had not been itself interested in participating in the common British Empire, it would have long since separated from it, since England could not have been able to retain it physically after the reforms of the 1860s and 1870s" [44, p. 95].

Similar considerations could be found in another Korf's works, devoted to the comparative characteristics of all British dominions. Speaking about the differences between Canada and other dominions, he underlines the gradual process of the formation of the Canadian statehood, which developed without any examples to follow.

"The metropolis first vigorously resisted, then began to give way, and by the end of the century stepped forward to meet the desires of the Canadians". "… Everything happened gradually, imperceptibly, concession after concession with no fixation on legalities. What other self-governing colonies were given by the metropolis as something natural, even necessary, was acquired by Canada, the first pioneer on this road to independence, only through a long and consistent struggle. Administrative and legislative functions had to be won step by step." [45, p. 95]

Generally speaking, the late nineteenth and early twentieth century Russian audience had access to a large variety of materials devoted to Canada and aimed at different readers—from specialists in various fields of knowledge to the general public. The latter was the targeted audience of a brochure written by Emilia Pimenova [65] and reprinted in several editions. In very simple language, it described the foundations of Canadian history and the state structure (the main source, apparently, being the above-mentioned work of Pavel Mizhuev). Pimenova emphasized the advantages of the social and economic system of Canada, where "farmers or peasants, small proprietors, represent ... the class that enjoys the greatest influence in the state" She further states that "for people engaged in self-sufficient agricultural work, the Canadian Federation offers many inducements. Climate and soil in Canada favor agriculture. There is still a plenty of free land" [65, p. 7].

The works mentioned above were not the only sources of information about Canada for the Russian reader. Canadian issues were also covered by the press, especially from the 1860s, as well as in fiction. However, until the middle of the nineteenth century, Canada had been perceived in Russia as a remote, "wild," and exotic country. After the 1850s, this perception gave way to a new approach: Canada regarded as a positive example for imitation and a possible source of positive experience (mainly in relation to railway construction in similar environmental conditions), the organization of colonization of new territories, and the development of agriculture.

CANADIAN STUDIES IN PRE-ISKRAN PERIOD: THE TIME OF CONTRASTS

In this section, we will discuss Canadian studies in the Soviet Union in the period preceding the creation of the Institute of the USA (later of the USA and Canada) as a part of the Academy of Sciences of the Soviet Union in 1967. The Institute would be renamed the Institute for the USA and Canadian Studies (ISKRAN) in 1967.

Before 1967, the Soviet Union produced relatively few works dedicated to Canada. The total list includes about 160 titles (excluding journal articles). However, the ones that got published became characteristic intellectual monuments of their era. They combined a Marxist theoretical approach, ideological clichés, and carefully worded information in a truly bizarre way.

We believe that during this period, Soviet Canadian studies were dominated by what might be called a class-opportunistic approach. Canada was portrayed as one of the capitalist countries developing in accordance with Marxist–Leninist theory. Depending on the situation, either Canada's dependence on the United States was highlighted, its achievements in certain areas, the problems it was facing, or its contribution to the struggle against fascism.

Very few works on Canada came out in the Soviet Union in the pre-World War II period, and these were of a purely applied nature. The most outstanding among them was Dmitry Pavlov's book on the Canadian grain economy [64]. It contained a lot of practical information and—unlike other publications of the time—it was absolutely free of Communist propaganda. It is due to this reason that a special comment from the publishing house was required as a foreword. It stated that the book of Comrade Pavlov gave the richest factual material about the grain economy of Canada. It portrayed Canada as a country bogged down in the economic crisis and suffering the "degradation of agriculture." It also claimed that it lacked "an exhaustive socio-economic analysis of the issues treated in the book" and did not "show ... the growing aggravation of the class struggle and revolutionary movement." In addition to Pavlov's research, several reference works devoted to navigation and hydrography of Canada were published in the pre-war years.

During the World War II, after Germany attacked the USSR on 22 June 1941, the Soviet Union and Canada became allies in the fight against fascism. As a consequence, Canada began to attract much more attention both from the Soviet public and the scientific community. In 1942, diplomatic relations were established between the two countries to facilitate further collaboration against the common enemy. The mutual interest in cooperation was obvious. On the Canadian side, the appointment of L. Dana Wilgress as ambassador to the USSR showed that Ottawa recognized the importance of economic cooperation with the Soviet Union in order to efficiently foster bilateral relations and to better engage with the USSR in international affairs [57].

From the Soviet side, the interest was no less evident. In the same year, 1942, under extreme wartime conditions, Alexander Goikhbarg's brochure entitled "Canada" was published with a large circulation [36]. It contained a lot of reference information regarding Canadian history, geography, and the political system. The overall tone of the study was very positive. In particular, it discussed the "people's representation" in Canada and the high level of its national economy. The brochure ends rather pompously. It stated that the Canadian people "are bowing to the heroic courage of the Red Army and the peoples of the USSR, who are fighting against Hitler's tyranny with such perseverance, endurance and courage."

A similar positive spirit toward Canada is found in a public lecture given by Prof. Isaak Zvavich at the Scientists' Club of Moscow in 1945, which was subsequently published [100]. This lecture emphasized that Canada was an arsenal of the British Empire and highlighted the scale of its military production. It was forecast that in the post-war world the role of Canada would grow, and that it should take an active part in international relations. The prospects of relations between Canada and the USSR were described with great optimism and rested upon the activities of the Canadian Aid to Russia Fund. Zvavich also stressed "the partnership of the Soviet and Canadian peoples, forged in the battles against the Hitler's Germany."

Unexpected and interesting is Zvavich's assessment of Slavic immigration to Canada: "Chased by police persecutions in Tsarist Russia, Russian and Ukrainian peasants brought their dreams of a better social order to the New World. Tolstoyans and Molokans went to Canada in search of truth and justice" [100, p. 8]. He writes that "Russians and Ukrainians have become Canadian citizens. They built up the prairies, constructed roads and cultivated virgin land; they built a region for wheat exports. They sent their representatives to the Parliament of the Canadian Federation—to Ottawa—in order to strengthen their ties with the world, to pursue a peaceful policy towards all friendly countries and resist aggression" [100, p. 9]. Despite the Gouzenko spy affair in 1945–1946 (which was widely publicized in Canada, but completely unheard of in the USSR) and the beginning of the Cold War, the positive trend of Canada's perception in the Soviet Union persisted for several years after World War II.

In the late 1940s, many reference and technical studies (concerning, for example, the aviation industry of Canada, its metal mining, exploration of North, use of water resources, etc.) were published in the Soviet Union.

They were mostly translated from English and, accordingly, free from propaganda. However, the highest achievement of Soviet Canadian studies in mid-twentieth century is "War and Economy of Canada" (1947) written by Isaak Sosenskiy [85]. Relying largely on British statistics, he correctly noted a number of the most important tendencies of post-war development in Canada, including its increasing dependence on trade with the United States. In general, this study is very objective and, surprisingly for the times, its 104 pages contain only a single reference to Stalin.

A turning point in the perception of Canada in the Soviet Union occurred after 1949 and was associated mainly with the escalation of the confrontation between the USSR and the West (the Berlin crisis, the creation of NATO, the emergence of the Soviet atom bomb). In addition, this turning point corresponded to the general tendency of a "tightening of the screws" in the USSR in the late years of Stalin's rule.

The first sharply negative work devoted to Canada was a collection of translated articles entitled "The American North" issued in 1950 [12]. The collection was prefaced by an editorial note and a long introductory article written by the Soviet journalist Isaak Yermashev. He condemned American military preparations in the Canadian North and the "bourgeois position" of the contributors: "Being bound by the interests of their class and the imperialist policy of their governments, expressing the desires of the big American monopolies, the authors had to ignore, embellish and distort much of the information they rely on" [12, p. 8].

In this same vein is the book "Canada: The Patrimony of American Imperialism," published in 1951 by Semyon Shcherbatykh [77]. It represents a striking contrast to the works of Goikhbarg, Zvavich, and Sosenskiy mentioned above. In the first pages of his book, Shcherbatykh claims that "Canada is an aggressive imperialist country, actively participating in the preparation of a new world war by the American–English bloc" [77, p. 3]. The first three chapters describe Canada's dependence on the United States, Canada's sins in the war against the freedom-loving Korean people, and its participation in the UN's aggression in the Korean War. The fourth chapter is devoted to the progressive forces in Canada, fighting for peace.

A sharp change in the tone of the Soviet perception of Canada also can be seen in the travel notes or sketches of persons who visited Canada, published in the USSR in mass editions for the general public. This was a fairly typical literature in the Soviet Union, which focused on what were claimed to be the sufferings of people in the capitalist countries and accordingly extolled the advantages of the Soviet socialist system and life in the USSR. Typical of the genre is a pocket brochure by Boris Zavadsky "Five Years Overseas," published in several editions, one of which involved 150,000 copies [98, 99]. It describes the toils of a common man in a capitalist country, culminating in his happy return to his Russian Homeland. Another such account, entitled "20 Years Overseas" [27], was composed as the story of a Russian migrant from Transcarpathia, who spent 20 years in Canada and in the United States. It should be noted that the reliability of these works and others of this genre is highly questionable. They were a clear product of the state propaganda machine, designed to set the Soviet society against the "saber-rattlers of a new war."

After Stalin's death and the beginning of the Khrushchev's Thaw in the USSR, the attitude towards capitalist countries in general and Canada in particular changed significantly. The "class" approach continued, but it became less belligerent and hardline. Four trends were dominant in Canadian studies during this post-Stalin era and in the general perception of Canada in the USSR. They included the following:

1. More publications of descriptive, technical or reference nature were published in the press;
2. The quality of works on social and human aspects of Canada (economics, history, politics, etc.) increased dramatically;
3. The tone of travel notes and sketches changed radically;
4. Propaganda and ideology still persisted in both academic and popular publications.

The first tendency is best illustrated by a 1957 reference brochure by the Soviet geographer Irina Antonova [8]. It is composed in a completely neutral way and far from ideology. Along with it, a number of directories on Canadian seed production, oil refining, forestry, grain farming, water power engineering, etc. were published in the same period.

The second tendency is represented by the work of A. Lidin, entitled "The State System of Canada" [51], and Rachik Faramazyan's "The Economy of Modern Canada" [30]. The latter is the most typical example of Soviet academic literature of the mid-1960s: on the one hand, it contains a lot of interesting scientific information, on the other hand, it is preceded by an overly ideologically-driven introduction (with quotations from Lenin's works, the CPSU Program, etc.). According to the author, Canada was "a vivid example of the law of uneven economic and political development of capitalist countries in the era of imperialism, discovered by the Great Lenin" [30, p. 5].

The highest achievement of Soviet Canadian studies during the pre-ISKRAN period is the encyclopedic book "Canada and Anglo-American Contradictions," written by Abram Mileikovskij [56]. It occupies a special place in the national historiography, since it was the first work to contain a very long historical essay and a detailed analysis of Canadian trade and economic policy.

The third trend in post-Stalin Canadian studies includes the book "Happiness on Credit: Essays on Canada," by Oleg Feofanov and published in several editions (the second edition had a publication run of 100,000 copies) [32, 33], and "Leaves Are Falling from the Maple Tree" [11] by Leon Bagramov, a man who would later come to embody Soviet Canadian studies. Both works are written in a completely different way than the sketches of the early 1950s cited above. They give a very detailed picture of Canadian life—from its politics, including anecdotes on the Rivard bribery affair to the prospects of forming a common American market. They also give insights into the Canadian people, clubs, and different political views.

Feofanov's and Bagramov's books reflected the trend that was taking shape in the Soviet Union during the years of the Thaw. After Stalin's death, the world (even in Soviet official propaganda) ceased to be "black and white." It became more nuanced and diverse. Foreign artists and musicians began to visit the USSR, European (and later even American) films appeared at the cinema. Foreign students began to study at Soviet universities, and the Soviet people began to take an interest in what was happening in the world.

Traveling abroad (especially to the "capitalist" countries) remained open to very few Soviet people. Therefore, any information about the life abroad (or, as they used to say in the USSR "there, across the pond") was very attractive and much in demand. Sketches by Soviet journalists about the Western countries were published in huge print runs and excerpts from them often were printed in magazines. The number of those wishing to read these books was enormous (they were in high demand in libraries, borrowed from acquaintances, etc.)

The last tendency during this era is represented by the ideology-driven works by Vladimir Sushchenko, who wrote a series of studies on the Canadian economy [86–88], and by Boris Altaev and Konstantin Lomov, who authored the book, "New in the Workers' Movement of Canada" [7]. However, even in their publications, Canada, unlike the United States, was never seen as a potential rival or enemy of the Soviet Union.

In addition, the period from the late 1940s to the early 1960s witnessed the publication of translations of some left-wing Canadian authors, including Stanley B. Ryerson [75], Watt H. Collum [55], and Tim Buck [17–21]. It should be noted that Soviet intellectuals did not swallow uncritically all of what such authors wrote. They had mastered the art of reading between the lines and extracting objective factual information even from such works as those just mentioned. Canada was perceived by most of them as a source of experiences worth studying, the embodiment of better life, and, in some sense, an ideal society.

Canadian Studies in the Soviet Union, 1967–1991

The period from the late 1960s into the 1970s was another turning point in Canadian Studies in the USSR and in the perception of Canada in this country. This was due in no small part to the creation of the Institute of the USA (ISAN), under the auspices of the Academy of Sciences of the USSR. ISAN was a specialized institution that engaged in scientific activities and expertise for the needs of the Soviet government. Although its main focus was on the United States, from the outset ISAN included a Canadian division. Originally, it was merely a sector devoted to the study of Canada. In 1972, however, it was transformed into the Department of Canada that exists to the present day and consists of both a political and an economic sector. In 1974, it was decided to rename the Institute. It became the Institute of the USA and Canada (ISKAN).

ISKAN immediately assumed one of the leading places among the Soviet "think tanks" dealing with foreign policy issues. Work at the Institute was prestigious and highly paid (by Soviet standards). The Institute received generous state funding as well as two buildings in the center of Moscow. Its employees had access to foreign scientific literature and periodicals as well as the opportunity to travel abroad (which was still a rarity in the USSR). Beginning in 1970 the Institute began to publish the monthly scientific journal "USA: Economy, Politics, Ideology," which from its earliest days also regularly published articles on Canadian topics.

From the beginning, the Institute differentiated itself from other Soviet era think tanks by hosting experts and scientists, not party functionaries. Therefore, their views and approaches were not so ideology-driven.

This fact was recognized by Canadians. For instance, Robert A. Ford, [34] Canada's Ambassador to the Soviet Union from 1964 to 1980, noted in his memoirs that, "The Institute of American Studies, headed by Georgij Arbatov, had a reasonably accurate idea of what was happening in the United States, but their reports normally had to pass through the American Department of the Central Committee Secretariat. It was staffed primarily by bureaucrats highly influenced by ideology, with little first-hand knowledge of the United States and interested in presenting analyses that were ideologically sound and satisfying to the leaders" [32, p. 262].

As a result of the Institute's activities, a small group of professional Americanists and Canadianists—mostly economists and political scientists—developed in the USSR (Officially there was no such discipline as political science in the USSR. Scientists dealing with political issues were often called historians or philosophers). The first head of ISKAN's Canadian Sector, then the Canadian Department, was the aforementioned Leon Bagramov He was an international journalist by training. Bagravov's staff included Sergej Molochkov, Arkadij Cherkasov, Sergej Danilov, Liudmila Nemova, Elena Komkova, Evgenija Issraelyan, Nikita Bantsekin, Konstantin Baranovskiy, and others. Some of them still work at the Institute, providing an interesting and important bridge spanning the Cold War and post-Cold War eras.

A second important factor influencing Canadian studies during these years involved significant geopolitical changes, Canada's growing role in international affairs, and changes in Soviet–Canadian relations in the late 1960s and especially in the early 1970s. It is important to note that the increased role of Canada in international affairs was observed and recognized in the USSR. The founder and the first director of ISKAN, Georgij Arbatov, wrote in the late 1970s: "Our interest in Canada is not purely academic. Improvement of Soviet-Canadian relations is an important part of those multilateral efforts that made possible a turn from the Cold War to détente in the early 1970s" [9, pp. 5–6]. Writing in 2002, Arbatov again commented on Canada's increasingly important role during the era of détente: "Canada and Pierre Trudeau personally played their part in the beginning of détente. Canada had an independent foreign policy regarding Cuba, arms control, and other issues... . Destiny intended Canada to be a significant actor in world politics. This country understands many issues better than other countries because of its history and the multinational nature of the state." [42, p. 77]

In the early 1970s, Canada was perceived by the Soviet people as an intermediary between the USSR and the USA. This positive turn was partly explained by the "hockey diplomacy" that began 1972, and the beginning of massive purchases of grain from Canada. These two developments drew Canada somewhat closer to the Soviet Union and separated it somewhat from other capitalist states, most notably the United States. This new tendency had an impact on scientific writing about Canada as well.

The team of the new Institute published its first general work in 1979. It was a collective monograph entitled, "Canada at the Onset of the 1980s" [9]. The book was devoted to a comprehensive analysis of Canada's general economic and political problems, as well as the most pressing issues of the country's development in the late 1970s: the place of foreign capital in the Canadian economy, the role of the state in the development of national energy and science, the development of the North, federal–provincial relations, the situation in the Franco-Canadian province of Quebec, the main features of the party system, the trade union movement, the specifics of foreign trade, and Canada's foreign and military policies.

One of the main tasks of this book, as seen by its authors, was to understand how the general patterns of capitalism were embodied in the concrete socio-economic and political conditions of Canada. The book ackowledged that Canada had become a large industrial capitalist state and had reached a high level of economic development. It concluded that despite being dominated by international, mostly American monopolies ("in the capitalist world there are no two other countries so closely linked as the USA and Canada") [9, p. 16], Canada managed to maintain its identity. The authors emphasize both the academic and practical significance of their study and its importance for the development of Soviet–Canadian cooperation. It was a good start, indeed. The book received positive reviews not only in the Soviet scientific community but, perhaps more important, in Canada too [93]. The reviews commented on the objective, non-ideological approach of the contributors to the analysis of the issues covered in the book.

It is noteworthy that this first monograph published by ISKAN was built on the traditional Marxist scheme, first addressing economic issues. Subsequent monographs prepared by the ISKAN/ISKRAN team were structured around this same model. This has continued to the present day.

"Canada at the Onset of the 1980s" was soon followed by several other overviews of different aspects of Canadian politics and economics, including "Canada–USA: Economical and Political Relations" [60], "The State and Economy of Canada" [10], and "Canada's Modern Domestic Politics" [59]. These books emphasized the importance of studying Canada and its special position of Canada as the northern neighbor of the USSR, a member of the G-7, a country with a unique political life (the coexistence of two nations), a center of the international labor movement, etc. They also detailed the specificity of development and priorities of federal government policy; the administrative processes of the Canadian government; constitutional reform and confrontation between Ottawa and the provinces; the Franco-Canadian problem and Canadian federalism; the existence and conditions of ethnic minorities and the policy of multiculturalism; the policy of the Canadian government towards the Indigenous peoples of the country; the attitude of the Canadian public to the problem of preventing nuclear war, and the development of the Canadian economy and its growing dependence on the United States.

Notwithstanding the important role played by ISKAN, Canadian studies in the USSR were not limited to the activities of that institute. From the early 1970s, serious publications on various aspects of Canadian society began to be published by other Moscow institutes, including Moscow State University, the Institute of General History, and the Institute of Ethnography of the Academy of Sciences, as well as in Leningrad. Notable contributions included the following:

1. *History.* The most outstanding contributions in this field were made by Valerij Tishkov [90], Leonid Koshelev [92], Vadim Koleneko, and Lidija Pozdeeva. Their books included two reference works—"The History of Canada" [84], and a very detailed work, "Canada, 1918–1945" [69]—as well as a number of monographs on such subjects as "The Liberation Movement in Colonial Canada" by Tishkov [91], "The Labor movement in Canada in the Late 1910s and Early 1920s" by Oleg Soroko-Tsyupa [83], and "The Quebec Issue in Post-war Canada" by Koleneko [39].

2. *Domestic and foreign policy.* These political matters were examined by Sergej Danilov in his books, "Canada's Two-Party System: Trends of Development" [23], "The Policy-Making and State Mechanism of Modern Canada" [26] and "Twelve Faces of Canada" [25], by Arkadij Cherkasov in "Foreign Experience

in Exploration and Reclamation of the North" [22], and by Viacheslav Shilo in "Canadian Federalism and International Relations" [78].

3. *Economics.* Late-Soviet works on the economic and trade policy of Canada included those by Boris Aljokhin "Soviet-Canadian Economic Co-operation" [5] and "Canada in World Trade" [6], Vladimir Popov's, "Canada: Features of Industrial Development" [67] and "USA - Canada: Interaction of Economic Cycles" [68], and Alexej Kvasov's "Military and Economic Integration of the USA and Canada" [48] and "Financial Capital and Financial Oligarchy of Canada" [49].

4. *National development.* This area of studies was explored by Lidija Fursova in "Immigration in Canada's National Development" [35] and by Veniamin Agamoglanov in "The Aggravation of the National Question under the Conditions of the General Crisis of Capitalism: the Case of Canada" [1].

5. *Literature.* A study of great importance was produced by the Leningrad linguist Elizaveta Referovskaia, entitled "The French Language in Canada" [71]. It focused not only on the language itself (features of pronunciation, word formation, borrowings, etc.), but also on the history and culture of French Canada. For a long time, this was one of the few books that contained detailed information about Canada during the era of French colonial rule.

In the late Soviet era, Canadian Studies also began to develop in Ukraine. The Kiev historians and ethnographers Arnold Shlepakov, Vadim Evtukh, and Oleg Shamshur published several works on the national question in Canada [76, 79, 97]. The Ukrainian presence in Canada goes back to significant immigration in the late nineteenth and early twentieth centuries. Canadians of Ukrainian ancestry had played an important role in the abandonment of the image of Canada as a bicultural nation and the embrace in the early 1970s of official multiculturalism.

We may say, therefore, that beginning in the late 1960s Canadian studies in the USSR reached a new level, both quantitatively and qualitatively. From a sporadic character, depending either on a momentary conjuncture of events or on the scientific interests of a relatively small number of persons, it developed into a profession.

In the years of Perestroika (1985–1991), the integration of Soviet Canadianists into international networks increased sharply. The number of academic exchanges rose dramatically and censorship restrictions and ideological pressure on scholars gradually disappeared. In 1989, the Soviet Association for Canadian Studies (SACS) was founded at the premises of ISKAN. Before the collapse of the USSR, it managed to hold a single convention at Chernivtsi University.

CANADIAN STUDIES IN POST-SOVIET RUSSIA: FROM CRISIS TO BLOOM

The late 1990s to the early 2000s were perceived by many Russians as a time of great hopes and expectations. It was seen as a period that would lead Russia to enter fully into the globalized economy, and to rapprochement with other countries and peoples, including Canada.

After the brief domestic political crisis of the early 1990s, Canadian studies in Russia began to develop even more rapidly than after the creation of ISKAN (which was renamed the Institute for the USA and Canadian Studies, ISKRAN, in 1991). It should also be noted that in 1999 the journal, "USA: Economics, Politics, Ideology,"was also renamed, becoming "USA-Canada: Economics, Politics, Culture." However, developments during this most recent period have differed dramatically from those that characterized the earlier periods of Canadian studies described above.

The first of these developments involves the loss of what had previously been ISKRAN's clear domination in Canadian studies. Initially this was caused by financial reasons and the general crisis of Russian science in the immediate post-Perestroika years. By the 2000s, however, this decline in ISKRAN's stature was a result of the departure of a galaxy of brilliant scientists who had been founders of the Institute. Nevertheless, the ISKRAN team continued its research and published a number of essential works that may be said to comprise the core of the national historiography of Canada [38, 40, 41, 43, 54, 61, 62].

The second most important development has been the emergence of new significant centers for studying Canada both in Moscow and other parts of Russia, and the distinctive division of interests and field of activity between them. ISKRAN has retained the status of a center for studying Canadian economic and political problems, and continues to work on themes that it has emphasized over the decades. Every several years it publishes general works that represent, in fact, high-quality updates of previous years' publications.

New centers of Canadian studies, formed in the regions nationwide, have focused on such topics as on history, philology, law, and studies of federalism. The largest centers arose in Volgograd, Saratov, Bryansk, Chelyabinsk, Magnitogorsk, Tambov, Yakutsk, and St. Petersburg (St. Petersburg University hosts the only department of American studies in Russia). Some specialists majoring in Canadian studies can also be found in Chita, Vladivostok, and Nizhnij Novgorod.

The third development has been the strengthening of the role of SACS, renamed the Russian Association for Canadian Studies (RACS) in 1992. Since its creation, RACS has carried out several important functions including: the promotion of Canadian studies in Russia (public lectures, screenings of movies, etc.); the organization of various scientific events dedicated to Canada in Moscow and the regions; and the coordination of contacts between Canadian studies centers in the regions.

It was RACS that supported the emergence of major centers of Canadian studies in St. Petersburg, Kazan, and Volgograd, with St. Petersburg being the most successful of these branches. St. Petersburg State University professor Yuriy Akimov was already exploring different aspects of Canadian history and political life in the early 1990s, well before the establishment of a RACS division there in 1999. The interest in Canadian research in the regions arose independently of RACS, but its continuation and development may to some important degree be attributed to that association.

At the present time, RACS brings together scientists, university professors, students, journalists, businessmen, and employees of state and public organizations. At its foundation, RACS was directed by the late head of the Canadian department of ISKRAN, Vasilij Sokolov, followed by Sergej Rogov, a member of the Russian Academy of Sciences. Today RACS is headed by Tatiana Kuzmina. The association has held major international and all-Russian conferences dedicated to Canada, not only in Moscow but also in other parts of Russia. Biennial conventions are held alternately in Moscow and St. Petersburg (usually in even years), and in odd years the Canadian conferences are organized in St. Petersburg.

During the first 20 years of RACS existence, its work depended crucially on financial support provided by the Canadian government and the International Council for Canadian Studies (ICCS). For example, many Russian Canada experts became ICCS and Canadian government scholarship holders and traveled to Canada for teaching (as visiting professors), for scientific internships, and for research work in Canadian archives and libraries. In 2011, Yury Akimov, who had more than once won ICCS scholarships, received the prestigious Pierre Savard award for the best scientific research publication on a Canadian topic in a foreign language [3].

After the 2012 decision of the Canadian government to end funding for Canadian studies abroad, the number of foreign trips by Russian Canadian experts and the scale of events dedicated to Canada decreased significantly. However, the old traditions are still alive. In April 2017, St. Petersburg State University held the Sixth Canadian Conference dedicated to the 150th anniversary of the Canadian Federation [4], and in December of 2017 RACS and ISKRAN organized a major scientific conference in celebration of the 50th anniversary of ISKRAN. This conference more or less coincided with the publication of a jointly authored monograph entitled, "Canada: Modern Development Tendencies" [80]. Russian experts on Canada are often aided by the Canadian Eurasia Russia Business Association (CERBA). The Chairman of the CERBA Moscow Board, Nathan Hunt, is a permanent participant at the Canadian conferences and round tables in Russia.

All regional offices of RACS, as well as the Canadian department of ISKRAN, continue to function successfully. Among the special interests of Russian Canadianists are Russia–Canada relations and their prospects for development, North American economic integration (NAFTA) and Canada-EU relations, Canadian economic and trade policy, Arctic studies, Canadian military policy, the para-diplomacy of the Canadian provinces in the global and regional context, Canada's political landscape, Canadian federalism, the comparative history of colonization (including the Jesuit missions in New France), Canadian military history, Canada's role in international organizations, multiculturalism in Canada, and Canadian literature. Russian Canadianists not only actively participate in the scientific life of RACS, but also successfully pass on their love and interest in Canada to their students, many of whom choose Canadian studies as topics for their bachelor's honors theses, and master's theses, and doctoral dissertations.

ISKRAN and RACS are also active in publishing books and journals reflecting the achievements of Canadian studies in Russia. In 1999–2002,

Russian Canadianists participated in the publication of the magazine "Canadian Passport" [94], which was distributed in hotels, large shopping centers, and tourist offices in Moscow and in large Canadian cities. It was designed mainly for potential emigrants to Canada and contained many interesting materials on the diverse spheres of Canadian public life. In the fall of 2000, the first issue of the new magazine "Canada", designed for a wide range of general readers, was published with much fanfare. As it happened, however, this promising initiative ended rather quickly when the magazine's editors moved to Canada for permanent residence.

At present, in addition to the monthly journal "USA–Canada: Economy, Politics, Culture," other scientific publications on Canada are regularly published in Russia. The most prominent of them are "Kanadskii ezhegodnik" (Annual Journal for Canadian Studies in Russia) and "Trudy ROIK" (Works of RACS). The former journal was established by Vadim Koleneko, a leading professional well known in Canada. For many years, he was a member of the editorial board of the International Journal for Canadian Studies. In recent years, monographs by Russian Canadianists have been authored not only by scholars in Moscow and St. Petersburg [2, 24, 37, 74], but also by their Canadian studies colleagues from the regions. Among these are works by Il'ia Sokov (Volgograd) [81, 82], Andrej Fedin (Briansk) [31], Ivan Nokhrin (Cheliabinsk) [63], etc. Mention should also be made of the memoirs of Andrej Belonogov, the Russian ambassador to Canada from 1992 to 1998, published in 2011 [13]. This book caused great interest not only in academia, but also among the general public.

In Russia, there also exists an organization that studies the distinct Canadian province of Quebec. Created in 1997, the Russian center "Moscow–Quebec" has been based at the Russian State University for Humanities (RGGU). The center is engaged in the comparative study of the history and culture of Quebec, as well as its modern social and cultural development. It was created with the assistance of the Ministry of Foreign Affairs of the Province of Quebec and the Université de Laval (Quebec). Since its creation it has been directed by Ekaterina Isaeva, whose great contribution to cultural cooperation between Russia and Quebec is recognized on both sides of the Atlantic. In 2015 the center, in collaboration with prominent colleagues from Université de Laval, published in both French and Russian a very interesting book entitled, "Quebec, Canada, Russia: 100 Mirrors" [14].

CONCLUSION

In this chapter, we examined what we believe to be the most important stages in the establishment of Canadian studies in Russia and the main trends in its development over time. Our conclusions may be summarized as follows:

1. The study and perception of Canada in the Russian Empire, the USSR, and today's Russian Federation was and continues to be closely related to the evolution of Russia and its self-representation (even more than to the evolution of Russian/Soviet–Canadian relations). Therefore, there is an obvious connection between the domestic and foreign policy agendas of the observer's society, on the one hand, and the formation of knowledge about the observed society, on the other.

2. During the periods of the Russian Empire, the USSR, and now the Russian Federation, Canada was and still is perceived as "the other," "an alien." At the same time, there has always been an awareness of the significant difference between Canada and its main "other," the United States.

3. The perception of Canada in the Russian Empire, followed by the USSR, and now the Russian Federation has been rather fluid and has undergone important changes over time (see Table 7.1). In our opinion, this is due to the fact that Canada was a young country and remained for a long time "in the shadows" of Britain and the USA. Hence, the Russian/Soviet people had no strong narratives regarding Canada as a distinctive society.

4. Individual scholars and researchers and their particular interests played an important role in the formation and the development of the Canadian Studies in Russia. They influenced the applied nature of early Canadian Studies in Russia and its subsequent professionalization.

5. Canadian studies in the USSR and post-Soviet Russia confirm the critical importance and significant role played by academic centers in the process of institutionalizing area studies. Such organizations as ISKRAN, the Center for North American Studies in the Institute of General History of the Russian Academy of Sciences, the Moscow–Quebec Center, and the Department of American Studies at St. Petersburg State University have been critical in bringing Canadian Studies in the USSR/Russia to its present professional level.

Table 7.1 Russian images of Canada and approaches to its study

Time period	Image	Approach	Dominating evaluation
Mid-XVIII c.–last third of the XIX c.	*Exotic:* Canada as a "wild" country	Amateur/dilettante	Neutral
Last third of the XIX c.–1917	*Progressive:* Canada as a rapidly developing country, as a paragon	Semi-professional/ practical	Positive
1917–1967 (Soviet-pre ISKAN period)	*Class/opportunistic:* Canada as one of the capitalist countries; as a country dependent on the USA; as an ally in WWII	Semi-professional/ professional	Negative/ neutral
1967–1991 (Soviet ISKAN period)	*Opportunistic/class:* Canada as one of the capitalist countries; as a country dependent on the USA; as a rival in the Cold War, as a "bridge" between two superpowers	Professional	Neutral/ negative
1991–to the present	*Progressive/opportunistic:* Canada as a rapidly developing country, as a paragon	Professional	Neutral/ positive

REFERENCES

1. Agamoglanov, Veniamin. 1976. *Obostrenie nacional'ogo voprosa v uslovijah obshhego krizisa kapitalizma (Na primere Kanady)* [The Aggravation of the National Question in the Conditions of the General Crisis of Capitalism (The Case of Canada)], 160. Moscow: University of People's Friendship Press (In Russian).
2. Aggeeva, Irina. *Kul'urnye svjazi jepohi holodnoj vojny: SSSR-Kanada (1950–1970-e gg.)* [Cultural Ties of the Cold War: USSR-Canada (1950–1970s)], 214. Moscow: IVI RAN (In Russian).
3. Akimov, Y.G. 2010. *Severnaja Amerika i Sibir'v konce XVI - seredine XVIII v.: ocherk sravnitel'oj istorii kolonizacij* [North America and Siberia in the Late XVI—Middle of the XVIII Century: An Essay on the Comparative History of Colonization], 369. St. Petersburg: St. Petersburg University Press (In Russian).

4. Akimov, Y.G., and K.V. Minkova (eds.). 2017. *150 let Kanadskoj Federatsii: ot britanskogo dominiona k global'nomu igroku: Materialy VI Kanadskikh chtenii* [150 Years of the Canadian Federation: From a British Dominion to a Global Player: Proceedings of the VI International Conference on Canadian Studies], St. Petersburg, 307, April 7–8. St. Petersburg: SKIFIA-Print (In Russian).

5. Aljokhin, Boris, and Igor Runov. 1983. *Sovetsko-kanadskoe jekonomicheskoe sotrudnichestvo* [Soviet-Canadian Economic Co-operation], 170. Moscow: ISKAN (In Russian).

6. Aljokhin, Boris, and Elena Komkova. 1986. *Kanada v mirovoj torgovle* [Canada in World Trade], 252. Moscow: Nauka (In Russian).

7. Altaev, Boris, and Konstantin Lomov. 1960. *Novoe v rabochem dvizhenii Kanady* [The New in the Canadian Labor Movement], 104. Moscow: Profizdat (In Russian).

8. Antonova, Irina. 1957. *Kanada* [Canada], 84. Moscow: Gosudarstvennoe izdatel'stvo geograficheskoi literatury (In Russian).

9. Bagramov, L.A. (ed.). 1979. *Kanada na poroge 80-h godov: jekonomika i politika* [Canada at the Onset of the 1980s: Economy and Politics], 400. Moscow: Nauka (In Russian).

10. Bagramov, L.A. (ed.). 1986. *Gosudarstvo i ekonomika Kanady* [The State and Economy of Canada], 317. Moscow: Nauka (In Russian).

11. Bagramov, Leon. 1967. *List'a padajut s klena* [Leaves Are Falling from the Maple Tree], 207. Moscow: Molodaja gvardija (In Russian).

12. Baranskij, N.N. (ed.). 1950. *Amerikanskij Sever: sbornik perevodnykh statei* [The American North: A Collection of Translated Articles] with an Introductory Note by I.I. Yermashev, 291. Moscow: Izdatel'stvo inostrannoi literatury (In Russian).

13. Belonogov, Aleksandr. 2011. *Missija v Kanadu* [Mission to Canada], 484. Moscow: MGIMO (In Russian).

14. Berthold, E., H. Dorion, E. Isaeva, and A. Lomakina. 2015. *Québec, Canada, Russie: 100 Miroirs*, 238. Quebec: Universite Laval.

15. Bolhovitinov, N.N. (ed.). 1983. *Istorija SShA* [History of the USA], 4 vols., vol. 1., 1607–1877, 687. Moscow: Nauka (In Russian).

16. Bossu, Jean-Bernard. 1783. *Novye puteshestvija v Zapadnuju Indiju* [Nouveaux voyages aux Indes occidentales], 2 vols. Moscow: N. Novikov.

17. Buck, Tim. 1950. *Pravda o Kanade* [The Truth about Canada], 172. Moscow: Izdatel'stvo inostrannoj literatury (In Russian).

18. Buck, Tim. 1954. *Tridcat'let kommunisticheskogo dvizhenija v Kanade (1922–1952)* [Thirty Years of the Communist Movement in Canada], 240. Moscow: Izdatel'stvo inostrannoj literatury (In Russian).

19. Buck, Tim. 1957. *Oktjabr'kaja revoljucija i kanadskoe rabochee dvizhenie* [The October Revolution and the Canadian Labor Movement], 24. Moscow: Gospolitizdat (In Russian).

20. Buck, Tim. 1966. *Narod Kanady protiv monopolij: Za novuju jekonomich-eskuju politiku Kanady* [The Canadian People Against Monopolies: For the New Economic Policy of Canada], 95. Moscow: Progress (In Russian).
21. Buck, Tim. 1972. *Lenin i Kanada* [Lenin and Canada], 184. Moscow: Progress (In Russian).
22. Cherkasov, Arkadij. 1985. *Zarubezhnyj opyt issledovanija i osvoenija Severa* [Foreign Experience in Exploration and Reclamation of the North], 181. Moscow: VINITI Press (In Russian).
23. Danilov, Sergej. 1982. *Dvuhpartijnaja sistema Kanady: tendencii razvitija* [Canada's Two-Party System: Trends of Development], 269. Moscow: Nauka (In Russian).
24. Danilov, Sergej. 2012. *Jevoljucija kanadskogo federalizma* [Evolution of Canadian Federalism], 303. Moscow: HSE Press (In Russian).
25. Danilov, Sergej, and Arkadij Cherkasov. 1987. *12 lic Kanady* [12 Faces of Canada], 300. Moscow: Mysl' (In Russian).
26. Danilov, Sergej, and Viacheslav Shilo. 1991. *Politiko-gosudarstvennyj meh-anizm sovremennoj Kanady* [Policy and State Mechanism of Modern Canada], 133. Moscow: Nauka (In Russian).
27. Dobra, Pyotr. 1955. *20 let za okeanom: Rasskazy zakarpatskogo kol-hoznika ob Amerike* [20 Years Overseas: The Stories of the Transcarpathian Collective Farmer About America], 147. Uzhgorod: Zakarpatskoe oblast-noe izdatel'stvo (In Russian).
28. Epanchin, Nikolaj. 1913. *Oroshenie i kolonizacija chernozemnyh prerij dal'ego zapada Kanady Obshhestvom Kanadskoj Tihookeanskoj zheleznoj dorogi: Otchet po komandirovke v Kanadu v 1912 g.* [Irrigation and Colonization of the Black Earth Prairies of the Canadian Far West by Canadian Pacific Railway Ltd: Report of Mission to Canada in 1912], 473. St. Petersburg: R. Golike & A. Wilborg (In Russian).
29. Epanchin, Nikolaj. 1914. *Kanadskij zakon o zerne izdanija 1912 goda: Materialy k jeleva-tornomu delu v Kanade* [Canada Grain Act, 1912: Materials on Grain Elevators in Canada], 136. St. Petersburg: R. Golike & A. Wilborg (In Russian).
30. Faramazyan, Rachik. 1963. *Jekonomika sovremennoj Kanady* [The Economy of Contemporary Canada], 224. Moscow: Izdatel'stvo inostran-noj literatury (In Russian).
31. Fedin, Andrej. 2016. *Iezuitskaja missija v Novoi Frantsii v pervoj polovine XVII v* [Jesuit Mission in New France in the First Half of the XVII c.], 432. Moscow: Izdatel'stvo Ippolitova (In Russian).
32. Feofanov, Oleg. 1963. *Schast'e v kredit. Zapiski o Kanade* [Happiness on Credit: Notes on Canada], 208. Moscow: Gospolitizdat (In Russian).
33. Feofanov, Oleg. 1966. *Schast'e v kredit. Zapiski o Kanade* [Happiness on Credit: Notes on Canada], 319. Moscow: Politizdat (In Russian).

34. Ford, Robert. 1989. *Our Man in Moscow: A Diplomat's Reflections on the Soviet Union*, 356. Toronto: University of Toronto Press.
35. Fursova, Lidija. 1975. *Immigracija i nacional'oe razvitie Kanady (1946–1970 gg.)* [Immigration in Canada's National Development (1946–1970)], 439. Moscow: Nauka (In Russian).
36. Goikhbarg, Aleksandr. 1942. *Kanada* [Canada], 48. Moscow: Gospolitizdat (In Russian).
37. Issraelyan, Evgenija, and Natalya Evtikhevich. 2013. *Gumanitarnye aspekty vneshnej politiki Kanady* [Humanitarian Aspects of Canadian Foreign Policy], 211. Moscow: ISKRAN (In Russian).
38. Klokov, Vasilij. 2004. *Slovar' francuzskogo jazyka v Kanade: Kvebek i Akadija* [Dictionary of the Canadian French: Quebec and Acadie], 524. Saratov: Saratov State University Press (In Russian).
39. Koleneko, Vadim. 1981. *Kvebekskaja problema v poslevoennoj Kanade* [The Quebec Issue in Post-war Canada], 279. Moscow: Nauka (In Russian).
40. Koleneko, Vadim. 2000. *Katolicheskij sindikalizm v Kanade: teorija i praktika (1920–1960)* [Catholic Syndicalism in Canada: Theory and Practice (1920–1960)], 224. Moscow: IVI RAN (In Russian).
41. Koleneko, Vadim. 2006. *Francuzskaja Kanada v proshlom i nastojashhem: ocherki istorii Kvebeka, XVII–XX v.* [French Canada in the Past and Present: Essays on the History of Quebec, XVII–XX century], 314. Moscow: Nauka (In Russian).
42. Komkova, Elena. 2002. *60 let diplomaticheskim otnoshenijam mezhdu SSSR/Rossiej i Kanadoj* [60 Years of Diplomatic Relations Between the USSR/Russia and Canada]. *SShA–Kanada: ekonomika, politika, kul'tura* (10): 74–86 (In Russian).
43. Komkova, Elena. 2005. *Kanada i NAFTA: itogi i perspektivy severoamerikanskoj jekonomicheskoj integracii* [Canada and NAFTA: Results and Prospects of North American Economic Integration], 349. Moscow: ISKRAN (In Russian).
44. Korf, Sergej. 1911. *Gosudarstvennyj stroj Kanady* [Political System of Canada], 101. Moscow: V. Chicherin (In Russian).
45. Korf, Sergej. 1914. *Avtonomnye kolonii Velikobritanii* [Autonomous Colonies of Great Britain], 453. St. Petersburg: Trenke & Fussneau (In Russian).
46. Krjukov, Nikolaj. 1897. *Kanada. Sel'skoe hozjajstvo v Kanade v svjazi s drugimi otras-ljami promyshlennosti* [Canada. Agricultural Sector in Canada in Relation to Other Sectors of Industry], 232. St. Petersburg: V. Kirschbaum (In Russian).
47. Kruglikov, Nikolaj, and Adam Imshenik-Kondratovich. 1891. *O Kanadskoj Tihookeanskoj zheleznoj doroge: «Zapiska» inzhenerov Kruglikova i Imshenik-Kondratovicha, predstavlennaja gospodinu ministru putej soobshhenija*

[On Canadian Pacific Railways: A Report, Presented to the Minister of Communications by Engineers Kruglikov and Imshenik-Kondratovich], 54. St. Petersburg: Panteleev (In Russian).

48. Kvasov, Alexej. 1985. *Voenno-jekonomicheskaja integracija SShA i Kanady* [Military and Economic Integration of the USA and Canada], 91. Moscow: ISKAN (In Russian).

49. Kvasov, Alexej. 1989. *Finansovyj kapital i finansovaja oligarhija Kanady* [Financial Capital and Financial Oligarchy of Canada], 135. Moscow: Nauka (In Russian).

50. Lakier, Aleksandr. 1859. *Puteshestvie po Severo-Amerikanskim Shtatam, Kanade i ost-rovu Kube* [Journey to the United States, Canada and Cuba Island], 2 vols., vol. 1, 374. St. Petersburg: C. Wulf (In Russian).

51 Lidin, A. 1960. *Gosudarstvennyj stroj Kanady* [The State System of Canada], 69. Москва: Gosjurizdat (In Russian).

52. Lodygin, Dmitrij. 1783. *Izvestie v Amerike o selenijah aglickih, v tom chisle nyne pod nazvaniem Soedinennyh provincij: Vybrano perechnem iz novejshih o tom prostranno sochinitelej* [Information on English Settlements in America, Including Those Who Are Known Now Under the Name of the United Provinces], 60. St. Petersburg: Tipografija Morskogo Kadetskogo Korpusa (In Russian).

53. Luzjanin, Gennadij. 2008. *Rossijsko-kanadskie otnoshenija v konsul'skij period 1900–1922 godov* [Russia–Canada Relations in the Consular Period, 1900–1922]. *Vestnik Cheljabinskogo gosudarstvennogo universiteta* 28 (35, 136): 166–179 (In Russian).

54. Marusenko, Mikhail. 2007–2008. *Frankofonija Severnoj Ameriki* [Francophonie of North America], 2 vols., vol. I, 2007, 353; vol. II, 2008, 290. St. Petersburg: St. Petersburg University Press (In Russian).

55. McCollum, Watt. 1948. *Kto vladeet Kanadoj: Fakty, harakterizujushhie koncentraciju kapitala i kontrol'monopolij nad sredstvami proizvodstva i finansami Kanady* [Who Owns Canada? Facts About the Concentration of Capital and the Control of Monopolies over the Means of Production and Finance of Canada], 195. Moscow: Izdatel'stvo inostrannoi literatury (In Russian).

56. Mileikovskij, Abram. 1958. *Kanada i anglo-amerikanskie protivorechija* [Canada and Anglo-American Contradictions], 503. Moscow: Gospolitizdat (In Russian).

57. Minkova, Kristina. 2017. *Jekonomicheskoe sotrudnichestvo Kanady i SSSR v gody Velikoj Otechestvennoj vojny* [Economic Co-operation Between Canada and Russia]: *Materialy VI kanadskih chtenij «150 let Kanadskoj Federacii: ot britanskogo dominiona k global'omu igroku»* [Proceedings of the VI International Conference on Canadian Studies], 125–142, St. Petersburg, April 7–8. St. Petersburg: SKIFIA.

58. Mizhuev, Pavel. 1905. *Krest'janskoe tsarstvo. Ocherk istorii i sovremennogo sostojanija Kanady* [A Peasants' Kingdom: An Essay on History and Present State of Canada], 118. St. Petersburg: L'vovich (In Russian).

59. Molochkov, S.F. (ed.). 1986. *Sovremennaia vnutreniaia politika Kanady* [Canada's Modern Domestic Politics], 240. Moscow: Nauka (In Russian).

60. Molochkov, S.F., and V.B. Povolotskij (eds.). 1983. *Kanada–SShA: ekonomicheskie i politicheskie otnoshenija* [Canada–USA: Economical and Political Relations], 304. Moscow: Nauka (In Russian).

61. Molochkov, Sergej, Liudmila Nemova, and Elena Komkova. 1999. *Aktual'ye problemy rossijsko-kanadskih otnoshenij* [Topical Issues in Russian–Canadian Relations], 166. Moscow: Nauka (In Russian).

62. Nemova, Liudmila. 2004. *Social'no-jekonomicheskaja politika gosudarstva v Kanade* [Socio-economic Policy of the Canadian State], 356. Moscow: ISKRAN (In Russian).

63. Nokhrin, Ivan. 2013. *Kanada: anglijskaja ili francuzskaja? Utverzhdenie britanskoj kolonial'oj administracii v Kvebeke i pervye popytki uregulirovanija mezhjetnicheskih protivorechij (1763–1791 gg.)* [Canada: English or French? Adoption of the British Colonial Administration in Quebec and the First Attempts to Settle Interethnic Contradictions (1763–1791)], 160. Chelyabinsk: Entsiklopedija (In Russian).

64. Pavlov, Dmitrij. 1934. *Jekonomika zernovogo hozjajstva Kanady* [Canada's Grain Economy], 246. Moscow: SOTSGIZ (In Russian).

65. Pimenova, Emilija. 1906. *Strana velikih ozer (Kanada)* [Country of Great Lakes (Canada)], 104. St. Petersburg: Slovo (In Russian).

66. Pokotilov, Dmitrij. 1894. *Kanadskaja tihookeanskaja zheleznaja doroga i vlijanie, oka-zannoe eju na rost jekonomicheskogo blagosostojanija Kanady* [Canadian Pacific Railway and Its Impact on the Economic Growth of Canada], 26. St. Petersburg: W. Kirschbaum (In Russian).

67. Popov, Vladimir. 1983. *Kanada: osobennosti promyshlennogo razvitija* [Canada: Features of Industrial Development], 200. Moscow: Nauka (In Russian).

68. Popov, Vladimir. 1988. *SShA - Kanada: vzaimodejstvie jekonomicheskih ciklov* [USA–Canada: Interaction of Economic Cycles], 205. Moscow: Mezhdunarodnye otnoshenija (In Russian).

69. Pozdeeva, L.V. (ed.). 1976. *Kanada, 1918–1945: Istoricheskij ocherk* [Canada, 1918–1945: An Historical Essay], 504. Moscow: Nauka (In Russian).

70. Raynal, Guillaume. 1805–1811. *Filosoficheskaja i politicheskaja istorija o zavedenijah i kommercii evropejcev v obeih Indijah* [Histoire philosophique et politique des établissemens & du commerce des européens dans les deux Indes], 6 vols. St. Petersburg: Schnor (In Russian).

71. Referovskaja, Elizaveta. 1972. *Frantsuzskij jazyk v Kanade* [The French Language in Canada], 215. Leningrad: Nauka (In Russian).
72. Robertson, William. 1784. *Izvestie o Amerike Villiama Robertsona, pervenstvujushhego professora v Universitete v Edinburge i korolevskogo istoriografa po Shotlandii* [The History of America]. St. Petersburg: Imperatorskaja Akademija Nauk.
73. Romanov, Dmitrij. 1862. *Monreal': Putevye vpechatlenija* [Montreal: Travel Notes], 23. St. Petersburg: Tipografija morskogo ministerstva (In Russian).
74. Romanov, Konstantin. 2017. *Introduction to Canadian Studies for Russian Students*, 314. Moscow: Mezhdunarodnye otnoshenija.
75. Ryerson, Stanley. 1963. *Osnovanie Kanady: Kanada s drevnejshih vremen do 1815 g* [The Founding of Canada: Beginnings to 1815], 350. Moscow: Izdatel'stvo inostrannoi literatury (In Russian).
76. Shamshur, Oleg. 1987. *"Zolotye dveri" immigracii: chto kroetsja za nimi?* ["Golden Doors" of Immigration: What Lies Behind Them?], 170. Kharkiv: Prapor (In Russian).
77. Shcherbatykh, Semyon. 1951. *Kanada – votchina amerikanskogo imperializma* [Canada—The Patrimony of American Imperialism], 76. Moscow: Gosudarstvennor izdatel'stvo politicheskoi literatury (In Russian).
78. Shilo, Viacheslav. 1985. *Kanadskij federalizm i mezhdunarodnye otnoshenija* [Canadian Federalism and International Relations], 193. Moscow: Nauka (In Russian).
79. Shlepakov, Arnold, Vladimir Yevtukh, and Oleg Shamshur. 1988. *Burzhuaznye koncepcii nacional'yh otnoshenij v razvityh kapitalisticheskih stranah* [Bourgeois Concepts of National Relations in Developed Capitalist Countries], 177. Kiev: Naukova dumka (In Russian).
80. Sokolov, V.I. (ed.). 2017. *Kanada: sovremennye tendentsii razvitija* [Canada: Modern Trends of Development], 432. Moscow: Ves' mir (In Russian).
81. Sokov, Ilya. 2011. *W.L.M. King and the Evolution of Canadian Liberalism in the First Half of the XX-th Century*, 512. Moscow: RIOR.
82. Sokov, Ilya. 2014. *Sovremennaja vnutrennjaja i vneshnjaja politika Kanady* [Domestic and Foreign Policy of Contemporary Canada], 647. Volgograd: Volgograd State University (In Russian).
83. Soroko-Tsyupa, Oleg. 1977. *Rabochee dvizhenie v Kanade (1929–1939)* [The Canadian Labor Movement, 1929–1939], 268. Moscow: Moscow State University Press (In Russian).
84. Soroko-Tsyupa, Oleg. 1985. *Istorija Kanady* [Canadian History], 304. Moscow: Vysshaja shkola (In Russian).
85. Sosenskij, Isaak. 1947. *Voina i ekonomika Kanady* [The War and Canadian Economy], 104. Moscow: OGIZ (In Russian).

86. Sushchenko, Vladimir. 1953. *Jekspansija amerikanskogo imperializma v Kanade posle vtoroj mirovoj vojny* [Expansion of American Imperialism in Canada After the Second World War], 256. Moscow: Izdatel'stvo Akademii Nauk SSSR (In Russian).

87. Sushchenko, Vladimir. 1956. *Anglo-amerikanskie protivorechija v Kanade posle vtoroj mirovoj vojny* [Anglo-American Contradictions in Canada After the Second World War], 184. Moscow: Gospolitizdat (In Russian).

88. Sushchenko, Vladimir. 1958. *Kanada* [Canada], 40. Moscow: Znanie (In Russian).

89. Taube, Friedrich. 1783. *Istorija o aglinskoj torgovle, manufakturah, selenijah i moreplavanii onye v drevnie, srednie i novejshie vremena do 1766 goda; s dostovernym pokazaniem spravedlivyh prichin nyneshnej vojny v Severnoj Amerike i prochih tomu podobnyh veshhej do 1776 goda* [*Geschichte der engländischen handelschaft, manufacturen, colonien und schiffarth in den alten, mittlern und neuern zeiten, bis auf das laufende jahr 1776*], 183. Moscow: N. Novikov.

90. Tishkov, Valerij. 1977. *Strana klenovogo lista: nachalo istorii* [The Maple Leaf Country: The Early History], 175. Moscow: Nauka (In Russian).

91. Tishkov, Valerij. 1978. *Osvoboditel'oe dvizhenie v kolonial'oj Kanade* [Liberation Movement in Colonial Canada], 384. Moscow: Nauka (In Russian).

92. Tishkov, Valerij, and L.V. Koshelev. 1982. *Istorija Kanady* [Canadian History], 268. Moscow: Mysl' (In Russian).

93. Weider G. 1983. *Kanada na poroge 80-kh godov* [Canada on the Threshold of the 1980s], ed. L.A. Bagramov (review). *The Canadian Historical Review* 64 (2): 255–256.

94. *Kanadskij pasport* [Canadian Passport]. http://www.niworld.ru/Statei/canad_pass/o_gurn.htm.

95. *Pis'mo odnogo anglichanina iz Kvebeka* [Letter of a Young Englishman from Quebec-City]. *Vestnik Evropy*, 1803, pt. 10 (16): 272–276 (In Russian).

96. *Pis'mo odnogo molodogo francuza iz Monrealja (Iz nem. zhurn)* [Letter of a Young Frenchmen from Montreal (From a German Review)]. *Vestnik Evropy*, 1803, pt. 11 (20): 279–283 (In Russian).

97. Yevtukh, Vladimir. 1982. *Istoriografija nacional'yh otnoshenij v SShA i Kanade (1960–70-e gody)* [Historiography of National Relations in the USA and Canada (1960–70s)], 160. Kiev: Naukova dumka (In Russian).

98. Zavadskij, Boris. 1952. *Pjat'let za okeanom (Iz kanadskih zapisok)* [Five Years Oversees: From Canadian Notes], 64. Moscow: Pravda (In Russian).

99. Zavadskij, Boris. 1961. *Pjat'let za okeanom (kanadskie zapiski)* [Five Years Oversees: The Canadian Notes], 350. Moscow: Sovetskij pisatel' (In Russian).

100. Zvavich, Isaak. 1945. *Stenogramma publichnoj lekcii professora I. S. Zvavicha, prochitannaja v Dome uchenyh v Moskve* [The Transcript of a Public Lecture Given by Prof. Isaak Zvavich at the Scientists' Club in Moscow], 21. Moscow: Tipografija imeni Stalina (In Russian).

CHAPTER 8

From Individual Scholarship to Academic Institution: Canadian Studies in the German-Speaking Countries and Cultural Diplomacy

Wolfgang Klooss

INTRODUCTION

When journalist, political analyst, and writer Bruce Hutchison (1942) published *The Unknown Country: Canada and Her People*, his book was aimed at an American readership. Canada's ally in the World War II, largely uninformed about its northern neighbor, was to be instructed about a physical and social space which until then had remained *terra incognita* on the American mindscape. Hutchison's pedagogic intentions might also have been and, to a certain extent, could still be addressed at a German readership, for whom Canada's public image remains reduced to a series of clichéd icons such as the maple leaf, hockey, the Mountie,

I am indebted to Konrad Gross and Dirk Hoerder for their groundbreaking work on the emergence and development of Canadian Studies in the German-speaking countries (see references). All English translations of German titles are mine.

W. Klooss (✉)
Trier University, Trier, Germany

© The Author(s) 2019   199
S. Brooks (ed.), *Promoting Canadian Studies Abroad*,
Palgrave Macmillan Series in Global Public Diplomacy,
https://doi.org/10.1007/978-3-319-74027-0_8

lakes, forests, wildlife, a frozen north, and endless space, all of which are repeatedly resorted to by travel bureaus and visitor guides in order to attract tourists to the "Other America." Compared to her powerful neighbor south of the border, Canada receives only limited coverage in Germany's public media so that her history, political, economic, and cultural development or ethnic composition have remained obscure for most Germans. The impact of the fur trade, the story of Québec, Native Canada, the legal system, bilingualism, multiculturalism, etc. are subjects for the academy. At the same time, it needs to be noted that from an institutional point of view Canadian Studies are only located in the peripheral sphere of higher education although the study of Canada— not least due to the impact of research and teaching programs aided by the federal government and the provincial government of Québec—has made it on numerous university curricula in Austria, Germany, and to a lesser extent in the German part of Switzerland.

This chapter will attempt to sketch the history and development of Canadian Studies in the German-speaking countries (taking into account both West- and East-Germany), looking at the role of individual scholars and disciplines in this process as well as the institutionalization of Canadian Studies within the broader framework of higher education and the way in which Canada's cultural diplomacy has been instrumental in promoting research and teaching facilities. This will be complemented by a brief discussion of the shifts in research paradigms that have accompanied the study of Canada in different academic fields and subject areas.

INDIVIDUAL SCHOLARSHIP AND FIRST BEGINNINGS: CANADIAN STUDIES IN GERMANY FROM THE LATE EIGHTEENTH CENTURY TO THE END OF WORLD WAR II

When the local ruler Elector George Augustus of Hanover, who was also King of England as George II, founded Georg-August-Universität, Göttingen, in 1734, the objective of this new university in Lower Saxony was to serve the goals of the Enlightenment. Subsequently, Georg-August-Universität became a center for the collection of travel and exploration accounts which also included reports on Canada. English as well as French texts and documents were quickly translated into German so that during the last two decades of the eighteenth-century Canada became a subject for scientific investigation. Since the German nation states had not participated in overseas expansion,

Göttingen provided second-hand information on a foreign territory for anthropologists, historians, and natural scientists. However, this did not lead to a *systematic* study of Canada (cf. Bitterli 1976: 255–258; Gross 1986: 31). It took another century until Canada became a proper subject of academic concern. The political and economic changes which the former British colony had undergone during the second half of the nineteenth century motivated German scholars to focus on the "Other America." Confederation (1867), the opening of the west and the completion of the transcontinental railway (CPR) in 1885, with their effects on the emergence of an agrarian economy, inspired disciplines such as geography, anthropology, economics, but also Romance Studies to extend their research activities to the northern part of North America.

A case in point is Albrecht Penck's expedition of 1897. Penck, a geographer and geologist from Leipzig, who later founded the famous Vienna School of Physical Geography, took his students to Canada and crossed the country from east to west. More than a decade earlier, Franz Boas, who had started his career as a geographer at Christian-Albrechts-Universität, Kiel, before he became one of North America's leading cultural anthropologists, had already traveled to the Eastern Arctic Archipelago. His journals of the Arctic were assembled at a critical period of change when industrialization challenged the relationship between Indigenous peoples, settler populations and the land. They are still significant documents in Canadian history. Among Boas's pioneering scholarly investigations was *The Central Eskimo* (1888). This Inuit study was the product of field work on Baffin Island which he had conducted in 1883–1884. Later Boas focused on the Kwiakutl of British Columbia and advanced his already previously formulated notion of cultural relativism as an axiom in anthropological research (cf. Boas 1887: 589), thus promoting the idea that "First Peoples' cultures [should] be understood only in their own terms of reference" (Hoerder 2005: 175).

After the turn of the century Romance linguistics and literatures appeared on the scene with a few single contributions. Between 1904 and 1912, for instance, an annual report about new releases in French Canadian writing was made available in the journal *Kritischer Jahresbericht über die Fortschritte der romanischen Philologie* [Annual Critical Report on the Progress of Romance Philology], and in the first volume of the renowned periodical *Germanisch-Romanische Monatsschrift* [Germanic-Romanesque Periodical] Wilhelm Meyer-Lübke who taught at Vienna published an article titled "Das Französische in Kanada" [The French Language in Canada].

By far the most interest in Canada though was seen in the economic sciences. As an immigrant country with a flourishing agricultural economy, Canada became a target for the export of German industrial products and attracted not only the attention of export-oriented companies, but also of those economists who wanted to give advice and pave the way for a more competitive German presence in the Canadian market. Since the *Kaiserreich* had entered the colonial race late, i.e. after England and France had staked their claims, it seemed high time to challenge the economic presence of Great Britain and the United States north of the 49th parallel. A scholarly work which reflected this develoment in scientific research and which spread the message was Anton Fleck's, *Kanada. Volkswirtschaftliche Grundlagen und weltwirtschaftliche Beziehungen* [Canada: Economic Foundations and Global Economic Relations] (1912), the first study of its kind. In his monograph Fleck, from Christian-Albrechts-Universität, took stock of Canada's economy and speculated that Canada might turn into an economic giant of the future. This idea was picked up again in an invective pamphlet against the United States by Egon Berg, published in Dresden shortly before the end of the World War I under the title *Kanada, das Land des 20. Jahrhunderts: Ein politischer und wirtschaftlicher* Ausblick [Canada, the Country of the Twentieth Century: A Political and Economic Prospect] (cf. Berg 1918).

Among the rare studies in the humanities with a Canadian Studies content that were undertaken during the war period was Johannes Kleefisch's doctoral thesis *Untersuchungen zur französischen Kolonialgeschichte in Nordamerika* [Studies in French Colonial History in North America] (1917). Kleefisch was a student of Ernst Robert Daenell, an eminent historian at Westfälische Wilhelms-Universität, Münster, who in 1910–1911 had held a guest professorship at Columbia University, New York. Another of Daenell's students was Helene Stehling who completed her dissertation *Beiträge zur Charakteristik der französischen Geschichtsschreiber des 17. und 18. Jahrhunderts über Französisch-Nordamerika* [Contributions to the Characterization of the French Historiographers of the 17th and 18th Centuries on French North America] in 1919. She was among the first female students who were permitted to enter university after Prussia had opened the 'academic gates' to women in 1908. With her thesis, she became the first German woman to contribute to the study of Canada.

After World War I, the economic sciences and geography were foremost in their investigations into Canadian subject matters, paying particular attention to questions concerning settlement geography, as, for example, W. Tuckermann from Mannheim's Handelshochschule [The Mannheim School of Commerce] proved with his brief study *Das Deutschtum in Kanada* [Germanness in Canada] (1928). In a similar vein works by Louis Hamilton (1920) and Heinz Lehmann (1931) looked at the history of French and German settlement in North America.

During the 1920s and 1930s, studies on Canada were influenced by the fact that Germany had lost the war. When Hamilton, who taught at the Handelshochschule in Berlin, presented a general survey on Canada (cf. Hamilton 1921), he criticized Germany for having underestimated Canada's economic potential and its meaning for the victory of the allied powers and, especially for England. In the following years, Germany's ignorance about North America and the English Dominions also caused a change of directions in English Studies. Subsequently, both the United States and Canada became targets for scholarly investigations—among them "Die Selbständigkeitsbestrebung in den englischen Kolonien" [The Striving for Independence in the English Colonies] (1925) by Anglicist Wilhelm Dibelius from Friedrich-Wilhelm-Universität, Berlin. In his article Dibelius claimed that "Germans before the war had naively believed that Britain would be deserted by her colonies and Dominions which would bring about the fall of the British Empire" (Gross 2014: 4). Dibelius from then on supported and promoted further studies in his field. This resulted in the first two doctoral dissertations on English-Canadian writing which were supervised by Dibelius's disciple Friedrich Schönemann (cf. von Mensenkampff 1935; von Kieseritzky 1935). In 1936, Schönemann was appointed first Chair of American Studies at Friedrich-Wilhelm-Universität, a position he lost immediately after the Second World due to his previous membership in the *National Socialist Party of Germany*. This also meant the end of Canadian Studies within the realm of English Studies. In hindsight, it becomes obvious that the humanities had remained in the background and only sporadically contributed to the advance of Canadian Studies in Germany during the first half of the twentieth century.

An exceptional case among Germany's "Canadianists" of that period was Carl Schott. His post-doctoral thesis (*Habilitationsschrift*) *Landnahme und Colonisation in Canada, am Beispiel Südontarios* [Land Claims and Colonisation in Canada. The Example of Southern Ontario] was published by the Department of Geography of Christian-Albrechts-Universität in 1936. This study in the field of physical and social geography quickly became a classic that was also favourably received in Canada where it exercised a significant influence on the institutionalization of geography as an academic discipline (cf. Lenz 1979). It appears safe to suggest that the contributions of Handelshochschule Mannheim and Schott's scholarship established the basis for the systematic study of Canada in the twentieth century.

After Germany had succumbed to the rise of fascism and a dictatorial regime that led the country into another world war, Canada more or less disappeared from the university syllabus. This scholarly neglect for the northern neighbor of the United States during the late 1930s and 1940s carried on well into the era of the Cold War which saw a paramount presence of the US in the Federal Republic of Germany (FRG) and of the Soviet Union in the German Democratic Republic (GDR). Canada did not even occupy a marginal position in public life or the academy.

THE DISAPPEARANCE OF CANADA IN POST-WAR GERMANY

Among the three Allied Powers (France, Great Britain, and the United States) that controlled West Germany after the World War II (cf. Stirk 2009), the United States was by far the strongest and most influential. The *European Recovery Program* (Marshall Plan) which became effective on 3 June, 1948, was essentially meant to provide American financial aid for Europe during post-war reconstruction in order to promote world peace and the general welfare. It was particularly important for the recovery of Germany, but only affected the Federal Republic. While the US exercised not only an overwhelming political, but also cultural influence on the orientation of the FRG during the following decades, the German Democratic Republic looked eastward. Beyond the Iron Curtain, where the fourth Allied Power, the Soviet Union, was in control, the America of Eisenhower, Kennedy, Johnson, Nixon, and their successors was perceived as a capitalist–imperialist threat and opponent of the USSR. Whereas it was this eastern orientation that prevented the implementation of Canadian Studies at universities in the GDR, it was, on the other hand, the close ties to the United States that pushed Canadian Studies to the margin at institutions of higher education in the FRG. In West Germany,

studies on Canada came under the spell of American Studies which identified North America largely with the US. Subsequently, interdisciplinary
programs focusing on the United States were institutionalized at Freie
Universität, Berlin, Johann Wolfgang Goethe-Universität, Frankfurt,
Johannes Gutenberg-Universität, Mainz, and Ludwig-Maximilians-
Universität, München, to name only some of the oldest and more prominent centers for American Studies. In 1946, the US had already started
its Fulbright programs of scholar and student exchanges "to spread the
message of democracy – and perhaps [its] hegemony – in post-World War
Two societies [...]" (Hoerder 2005: 247).

Simultaneously, the US fostered the establishment of Amerika-
Häuser (America Houses), later named Kennedy-Häuser, in cities such
as Darmstadt, Frankfurt, Freiburg, Hamburg, Hannover, Heidelberg,
Köln, München, Nürnberg, Stuttgart, Tübingen, Vienna, West-Berlin
et al. This was clearly an act of cultural diplomacy. As American government institutions they were to provide the opportunity for German
and Austrian citizens to learn more about American culture and politics in order to strengthen transatlantic relationships. In these circumstances, it comes as no surprise that only a few German scholars
included Canadian issues in their research and teaching. Among
them was again Carl Schott, who accepted an offer from Philipps-
Universität, Marburg, in 1955. His appointment marked the beginning
of Marburg's "Canada School of Geography" which paved the way for
"Marburg University as a later center for Canadian Studies" (Gross
2014: 5) in Germany.

Furthermore, it turned out to be a favourable coincidence that Alan
Coatsworth, a Canadian businessman, donated a substantial amount of
Canadiana to the library of Philipps-Universität which was systematically
complemented during the following decades to become Germany's first
interdisciplinary Canadian Studies library. In addition, Coatsworth provided free accommodation for Marburg students in his Toronto home.
Among them was Paul Goetsch, a student of English, who in 1961
completed the first postwar German PhD in Anglo-Canadian Studies
with a dissertation on Hugh MacLennan (cf. Goetsch 1961) and who
became a leading scholar in the field of English-Canadian writing. Two
decades later, Anglicist Walter Pache from the Universität zu Köln presented *Einführung in die Kanadistik* [Introduction to Canadian Studies]
(1981), another basic study and pioneering work.

Goetsch's investigation was largely concerned with questions of identity construction and national self projections, a focus which was then also at the center of historical studies, namely those which looked at Canada's "two solitudes" (cf. Hauser 1964; Jürgensen 1967, 1968, 1971). As Konrad Gross from Christian-Albrechts-Universität, another pioneer among the German Canadianists, has argued, it was the Revolution tranquille of the 1960s and De Gaulle's controversial exclamation "Vive le Québec libre!" in Montréal (1967) which not only registered in Germany, but put Canada on the public as well as academic map and subsequently also determined the orientation of French–Canadian Studies (cf. Gross 1986: 34). As a consequence of the ongoing language debate in Québec, the emphasis was clearly on linguistics. Hans-Josef Niederehe from Universität Trier (cf. Niederehe and Schroeder-Lanz 1977) and Lothar Wolf, Universität Augsburg, (cf. Wolf 1981) were among the first to conduct studies on the French language in Canada. Interestingly, it took another ten years until the political sciences appeared on the scene. When Rainer-Olaf Schultze's (1977) dissertation *Politik und Gesellschaft in Kanada* [Politics and Society in Canada] appeared, this monograph opened the path for further comparative research on Canada's and Germany's social and political systems.

The aforementioned works from different disciplines, published between 1961 and 1981, demonstrate that this was a period when Canadian Studies became more visible in the West-German academy. *Anglistentag*, the association of German professors of English, had been a closed shop with little inclination to open its annual conventions to Canadian topics. Now things began to change and Canadian Studies slowly began to mature—a development that could also be observed in Austria and the German part of Switzerland, although on a smaller scale. To a much lesser degree, this holds true for the GDR which until the end of the Cold War had shown interest in North America's First Nations and their struggle for sovereignty (cf. Toth, esp. 2012: 183–221), while, on the other hand, scholarly investigations with a Canadian Studies content were hardly undertaken. When academic works on Canada recorded a significant increase in the 1980s, among them were a general introductory volume by GDR author Robert Riem, entitled *Die Länder der Erde: Kanada* [The Countries of the Earth: Canada] (1985), and a scholarly essay collection (1987) edited by Erhard Rosenkranz from Friedrich-Schiller-Universität, Jena, which covered areas such as Physical Geography, Sociology, Urban Studies, Architecture, Economics, History, Literature,

Media, the Fine Arts and Languages (cf. Rosenkranz 1987). It was also during this decade when mutual perceptions between Canada and the German Democratic Republic evolved more strongly (cf. Meune 2010).

What has not been mentioned yet is the impact of the Vietnam War on the German perception of the United States. The war led to a widespread anti-Americanism and in turn moved Canada more to the foreground. The need to differentiate more accurately between the two North-American states had also a favourable influence on the development of Canadian Studies.

As this brief overview indicates, it took nearly 35 years after the end of the World War II to integrate Canada into the academic syllabus in the German-speaking countries. During this period, Canadian cultural diplomacy functioned as a major driving force.

The Institutionalization of Canadian Studies and Cultural Diplomacy

When approximately 50 scholars, all of them commited to the study of Canada, assembled at Theodor-Heuss-Akademie in the small town of Gummersbach near Cologne in February 1977, this marked a first step towards the institutionalization of Canadian Studies in the German-speaking countries. The meeting had been initiated by the Canadian Embassy at Bonn and can be considered a first act of cultural diplomacy responding to the post-war cultural policy of the US in the Federal Republic of Germany. Previously, the Embassy had undertaken a survey with the objective "to trace the Canadian Studies potential in German cultural and academic institutions" (Gross 2004: 12). Among the discoveries was the University of Trier where Hans-Josef Niederehe (French linguistics) and Hellmut Schroeder-Lanz (geography) were active at the time. They had already organized a Québec week with the financial aid of the Government of Québec in June 1976. The focus of the follow-up symposium in October of the same year was on "Canada and the Canadian Arctic." This time the embassy provided generous support. And in 1977, with the support of La Délégation générale du Québec at Düsseldorf, the *Centre d'Études Québécoise à l'Université de Trèves* was founded. In this way, the University of Trier emerged as an institution of higher education which set an early example for the further development of Canadian Studies in the FRG.

A few months later, at the Gummersbach meeting, the scope of disciplines was much broader. It comprised numerous fields including Anglophone and Romance Studies, Geography, History, Economics as well as Political Science, and indicated the potential for a future treatment of Canada in the academy. Fortunately, Ambassador John G.H. Halstead was not only convinced of the long-term effects of cultural diplomacy, but even became a highly committed supporter of Canadian Studies. During his years at Bonn, the Embassy reacted towards what Thomas Symons, the founding president of Trent University, had complained about in *To Know Ourselves: The Report of the Commission on Canadian Studies* [CCS] (1975), namely that "the general domestic neglect of Canadian studies ha[d] [...] been closely paralleled by a neglect of Canadian studies abroad" because "[t]here ha[d] been a basic failure to recognize the importance of external cultural policy and to provide adequately for its support" (Symons 1975: 290). According to the CCS, "self-knowledge was not to imply self-centredness, it was to place state and society in the wider [western] world" (Hoerder 2005: 237).

Canada's new self-awareness and the acknowledgement of a policy that would foster her perception and recognition abroad built on previous investigative activities, notably the *Royal Commission on National Development in the Arts, Letters and Sciences* (Massey Commission) of 1949 and measures like the establishment of the Canada Council in 1957. Foremost, however, it was the optimistic spirit of the Centennial celebrations (1967) which showed a matured and self-conscious Canada and that helped to encourage Canadian Studies outside Canada. The first meeting at Gummersbach took place a decade later and was followed by two additional conventions with even greater participation in 1978 and 1979. It was on 22 February 1979, after extensive debates, that the unanimous decision was made to form a German-speaking association. As Gross writes,

The name *Gesellschaft für Kanada-Studien in deutschsprachigen Ländern/ Association for Canadian Studies in German-Speaking Countries* was chosen with care, because authorities in the German Democratic Republic unfortunately barred their Canadianists from joining, although they gave permission to some to attend the annual conferences. 68 founding members from Austria, the Federal Republic of Germany, Switzerland and Denmark elected Rainer-Olaf Schultze [...] as President with Karl Lenz and Franz K. Stanzel as Vice-Presidents during the fourth Gummersbach conference in 1980. At this meeting Ambassador Halstead as "godfather" of the GKS was offered the first honorary membership. (Gross 2004: 14)

Not least among the doubts and uncertainties that had preceded the foundation of GKS was the question of the appropriateness of an academic forum devoted to the study of a country that was only a middle power. Would the association be able to attract enough scholars or would it not be advisable to integrate a Canada section in the *Deutsche Gesellschaft für Amerika-Studien/German Association for American Studies?*

Fortunately, such doubts were soon cast aside. It became quickly obvious that the "Other America" offered itself for comparative studies with Germany and Europe in a variety of fields, while at the same time the differences in the historical, political, social, legal, and linguistic formation of Canada and the United States also became subjects for scholarly scrutiny. "In addition, Canada served as an interesting case study for the history and management of immigration, multicultural policies, the English-French dualism, bilingualism, Quebec seperatism, regionalism, and First Nations and Inuit cultures" (Gross 2004: 13). Moreover, Canada's literary production was steadily increasing. When Margaret Atwood delivered an address to the participants of the 1979 Gummersbach conference, this gave further impetus for the foundation of the trilingual *Gesellschaft für Kanada-Studien in deutschsprachigen Ländern/Association for Canadian Studies in German-Speaking Countries/Association d'Études Canadiennes dans les pays de lange allemande* (GKS) the following year.

Although the Canadian Embassy remained highly supportive, it retreated to the background, having played an important role in facilitating the birth of the GKS. The seat of the association moved from Gummersbach to Grainau at the bottom of Germany's highest mountain, the Zugspitze. Since 1981 its annual conventions (with only one exception) have taken place at Grainau. Together with six other Canadian Studies associations, GKS became a founding member of the *International Council for Canadian Studies/Conseil international d'études canadiennes* (established at Halifax in 1981). As an association representing more than one country, it set the example for the *Nordic Association for Canadian Studies* which was founded at Aarhus (Denmark) in 1984.

While the few German Canadianists working in the GDR had not been allowed by their government to participate in the Gummersbach meetings, they were now permitted to attend the Grainau conferences. However, the ideological gap between the FRG and GDR remained quite noticeable: the East-German colleagues had to register under

Kanadaistischer Arbeitskreis der DDR [Canadian Working Group of the GDR]. After the fall of the Berlin Wall in November 1989, they joined GKS at the Grainau conference in February 1990.

CANADIAN STUDIES IN THE ERA OF GKS

When Canada had been studied at all at German universities after the World War II, this had happened under the umbrella of North American Studies, Commonwealth Studies (later Postcolonial Studies) or Francophone Studies worldwide. Although with the birth of GKS this contextual positioning of Canadian Studies did not change rapidly, the foundation of the association marked a visible shift in paradigm as Canada was increasingly conceived of as an academic subject in its own right and where interdisciplinarity stood out as a distinct feature of this particular area of research and teaching. Accordingly, from the first Grainau symposium on "Kanada und die Probleme der 80er Jahre / Canada and the Problems of the 80s / Le Canada et les problèmes des années 80" (1981) to the most recent on "GeschichteN / HiStories / HistoireS" (2018) the convenors have subscribed to this notion by a theme-oriented conference design with numerous disciplines contributing to the annually changing topics. These conference topics have often focused on current public debates in Canada. Therefore, the anglophone-francophone binary as well as Québec culture, Indigenous and gender issues, the Canadian north, climate change, regionalism, globalization, but also technological advance and the media have repeatedly received attention. In addition, the conferences have followed a cross-hermeneutic approach which has had German and other non-Canadian participants as well as Canadian scholars share their views. Unlike the *Canadian Association for Canadian Studies*, founded in 1973, which had "restricted itself to Canadian Studies by Canadian scholars [...] and [had] remained aloof from outside perspectives" (Hoerder 2005: 243–244), GKS has lived up to its credo and has always offered multiple and transnational perspectives on the issues at stake. (For conference topics and international participation see GKS website and Gross 2004: 16–20.)

Moreover, Grainau has become a meeting place for Canadianists and cultural diplomats from abroad. It is there where, with the help of a special *Outreach Program*, introduced by the *Department of Foreign Affairs and International Trade* (DFAIT) in 2003, East European Canadianists have gathered for many years. It is there where the *European Network for Canadian Studies* and the Executive Board of the *International Council for Canadian Studies* met in February 2004. Grainau has also regularly hosted the representatives of various Canadian diplomatic missions in Europe or officers from DFAIT in Ottawa, among them the former Minister of Foreign Affairs and current Ambassador to Germany as well as special envoy to the European Union, political scientist Stéphane Dion. Already in 1992 Dion gave the keynote on "Les mesures pour accroître la proportion de femmes dans la fonction publique," when the newly formed Women Studies section was responsible for the general conference theme, "Geschlechterrollen und Institutionen in Kanada / Gender Differences and Institutions in Canada / Différences du sexe et institutions au Canada." Other keynote speakers from Canada have included the Québec politician Jacques Parizeau (1986), the *Globe and Mail* columnist Jeffrey Simpson (1987), Naullaq Arnaquq from the Baffin Divisional Board of Eduction (1994), Mary Simon, Ambassador for Circumpolar Affairs (1996), and former Governor General Edward Schreyer (2001). Among the prominent writers and artists who have visited Grainau are Jeannette Armstrong, Margaret Atwood, Herménégilde Chiasson, George Elliott Clarke, Ken Gass, Aritha van Herk, Adeena Karasick, Janice Kulyk Keefer, Robert Kroetsch, Antonine Maillet, Eli Mandel, Pierre Mathieu, Marco Micone, David Adam Richard, Rick Salutin, Stephen Scobie, Drew Hayden Taylor, Judith Thompson, Guillermo Verdecchia, Fred Wah, and Rudi Wiebe.

Grainau has also become the site where serious research on Canada is an expectation and where outstanding contributions to research and teaching in Canadian Studies receive special recognition. For instance, GKS provides travel grants to Canada for students who work on a master thesis with a Canadian Studies content, while the Gouvernement du Québec awards a *Prix d'excellence* for an examination thesis dealing with francophone Canada. A special travel fellowship is awarded by the Gallery CreARTion of the late Jürgen Sasse for a graduate study on First Nations and the Inuit. Complementing these annual funding activities, the *Stiftung für Kanada-Studien* [German Foundation for Canadian Studies], which was established upon the initiative of GKS and the Canadian Embassy in 1996, generously supports academic, artistic or journalistic ventures for which research in Canada is indispensable. This includes projects in the Natural Sciences as well as Medical Studies. Apart from non-scholarly investigations, since 2008 the foundation has exclusively funded PhD and postdoctoral theses. All in all, more than 100 projects have been promoted so far.

During the course of GKS's almost forty-year history numerous adjustments had to be made. Since the individual disciplines involved pursue different theoretical, methodological, and empirical strategies, they have been repeatedly reviewed and recast according to changes in research paradigms, and new subject areas have been added. This development is shown, for instance, by the example of economics. Notwithstanding that Germany's economic sciences contributed significantly to the study of Canada in the first part of the twentieth century, German economists have played a limited role in the activities of GKS. In contrast to the humanities or social sciences, economics employs a methodological rather than an area studies approach that is not especially interested in particular nations or societies. Although economic topics have regularly appeared on the association's conference programs it has been mostly Canadian speakers who addressed these problems, some of whom also held visiting professorships at local Canadian Studies Centres in Germany or Austria. On the other hand, Women and Gender Studies as well as Indigenous Studies are prominent among those subject matters that have extended the scope of GKS so that nowadays the association comprises six cross-area sections in which different disciplines are paired: (1) Language, Literature and Culture in Anglophone Canada; (2) Language, Literature and Culture in Francophone Canada; (3) Women and Gender Studies; (4) Geography and Economics; (5) Political Science and Sociology; (6) Indigenous and Cultural Studies. A seventh section is devoted to History. In addition a Young Scholars Forum, initiated by students in 2001 and subsidized by an annual grant from the *Foundation for Canadian Studies,* complements the range of activities at the annual conventions. At the same time, the Young Scholars Forum organizes its own theme-based conferences at different universities in Austria and Germany (cf. Banauch et al. 2010). Mention should also be made of the Teachers Workgroup which also meets at Grainau where it discusses issues relevant to the teaching of Canadian subject matters in high schools. The group's chairman, Albert Rau, has collected and continuously updated material that is available in online data bases. (See also contributions of the 1980s and 1990s by Düsterhaus, Franzbecker, Glaap, Gulden, and Rau).

Soon after its creation GKS launched both a newsletter and the scholarly periodical *Zeitschrift der Gesellschaft für Kanada-Studien* (1981). With the release of the 21st volume in 1992, the journal was renamed *Zeitschrift für Kanada-Studien.* A third publication of the

GKS, the series *Schriftenreihe der Gesellschaft für Kanada-Studien*, was launched in 1991. The first volume was a collaborative effort involving members of the *British Association for Canadian Studies* (BACS) and GKS. (See Easingwood et al. 1991.)

Since 2005 GKS has offered a set of virtual Canadian Studies courses in fields such as Anglophone and Francophone Canadian Languages, Literatures and Cultures, Geography, History or Native Studies, administered by Verena Schnabel from the University of Würzburg and Annekatrin Metz from the Centre for Canadian Studies at Trier University. These online courses are taught by colleagues from different universities and have been well received. They are aimed also at students who are not necessarily enrolled in a Canadian Studies programme.

The year 1989 marked a significant change in the history of GKS, when in the autumn the Iron Curtain was opened and the Berlin Wall came down. In the course of Germany's re-unification more and more colleagues from the former GDR joined the association, and in November 1991, upon the request of the Canadian Embassy, the interdisciplinary *Zentrum für Kanada-Studien an der Universität Trier*, which had been officially established as a central scientific institution of the university earlier that year, offered a special cross-area workshop to the "newcomers" from Chemnitz, Dresden, (East) Berlin, Greifswald, Jena, Leipzig, Rostock, etc. Generously supported by the Embassy, this particular event turned into a successful introductory seminar on Canada and resulted in a special publication by Canadianists from Trier and four other German universities (cf. Braun and Klooss 1992). Again, cultural diplomacy had played an important role in the dissemination of knowledge about Canada and for the future establishment of academic institutions in the new *Bundesländer* (New Federal States). Cultural diplomacy was again evident when the Embassy in Berlin suggested that three visiting professorships be established at East German universities. Upon the recommendation of two GKS jurors (Konrad Gross, Kiel, and Theo Schiller, Marburg), it was decided to allot these professorships jointly to the universities of Rostock and Greiswald, Jena and Erfurt, as well as Leipzig and Dresden. They were to be co-financed by the Canadian government and the receiving universities.

Moreover, it goes without saying that cultural diplomacy had already been instrumental in the foundation of numerous Canadian and Québec Studies centers at Austrian and German institutions of higher education that have emerged since the foundation of GKS (see Appendix). Most of these are informed by an Area Studies concept which allows for a partially cross-disciplinary approach to the study of pertinent subject matters. Among the earliest and most thriving centers the *Zentrum für Nordamerikastudien* at Kiel (1987), the *Zentrum für Kanada-Studien* at Trier (1991), and the *Zentrum für Kanada-Studien* at Marburg (2001) deserve special mention. The establishment of these institutions was preceded by long-term Canadian Studies activities at these universitis in various areas of research and teaching. At Kiel, for example, the first German *Habilitationsschrift* (doctoral thesis) in the field of Anglophone Canadian Studies was completed in 1985 and awarded a prize by DFAIT at the 1986 Grainau conference—upon the same occasion the first German *Habilitationsschrift* in Geography received a special GKS award (cf. Klooss 1989; Wieger 1990)—and geographer Alfred Pletsch from Marburg was the first to receive the prestigious Diefenbaker Award in 1992. Among the centers in the new *Bundesländer*, Greifswald's American and English Studies Department is rather unique, as one of the world's leading Native Studies experts, Hartmut Lutz, has made the institute's Canadian Studies Programme (1994) a stronghold of Canadian Aboriginal literature and other Canadian minority literatures. The three Austrian Canadian Studies Centres at Innsbruck (1997), Vienna (1998) and Graz (1999) have a distinct Cultural Studies orientation with an emphasis on Anglophone and Francophone Linguistics and Literature. Additionally, Leopold-Franzens-Universität at Innsbruck is the home of a *Centre d'étude de la chanson québécoise*, founded by Ursula Moser in 1995 (cf. for a closer scrutiny of Austria's Canadian Studies Centres Völkl 2017: esp. 3–5).

An especially noteworthy case is the *Institut für Kanada-Studien* at the University of Augsburg which was opened in December 1985. It is the first and still the only case of, "a project which was funded jointly by the Volkswagen Foundation, the Government of Canada, and the Bavarian Government." (Gross 2004: 21) Due to the number of disciplines originally involved (English, French, Geography, History, Law, Political Science, and Sociology), the University of Augsburg, which was only founded in 1970, took what was then the unusual step of creating a special Masters programme. Its Canadian Studies institute is the only one that offers a degree specifically in Canadian Studies. Generally, in German-speaking countries, Canadian Studies diplomas are offered under the umbrella of classical disciplines such as English, French, History, Political Science, Geography, etc.

Most of the local Canadian Studies Centres as well as individual Canadianists have benefitted from the long-term support by DFAIT and the Canadian embassies in Austria, Germany, and Switzerland, especially from the funding of visiting professorships and annual book donations. Many of the centers have partnerships with Canadian universities and participate in close collaborations with Canadian colleagues. To this end, the Centre for Canadian Studies at Trier University, for instance, has maintained a partnership with the University of Manitoba since 1985. This partnership has borne fruit in 17 thematic conferences conducted in either Winnipeg or Trier, and in numerous joint publications. Other Canadian Studies centers in Austria and Germany provide similar examples of fruitful collaboration.

Whereas some GKS members are also members of the non-scientific *Deutsch-Kanadische Gesellschaft* (German–Canadian Association) and while the two associations maintain a mutual relationship that involves occasional collaborations, the story of the German Canadian Alumni Club is one that is not particularly successful. The idea to identify alumni and form an alumni group was first put forward in 1992. It took six years to establish the club and it never really became viable or met its objectives.

When GKS was founded in 1980, it had only 68 founding members. Enrolment grew steadily and reached a high point of 714 members in 1997. Distribution according to disciplines was and has remained rather uneven, with Anglophone and Francophone Canadian Studies always in the lead and economics at the end of the line. In recent years, registration has fallen, such that in the spring of 2017 GKS could identify only 506 members. The reasons for this decline are manifold, involving both internal and external factors.

Canadian Studies 'After Bologna' and the End of the Understanding Canada Programme

In June 1999, Europe's ministers of culture met in Bologna to decide upon a common European system of higher education. During the following ten years German universities were forced to change their traditional teaching system, which had been based on the Humboldtian ideal of the unity of research and teaching. The Bologna process led to the adoption of a structured two-stage design with a clearly defined, yet comparatively narrow, consecutive course programme leading to BA and MA degrees. This development is generally referred to as the Bologna process (see Klooss 2007). Subsequently, an already marginal and mostly interdisciplinary subject such as Canadian Studies came under pressure, especially at institutions without a formal Canadian Studies center. More so than prior to the Bologna reforms, it now takes an exceptional individual commitment and an enhanced effort to integrate Canadian content into the regular syllabus.

An even more serious blow to the vitality of Canadian Studies was dealt by the abolition of the Understanding Canada programme. On 1 May 2012 DFAIT announced:

> In the current fiscal context, the decision was made to focus our programming on the department's core mandate first. As a result, we are phasing out the international Canadian studies program, and will be reducing the funding and geographic scope of the International Scholarships Program. (qt. after Thunert 2013: 170)

Although the preceding support measures which included the Faculty Enrichment and Faculty Research grants had been favorably reviewed, adjusted, and approved by the government, the same government canceled the succeeding Understanding Canada effective March 2013. The abolition of this center-piece of Canadian cultural diplomacy (cf. Thunert 2013), which had provided for book acquisitions, visiting professorships, conferences, readings, and artistic performances, and which had given so many Canadianists in the German-speaking countries an opportunity to conduct research on Canada that would later make it into the classroom or into scholarly publications has seriously affected the attraction of Canadian Studies for beginning university teachers, researchers, and students. Therefore, the board of the Foundation for Canadian Studies decided in November 2017 to include in its portfolio travel grants for high school teachers and young scholars as a small compensation for the loss of DFAIT's support.

Nevertheless, even though the future of Canadian Studies in the German-speaking countries does not appear quite as promising as during the thriving three decades that preceded the termination of Understanding Canada, the current picture does not look entirely bleak and lament would be an inappropriate way of coping with the new reality. The post-Understanding Canada situation requires more initiatives independent from Canadian government funding in order to allow Canadian Studies to keep its momentum and remain attractive for scholars and students alike. Due to the activities of the GKS board, the Grainau conferences are nowadays sponsored with bi-annual funding by *Deutsche Forschungsgemeinschaft* (German Research Foundation).

An especially noteworthy project, financed on a large scale by *Deutsche Forschungsgemeinschaft* and Canada's Social Sciences and Humanities Research Council, is the International Research Training Group "Diversity" (IRTG), which brings together scholars and PhD students from the universities of Montréal, Trier, and Saarbrücken. IRTG's website describes the program as follows:

> [It] proposes an innovative research program in the contested fields of diversity, multiculturalism, and transnationalism by examining paradigmatic changes and historical transformations in interpreting multicultural realities in North America (Québec and Canada in particular) and Europe (Germany and France in particular) since the 18th century.
>
> The IRTG Diversity is characterized by regular transatlantic exchanges between academics and doctoral candidates; the exploration of diversity in all its complexities, taking into account the individual, societal, political, and communicative level; taking into account historical developments and path-dependencies shaping current developments and phenomena. (IRTG website)

The IRTG and its principal spokesperson, historian Ursula Lehmkuhl, are based at the University of Trier. It is the home of 18 doctoral students—already the second cohort—who are generously funded for a three-year period. The individual theses are collaboratively supervised by Canadian and German scholars. A third cohort will be recruited in 2019. Regardless of the fact that this is a rather unique programme, it shows that Canada is still conceived as a country worth being studied by academics from abroad and that there are ways to integrate young scholars into this venture, thus guaranteeing the future of Canadian Studies.

Cultural Diplomacy and Academic Independence

Upon first sight and from an external point of view the involvement of the Canadian government in the development of Canadian Studies might appear problematic. It seems to suggest that the study of Canada is a sort of contract research with a predetermined and self-serving objective. The reality is, however, that in the humanities in particular, third party funding by sources outside the academy is not easily accessible. It demands extraordinary efforts to convince university administrations and state institutions of the validity of special study programs such as Canadian Studies. The Canadian Studies community in the German-speaking countries, which has never operated as a mouthpiece for governmental concerns, is therefore grateful for the support it has received from DFAIT and the Canadian embassies in Austria, Germany, and Switzerland. This gratitude is made all the greater by the fact that the Canadian government, through its academic and other cultural diplomacy programs, has never tried to interfere with the findings and teachings of researchers and university instructors, regardless of how critical their view on Canada might have been. Academic independence has never been at risk.

APPENDIX

Canadian Studies Centres in Austria and Germany

Augsburg: Institut für Kanada-Studien
Berlin: John-F.-Kennedy-Institut für Nordamerikastudien
Bonn: Deutsch-Kanadisches Zentrum/German–Canadian Centre
Bremen: Institut für Kanada- und Québec-Studien (BIKQS)
Graz: Zentrum für Kanada-Studien
Greifswald: Canadian Studies Programme
Innsbruck: Zentrum für Kanadastudien
Jena: CanStudies
Kiel: Zentrum für Nordamerikastudien
Lüneburg: Zentraleinrichtung Moderne Sprachen (Abteilung Nordamerikastudien)
Mainz: TransCanada Forum
Marburg: Zentrum für Kanada-Studien
Saarbrücken: Forum Canada
Trier: Zentrum für Kanada-Studien an der Universität Trier
Wien: Zentrum für Kanada-Studien der Universität Wien

Québec Studies Centres in Austria and Germany

Dresden: Zentrum für Interdisziplinäre Franko-Kanadische und Franko-Amerikanische Forschungen/Québec-Sachsen (CIFRAQS)
Innsbruck: Centre d'étude de la chanson québécoise
Leipzig: Québec-Studien-Zentrum
Saarbrücken: Arbeitsstelle für Interkulturelle Québec-Studien und Nordamerikanische Frankophonie

GKS-Presidents

1980–1984: Rainer-Olaf Schultze (Augsburg; Political Science)
1984–1987: Konrad Gross (Kiel; American and Canadian Studies)
1987–1990: Hans-Josef Niederehe (Trier; Romance Linguistics)
1990–1993: Roland Vogelsang (Augsburg; Geography)
1993–1995: Dietrich Soyez (Köln; Geography)
1995–1997: Ursula Moser (Innsbruck; Romance Literatures)
1997–1999: Wolfgang Klooss (Trier; English and Canadian Studies)
1999–2001: Wilfried von Bredow (Marburg; Political Science)
2001–2003: Elke Nowak (Leipzig; Cultural Anthropology)
2003–2005: Dirk Hoerder (Bremen; History)
2005–2007: Alfred Pletsch (Marburg; Geography)
2007–2009: Klaus Ertler (Graz; Romance Literatures)
2009–2011: Hartmut Lutz (Greifswald; American and Native Studies)
2011–2013: Martin Kuester (Marburg; English and Canadian Studies)
2013–2015: Ursula Lehmkuhl (Trier; History)
2015–2017: Caroline Rosenthal (Jena; American and Canadian Studies)

German ICCS Presidents

1991–1993: Hans Josef Niederehe (Trier; Romance Linguistics)
2009–2011: Klaus Ertler (Graz; Romance Linguistics)
2017–2019: Kerstin Knopf (Bremen; American and Native Studies)

Northern Telecom Five Continents Award in Canadian Studies

1985: Walter Pache (Köln; English and Canadian Studies)
1991: Konrad Gross (Kiel; American and Canadian Studies)

Governor General's International Award for Canadian Studies

2015: Wolfgang Klooss (Trier; English and Canadian Studies)

Ordre National du Québec

2005: Ingo Kolboom (Dresden; Romance Studies)
2017: Peter Klaus (Berlin; Romance Studies)

John G. Diefenbaker Award

1992: Alfred Pletsch (Marburg; Geography)
1993: Jürgen Erfurt, (Leipzig; Romance Linguistics)
1994: Wilfried von Bredow (Marburg; Political Science)
1996: Dirk Hoerder (Bremen; History)
2001: Hans-Jürgen Luesebrink (Saarbrücken; Romance Cultural Studies and Intercultural Communication)
2003: Hartmut Lutz (Greifswald; Native Studies)
2004: Christiane Harzig (Erfurt; History)
2014: Helga E. Boris-Sawala (Bremen; Romance Studies and History)

ICCS Certificate of Merit

1994: Hans-Josef Niederehe (Trier; Romance Linguistics)
1997: Claudia Glöckner (Augsburg; Institut für Kanada-Studien)
1998: Annekatrin Metz (Trier; Centre for Canadian Studies)
2010: Albert Rau (Brühl; Teachers Workgroup)
2012: Hartmut Lutz (Greifswald; American and Native Studies)
2017: Bernhard Metz (Freiburg; GKS Treasurer)

REFERENCES

Banauch, Eugen, Elisabeth Damböck, Anca-Raluca Radu, Nora Tunkel, and Daniel Winkler (eds.). 2010. *Apropos Canada/À propos du Canada. Fünf Jahre Graduiertentagungen der Kanada-Studien*. Frankfurt: Peter Lang. Print.

Berg, Egon. 1918. *Kanada, das Land des 20. Jahrhunderts: Ein politischer und wirtschaftlicher Ausblick*. Dresden: Bibliothek für Volks- und Weltwirtschaft 59. Print.

Bitterli, Urs. 1976, republished 1991. *Die "Wilden" und die "Zivilisierten": Grundzüge einer Geistes- und Kulturgeschichte der europäisch-überseeischen Begegnung*. München: C.H. Beck, 1991. Print.

Boas, Franz. 1887. "Museums of Ethnology and Their Classification," *Science* 9 (228): 587–589. Web.

———. 1888. *The Central Eskimo*. Washington: Smithsonian. Print.

Braun, Hans, and Wolfgang Klooss, (eds.). 1992, republished 1994. *Kanada: Eine interdisziplinäre Einführung*. Trier: Wissenschaftlicher Verlag. Print.

Dibelius, Wilhelm. 1925. Die Selbständigkeitsbestrebung in den englischen Kolonien. *Anglia* 147: 104–157. Print.

Easingwood, Peter, Konrad Gross, and Wolfgang Klooss, (eds.). 1991. *Probing Canadian Culture*. Beiträge zur Kanadistik 1. Schriftenreihe der Gesellschaft für Kanada-Studien. Augsburg: AV-Verlag. Print.

Fleck, Anton. 1912. *Kanada. Volkswirtschaftliche Grundlagen und weltwirtschaftliche Beziehungen*. Schriften des Instituts für Seeverkehr und Weltwirtschaft an der Universität Kiel X. Jena: Verlag von Gustav Fischer. Print.

Gesellschaft für Kanada-Studien. www.kanada-studien.org.Web.

Goetsch, Paul. 1961. *Das Romanwerk Hugh MacLennans. Eine Studie zum literarischen Nationalismus in Kanada*. Hamburg: Cram, de Gruyter. Print.

Gross, Konrad. 1986. Die Entwicklung der Kanadastudien. In *Kanada: Geschichte. Politik. Kultur*. Gulliver 19, ed. Wolfgang Klooss and Hartmut Lutz, 30–36. Berlin: Argument-Verlag. Print.

———. With the Assistance from Albert-Reiner Glaap and Marcel M. Feil. 2004. Twenty-Five Years Gesellschaft für Kanada-Studien: Institutional Memory. In *Twenty-Five Years Gesellschaft für Kanada-Studien: Achievements and Perspectives*, ed. Dirk Hoerder and Konrad Gross, 11–29. Beiträge zur Kanadistik 12. Schriftenreihe der Gesellschaft für Kanada-Studien. Augsburg: Wißner-Verlag. Print.

———. 2014. Canadian Studies in Germany and Europe. Ms. Kiel, p. 14. Print.

Grünsteudel, Günther (ed.). 1989. *Canadiana-Bibliographie*. Bochum: Brockmeyer. Print.

Hamilton, Louis. 1920. *Der Ursprung der französischen Bevölkerung Canadas: Ein Beitrag zur Siedlungsgeschichte Nordamerikas*. Berlin: Neufeld & Henius. Print.

———. 1921. *Canada.* Gotha: Perthes. Print.

Hauser, Oswald. 1964. Kanada als nationales Problem. *Saeculum* 15: 74–102. Print.

Hoerder, Dirk. 2005, republished 2010. *To Know Our Many Selves Changing Across Time and Space: From the Study of Canada to Canadian Studies.* Beiträge zur Kanadistik 13. Schriftenreihe der Gesellschaft für Kanada-Studien. Augsburg: Wißner-Verlag. Print.

Hutchison, Bruce. 1942, republished 2010. *The Unknown Country: Canada and Her People.* Don Mills, ON: Oxford University Press. Print.

International Research Training Group. "Diversity" (IRTG). www.irtg-diversity. com. Web.

Jürgensen, Kurt. 1967. Die kanadische Konföderation in der Zerreißprobe. *Geschichte in Wissenschaft und Unterricht* 18: 153–170. Print.

———. 1968. Kanada am Scheideweg. Verschärfter Nationalitätengegensatz in der kanadischen Konföderation. *Europa Archiv* 1: 21–29. Print.

———. 1971. Der Nationalitätenkonflikt in Kanada. *Das Parlament,* 5 (June): 13–30. Print.

Kieseritzky, Helene von. 1935. *Englische Tierdichtung. Eine Untersuchung über Rudyard Kipling, Charles G.D. Roberts und Ernst [sic] Thompson Seaton.* Jena: Neuenhahn. Print.

Kleefisch, Johannes. 1917. *Untersuchungen zur französischen Kolonialgeschichte in Nordamerika,* 89. Münster: Westfälische Vereinsdruckerei. Print.

Klooss, Wolfgang. 1989. *Geschichte und Mythos in der Literatur Kanadas. Die englischsprachige Métis- und Riel-Rezeption.* Heidelberg: Carl Winter-Universitätsverlag. Print.

———. 2007. 'Survival of the Fittest'? Die Kultur-und Geisteswissenschaften im Zeichen von Bologna. *kritische berichte. Zeitschrift für Kunst- und Kulturwissenschaften* 35 (2): 19–31. Print.

Lehmann, Heinz. 1931. *Zur Geschichte des Deutschtums in Kanada.* Stuttgart: Ausland und Heimat Verlags-Aktiengesellschaft. Print.

Lenz, Karl. 1979. Entwicklung und Stand der geographischen Kanada-Forschung anhand deutschsprachiger Literatur. In *Kanada und das Nordpolargebiet,* ed. Ludger Müller-Wille and Hellmut Schroeder-Lanz, 11–27. Trierer Geographische Studien, Sonderheft 1. Trier: Geographische Gesellschaft. Print.

von Mensenkampff, Ursula. 1935. *Die 'Grenze' in der anglokanadischen Literatur.* Riga: Plates. Print.

Meune, Manuel. 2010. Der transatlantische Magnet. DDR—Kanada. Die unmögliche Nähe. *Zeitschrift für Kanada-Studien* 30 (2): 11–27. Print.

Müller-Wille, Ludger, and Hellmut Schroeder-Lanz (eds.). 1979. *Kanada und das Nordpolargebiet. Trierer Geographische Studien.* Trier: Geographische Gesellschaft. Print.

Niederehe, Hans-Josef, and Hellmut Schroeder-Lanz (eds.). 1977. *Beiträge zur landeskundlich-linguistischen Kenntnis von Quebec.* Trierer Geographische Studien. Trier: Geographische Gesellschaft. Print.

Pache, Walter. 1981. *Einführung in die Kanadistik.* Darmstadt: Wissenschaftliche Buchgesellschaft. Print.

Riem, Robert. 1985. *Länder der Erde: Kanada.* Berlin-Ost: Die Wirtschaft. Print.

Rosenkranz, Erhard (ed.). 1987. *Kanada: Landeskundlicher Überblick.* Leipzig: Brockhaus. Print.

Schott, Carl. 1936. *Landnahme und Colonisation in Canada am Beispiel Südontarios.* Schriftenreihe des Geographischen Instituts VI. Kiel: Universität Kiel. Print.

Schultze, Rainer-Olaf. 1977. *Politik und Gesellschaft in Kanada.* Meisenheim am Glan: Hain. Print.

Stehling, Helene. 1919. *Beiträge zur Charakteristik der französischen Geschichtsschreiber des 17. und 18. Jahrhunderts über Französisch-Nordamerika,* 160. Diss. Ms. Münster: Universität Münster. Print.

Stirk, Peter. 2009. *The Politics of Military Occupation.* Edinburgh: Edinburgh University Press. Print.

Symons, Thomas H.B. 1975. *To Know Ourselves: The Report of the Commission on Canadian Studies.* Ottawa: Association of Universities and Colleges of Canada. Print.

Thunert, Martin. 2013. Understanding Canada? Zur Beendigung des Förderprogramms für Kanadastudien durch die kanadische Regierung. *Zeitschrift für Kanada-Studien* 33 (1): 169–174. Print.

Toth, Gyorgy Ferenc. 2012. *Red Nations: The Transatlantic Relations of the American Indian Radical Sovereignty Movement in the Late Cold War.* Diss. Iowa City: University of Iowa. Web.

Tuckermann, W. 1928. *Das Deutschtum in Kanada.* Stuttgart: Kohlhammer. Print.

Völkl, Yvonne. 2017. Canadian Studies in the Alps? On the Development and Thriving of Austria's Canadian Studies Centres. Ms. Graz, p. 14. Print.

Wieger, Axel. 1990. *Agrarkolonisation, Landnutzung und Kulturlandschaftsverfall in der Provinz New Brunswick (Kanada).* Aachener geographische Arbeiten 22. Aachen: Geographisches Institut. Print.

CHAPTER 9

Canadian Studies in the Nordic Countries

Robert C. Thomsen and Janne Korkka

INTRODUCTION

The Nordic Association for Canadian Studies/l'Association nordique d'études canadiennes (NACS) operates across all the Nordic Countries—Denmark, Finland, Iceland, Norway, and Sweden. These countries share some historical experiences and cultural traditions, but differ in other respects: for example, the association operates over the boundaries of five different national languages spoken in the Nordic region. As chapters and individual members bring varying national viewpoints to the table, within NACS we remain committed to the study of Canada both on its own and within various comparative frameworks where the rest of North America, the Arctic and the European Union also figure prominently. This shared passion for Canadian Studies has made it possible for us to cooperate closely for over thirty years across five different countries and to form solid ties with many different institutions and sister associations.

NACS covers a very large geographic area: over 3.4 million km², including *Kalaallit Nunaat* (Greenland), that stretches from the Kola

R. C. Thomsen (✉)
Aalborg University, Aalborg, Denmark

J. Korkka
University of Turku, Turku, Finland

© The Author(s) 2019
S. Brooks (ed.), *Promoting Canadian Studies Abroad*,
Palgrave Macmillan Series in Global Public Diplomacy,
https://doi.org/10.1007/978-3-319-74027-0_9

Peninsula to halfway across the ocean on the way to North America. This has always made it a challenge to bring together our members in great numbers. Only one university-level program leading to an MA degree in Canadian Studies has been established in the Nordic Countries, which means that scholars and students working on Canada usually do so within larger programs of History, Political Science, and English or French language and literature. Long distances and the sporadic national and regional division of scholars working on Canada have shaped NACS activities from the early days of the association: its work has been based on the efforts of persistent individual researchers and small groups working at various universities, not on a close-knit network of formally established Canadian Studies Centers. Consequently, students and scholars within the field have all made an extra effort to enable themselves to pursue the study of Canada. When little has been available in terms of a comfortably settled pool of Canadian Studies programs or university jobs, Nordic 'Canadianists' have been used to carving out space for Canada in the context of larger fields of study. In the short term, this perhaps enabled the Nordic Canadian Studies community to better withstand the otherwise devastating impact of the discontinuation of the Understanding Canada programme in 2012. Individuals and small working groups were already used to certain challenges in funding and cooperation between universities and interest groups that other networks then faced for the first time. Increasingly, however, the impact and of the 2012 decision is being felt, and in the long run there can be little doubt that the range of Canadian Studies activities will keep shrinking in the Nordic Countries if the situation remains unchanged.

CANADA AND THE NORDIC COUNTRIES—SIMILARITIES AND DIFFERENCES

Researchers working in the Nordic countries can identify many similarities which motivate closer, multidisciplinary analysis between their corner of the world and Canada.[1] The Nordic region is not one but five countries, but they share an identity-bearing history of developing well-functioning welfare states after World War II, with center-left parties having played major roles in each national parliament. The multi-party systems typical of the region mean that it is considered near-impossible for any one party to emerge as a "natural governing party," as the Liberal

Party of Canada has been sometimes dubbed. Still, the biggest Nordic center-left parties—the various Social Democratic Parties (in Finland, Norway, and Sweden) and Norway's Labour—frequently figure in respective post-war national governments, which typically extend beyond the traditional dividing point between left and the right.

In addition to the commitment to the modern welfare state, the Nordic Countries also share with Canada the geopolitical position of being neighbors to much larger political entities. In the past 200 years, Canada has enjoyed a more stable relationship with the United States than Finland with Russia and the Soviet Union, or Denmark and Norway with Germany. Since the War of 1812, the Canada–US border has not been tension-free, but it has not seen war or military occupation, such as Finland, Denmark and Norway faced from larger neighbors during World War II. The Nordic Countries differ in their post-war alliances: Denmark, Iceland, and Norway are, like Canada, founding members of NATO, whereas Finland and Sweden have remained formally neutral and outside multinational alliances. The latter two, however, continue to deepen their cooperation with NATO, recently through signing a host nation support agreement (in 2014). Denmark joined the EEC (later the EU) in 1973, Finland and Sweden in 1995, and Iceland and Norway remain outside, although Norway in particular has had its legislation and trade relations harmonized with EU legislation and practices. Despite formal differences, the post-war Nordic tendency to deepen ties with international organizations which include Canada, or work in close cooperation with Canada in other regards in pursuit of multilateralism, free trade, and peaceful coexistence, is clear. It provides scholars a multitude of opportunities to examine the long-term subtle differences in the development of societies which seem to be working towards largely similar goals.

One fruitful area in the study of Canada which sparks the interest of Nordic researchers is the analysis of multilingual societies. Finns in particular recognize something very familiar in Canada's formal bilingualism, as Finnish law recognizes both Finnish and Swedish as the nation's official languages. There is also something familiar in how the nationally recognized minority language—Swedish in Finland—is in fact widely used only in some areas of the country. The other Nordic Countries may seem to be officially monolingual, but actually there are two formally recognized versions of the Norwegian language, and while Sweden only recognizes Finnish as a regional language, the number of people living in Sweden who have recent Finnish ancestry and speak some form of Finnish is larger than the number of people who live in Finland and speak Swedish. When one considers the group of indigenous Sami languages spoken across Northern Finland, Norway, and Sweden, as well as the Faroese and Greenlandic languages spoken in the northern parts of the Danish realm, the situation begins to look even more "Canadian": an historically troubled relationship between dominant and indigenous languages has shifted towards a degree of respect and institutionalized usage that, nevertheless, still has indigenous languages struggling to achieve equal status with the majority languages.

In summary, the Nordic Countries and Canada compare well in many respects, such as their status as multilingual and multicultural societies known for their commitment to social justice. In several others, of course, they differ, and it is this unique blend of similarities and differences that make comparative research between Nordic and Canadian cases and situations so valuable. To many scholars and policy-makers in Canada and the Nordic Countries, however, this fruitful 'laboratory' for comparative studies has often remained an unobvious one. Unfortunately, Nordic publics have limited exposure to Canada in the media and their national education systems, so NACS/ANEC initiatives in the member countries offer vital conduits of information about Canada, its society, culture and peoples. Due to limited exposure to Canada, Nordic audiences may still approach Canada primarily as a neighbor of the United States, and view its culture as a reflection of that of its southern neighbor.

That perception can only be challenged through active cultural diplomacy, and since 1984 NACS/ANEC initiatives have inspired new generations of researchers, teachers, and students to engage in Canadian Studies and served to highlight the distinctiveness of Canadian society for a variety of Nordic audiences.

ORIGINS AND FOUNDERS

When academics from four Nordic countries[2] met at Aarhus University, Denmark, to launch the Nordic Association for Canadian Studies, youth around the world were listening to Bruce Springsteen's "Born in the USA" on their Sony Walkmen, then state of the art technology, and Jeopardy was the latest fashion in television entertainment.

Although Apple introduced the Macintosh computer to the market that year, it was still at least a decade until word processing, the Internet, and email became common working tools in university and everyday communication. Thus, the first statutes of the association were typed on a well-worn typewriter, by tenacious university professors exchanging drafts by handwritten letters, and ideas over landline telephone. Launching and running a transnational NGO in 1984, in other words, took determination, time, and a lot of patience. Clearly, the founders were motivated by more than a whim or the desire to boost their own CVs.

Happily, George Orwell's dystopia had not materialized but there were plenty of political, economic, and security issues to be concerned about in 1984. It was the height of the Cold War that saw the United States (with its NATO allies) and the Soviet Union (with its Warsaw Pact allies) locked as enemies in an ideological, seemingly never-ending standoff. Much more serious than the Soviet Union boycott of the Summer Olympics in Los Angeles that year were the numerous local armed conflicts in the Middle East, South America, Africa, and Asia, in which antagonists were supported by one or the other superpower—not least because any such conflict threatened to spread and plunge the world into an apocalyptic nuclear world war. Civil and ethnic wars were also aplenty: in Sri Lanka, for example, the separatist Tamil Tigers were fighting the government to create their own state, and in Northern Ireland "The Troubles" saw Catholic and Protestant paramilitaries on killing sprees in the name of their respective faiths.

In the Western hemisphere, the mid-1980s was characterized by the consolidation of neoliberal political power. Ronald Reagan was re-elected for his second term as President of the United States, while Pierre Elliott Trudeau was stepping down as Prime Minister of Canada, allowing Brian Mulroney and the Progressive Conservative Party to win a majority government. In the United Kingdom, Margaret Thatcher reigned supreme and, as elsewhere, the trenches on the left and right sides of the political spectrum were dug deeper, the tone of ideological struggle becoming increasingly unforgiving.

It was in this environment of international hostility and conflict that the founders of NACS found the impetus to develop a transnational, apolitical association that would focus on collaboration across national and ethnic divides, dialog and co-creation of knowledge, and the sharing of best practices. The "pioneers" who created NACS had themselves witnessed the independent international stance, the reason, and inclusiveness that was characteristic of Canada at the time, and saw in that many of the similarities with the Nordic Countries discussed above. NACS's founders were not themselves high-level political operators. The organization that they created would become an example of how to overcome differences of language and national perspective and of cooperation across national boundaries. Approaching four decades of transnational collaboration, the ties that were created between Nordic scholars and students from all five countries remain strong.

The founding of NACS coincided with a period during which the Canadian government engaged actively in what later would become commonly known as "public diplomacy" (see e.g. Cowan and Cull 2008). In 1987, Canada launched its "Canadian Studies Abroad" program (which became the "Understanding Canada" program in 2006), offering valuable support to both new and more established Canadian studies communities around the world. Compared to similar programs available to Nordic scholars, Canada's was comparatively much more generous in two ways: it offered substantial financial support, and it offered this support with few restrictions regarding research topics, approaches, or, importantly, conclusions.

As part of the establishment of an international Canadian Studies community, through Canada's Nordic embassies, the fledgling association of Nordic Canadianists thus received both moral and economic support from the Ministry of Foreign Affairs. Support for NACS also came from the International Council for Canadian Studies (ICCS)—of which NACS was a co-founder—and from the *Délégation générale du Québec* in London. From its inception, NACS has been a bilingual association—l'Association nordiques d'études canadiennes—and the funding provided by the Government of Quebec helped finance its Quebec-related activities.

Nevertheless, the first decade of existence remained an up-hill struggle, with much effort put into persuading environments at the university and high school levels in Denmark, Sweden, Norway, Finland, and, since 1993, Iceland[3] that Canadian society and its cultures were worth studying in their own right—and not merely as part of British, American, or Postcolonial Studies (the latter being very much in vogue at the time). The task of spreading the gospel of Canada as a truly unique society and an intriguing laboratory for progressive social and cultural practice was made easier, however, by the increasingly independent international role and identity that Canadian governments were busy forging for their country.

NACS and the interest in Canadian studies that its activities generated provided fertile ground for the establishment of the Canadian Studies Centre (CSC) in the Department of English of Aarhus University in 1991. For the majority of the association's existence, the CSC has functioned as the administrative hub of NACS. The center has hosted several Canadian visiting professors as well as many Canadian student interns. Moreover, it was at Aarhus that the first Nordic Master's degree specialization in Canadian Studies saw the light of day.

In Finland, the University of Helsinki has for decades run a North American Studies Program. While it emphasizes teaching and research on the United States, as its name implies, the program also incorporates the study of Canada. In Sweden, in 1997, the Institute for Canadian Studies was established under the Department of Romance and Classical Languages at the University of Stockholm, with a focus on research into Francophone Canadian culture and society.

Elsewhere in the Nordic Countries, university professors found the opportunity within already existing job and course descriptions and, increasingly, in newly established positions, to expand the size and scope of Canadian Studies within numerous different fields of research and teaching. The contribution to the new field of research and education by Nordic universities can thus be said to have been mainly in-kind—in the form of person hours, office space, administrative support, etc. Still, the total value of this contribution exceeded by many times the generous and essential, but comparatively small, contribution to Canadian Studies provided by Canadian governments.

THE CHANGING NATURE OF CANADIAN STUDIES IN THE NORDIC COUNTRIES

In its early years, Canadian Studies in the Nordic Countries was characterized by an emphasis on literary studies. Most of the early members of NACS came from literary backgrounds and soon students graduated from Nordic universities having written Master's theses on Atwood, Davies, Wiebe, van Herk, Richler, Gallant, and other great Canadian writers. Since the 1990s, however, new generations of Canadianists have brought into NACS their research and teaching in sociology, media studies, geography, history, linguistics, Indigenous Studies, migration and heritage studies, and political theory, thus making the study of Canada in the Nordic Countries increasingly multifaceted and comprehensive.

With many hundreds of members added to the four who inaugurated the association in 1984, NACS has changed its scope to comprise all imaginable aspects of Canadian Studies. A highly valued group of members is made up of high school teachers, as well as others who were taught Canadian Studies at university and have now themselves become teachers at post-secondary and secondary educational institutions.

Size and activity levels of the five national chapters have waxed and waned, very much depending on the availability of fiery souls within the scholarly community committed to "the cause." In addition to national, ethnic, and regional identity issues in Canadian literature, popular and recurring themes have been Canada's constitutional problems (including Québec secessionism and Indigenous rights), Canada's role in international politics (e.g. as a pioneer and major contributor over the years to global peacekeeping), immigration and multiculturalism policies, and the US–Canada relationship. On these issues and others, Nordic academics have contributed to debates as experts in their respective national media and internationally (Mikkelsen et al. 2008).

Throughout the 1990s and 2000s, the activities of the association continued to develop to assist those involved in Canadian Studies in the Nordic Countries. These included NACS Student Travel Grants (since 2000), and conference support and summer school grants enabling students and faculty to travel to Canada and to relevant Canadian Studies gatherings to increase their network and knowledge of Canada, thus nurturing a new generation of Nordic Canadianists. It should also be mentioned that Nordic universities have signed exchange agreements with more than twenty-five Canadian universities and that NACS members have been instrumental in setting up most of these agreements.

An academic journal, the *NACS Text Series*, replaced occasional conference proceedings in 1992 to provide a regional medium for scholarly articles as well as these proceedings, and Triennial Conferences—large, three-day events hosted by shifting Nordic chapters, with a range of prominent keynote speakers and workshop/seminar sessions—have brought together Canadianists from the Nordic Countries, Canada, and other parts of the world for fruitful exchange and collaboration since 1987. Another successful and fruitful creation of NACS has been its seminar tours (since 2003 the 'Bifrost Seminars in Canadian Studies'), which bring prominent Canadian writers, scholars, politicians, and civil servants on one- or two-week speaking tours/seminars to different destinations in the Nordic Countries. With local contributions in the form of student workshops and paper presentations, the topics have included Canada and the USA, gender and ethnicity in Canadian literature, postcolonial Canada, Atlantic Canada and regional development, Québec within the Canadian federation, Nunavut and Indigenous peoples in Canada, Canadian–European constitutional issues, Métis culture, language and history, heritage and change in the Arctic, and much more.

Between 1988 and 2008, the printed twice-annual newsletter, *NACS Bulletin ANEC*, was the main medium for communication between members and between the board/secretariat and the members of the association. To facilitate the growing demand for instant, international and more cost-efficient communication, however, in 1997 NACS launched its first website[4] and gradually switched entirely to electronic communication. This significantly increased the opportunity for further collaboration with new Nordic and extra-Nordic partners, such as *Gesellschaft für Kanada-studien* (the German-speaking association for Canadian studies; GKS), the British Association for Canadian Studies (BACS), the American Studies Association of Norway (ASANOR), the Maple Leaf and Eagle Conference series,[5] l'Association internationale des études québécoises (AIEQ), the University of the Arctic (UArctic), Centre for Innovation and Research in Culture and Living in the Arctic (CIRCLA), the University of Greenland, the European Network for Canadian Studies (ENCS), and the Network in Canadian Heritage and Environment (NiCHE). In the early 2000s, with two decades of activities to its name, NACS had reached a point of maturity from which it could be used as a platform for launching and assisting new Canadian Studies associations that emerged in the Baltic Countries.

NACS TODAY

Although met with disbelief and frustration by Nordic Canadianists, the termination of the 'Understanding Canada' program in 2012 did not have immediate significantly negative effects on the Nordic Association and its activities. Knowing that the program might be in jeopardy, the executive board had for awhile, with other associations, actively campaigned to dissuade the Canadian government from carrying out this decision, while also reducing activity levels and setting aside any funds possible to soften the anticipated blow. Since the early 1990s NACS had also invested in bonds, the interests on which provided continual funding for the Student Travel Grants. Hence, with smaller conferences, fewer seminars and publications, and the increased use of video chat technology for board meetings, NACS has been adapting to remain in existence, albeit with less smoke coming from its chimney. This new, scaled-back existence is, however, having some highly regrettable consequences, not least for Canada.

As Simon Anholt, the world's leading expert on nation branding, has famously stated, in this age of globalization there is only one remaining global superpower: the public opinion of the world's population (see e.g. *Guardian* 30 November 2014). Consequently, public diplomacy has become central to efficient, beneficial international relations, now and for the future. No doubt the NACS brand—and with it, Canada's national brand—has suffered from less visibility at universities, in journals, in the mass media of the Nordic countries, etc. In political and economic terms, the withdrawal of the Canadian government from this aspect of public diplomacy means the inability to tap into the great "soft power" potential (Nye 2004) in Nordic Countries–Canada partnerships. Nation branding and public diplomacy rely on a ready audience (Olins 2005; Dinnie 2016). After several decades of careful construction, today that audience is steadily disappearing in the Nordic Countries.

In the 1990s, when the founding fathers of Nordic Canadian studies were retiring and NACS needed a new generation of scholars to take over, a young cadre of enthusiastic Canadian Studies-trained scholars stood ready. The transition went smoothly, as older values and experiences merged with newer ideas and research fields into 'NACS 2.0'. Today (2018), after almost a decade of down-scaling activities, enthusiastic young Canadianists are still present, but they are fewer and farther between than in the past. While some courageously insist on following their scholarly conviction, others whose professional identity involved being Canadian Studies researchers and NACS members have been forced to seek greener pastures in such fields as Arctic or American Studies.

With some minor alterations to Pross's model of interest groups (Pross 1992; see also Chapter 2 in this book), the stages of development of Canadian Studies in the Nordic countries would include not only rapid and positive development towards institutionalization but, more recently, signs of stagnation and also gradual deinstitutionalization (see Table 9.1, based partly on Mikkelsen et al. 2008).

More than would seem to be the case elsewhere, NACS was not so much a product of a nascent or 'fledgling' Canadian Studies community as the instigator of it. Through the institutionalization of its

Table 9.1 Stages of development of Canadian studies in the Nordic countries

Fledgling	Mature	Institutionalized	Deinstitutionalization?
Few and unconnected pockets of university and high school teaching and university research environments concerned with Canadian culture and society. Mostly individuals with coincidental relations to Canada (family or colleagues). Usually sub-segments of larger North American, English, or French Language Studies	• NACS/ANEC is founded 1984 (Danish, Swedish, Norwegian, and Finnish chapters) • Triennial conferences and seminar tours • Conference proceedings published • *NACS Bulletin ANEC* est. 1988 • Focus remains, primarily, on literary studies and multiculturalism • Early collaboration with other Canadian Studies associations	• Continuation of successful activities at same or increased frequency • NACS/ANEC membership reaches 300. Many enthusiastic high school teachers engage in the field • Canadian Studies Centre, Aarhus University, est. 1991 • *NACS/ANEC Text Series* launched 1992 • Icelandic chapter of NACS/ANEC est. in 1993 • NACS/ANEC launches its first website, 1997 • Institute (since 2017 Center) for Canadian Studies, University of Stockholm, est. 1997 • Student Travel Grant est. 2000 • NACS/ANEC assists in establishing Canadian Studies associations in the Baltic countries • Focus expands to include sociology, politics (domestic and international), economics, Indigenous and Arctic studies	• Canadian government funding is discontinued, leading to reduced NACS/ANEC budgets and down-scaling • Seminar tours become smaller and less frequent • Triennial conferences, minor events, and student travel grants remain but activities are gradually depleting association savings • The high school teachers segment of NACS/ANEC membership diminishes • Younger scholars show interest in several disciplines describable as 'Canadian Studies,' but exercise it in neighboring fields of research/teaching
1970s–1984	1984–1990	1990–2000s	2010s

activities (seminars, conferences etc.), its mediums of communication, publications, and the growth of its membership, a vibrant, internationally engaged community has developed. Institutionalization, however, is no guarantee of continued influence, success or, indeed, existence. When fruitful collaboration with the Canadian state declined, including an end to support financial support, NACS began to slide backwards into an intermediate stage of institutional development.

THE FUTURE OF CANADIAN STUDIES: NORDIC NOIR?

There can be little doubt that Canadian Studies abroad is highly beneficial to Canada. Regardless of one's stance on the wisdom of current neoliberal political desires to view all or most functions of society in terms financial sustainability, it can be easily argued that the Canadian government programme for supporting this form of cultural-academic diplomacy was a highly cost-effective endeavor. When NACS received Canadian government funding, the association treated the Canadian contribution as seed money that provided leverage to attract significant local sources of funding. An example would be when NACS co-organized a major conference for teacher trainers on multiculturalism in Norway and Denmark and brought in Canadian experts to showcase Canada's experiences in order to suggest what Norway and Denmark might learn from Canada. The conference had a budget of well over CAD $100,000. The Canadian government's contribution was limited to the cost of four Canadian speakers.

With the loss of the modest but continuous and symbolically prestigious Canadian funding in 2012, such collaborative networks began to crumble. Nordic universities, particularly the ones where the association's current executive board members are based,[6] continue to support the association's activities. Nevertheless, holding on to the mosaic of public and private funding networks is becoming increasingly precarious without direct support from Canada.

At the time of writing (2018), NACS is planning its 12th Triennial Canadian Studies Conference in Akureyri, Iceland, organized in collaboration with the Stefansson Arctic Institute at the University of Akureyri. The expenses will further strain the association's coffers; hence, the continued position of the association as an active, well-known institution in Nordic academia would appear uncertain indeed. Yet the Akureyri conference, to be opened by the President of Iceland, promises to more than double the number of papers from the previous Triennial Conference in 2015, and the mix of long-time NACS collaborators and younger scholars from adjacent area studies coming to the conference has convinced us that the popularity is about more than the pull of Northern Iceland as an attractive venue. Despite the loss of Canadian funding, Canadianists continue the search for ways to maintain the global Canadian Studies community. This bodes well for an association still capable of re-igniting a wide range of activities in case the Canadian government decides to reinstitute its funding for cultural diplomacy.

In the unexpected twists and turns of North American and global politics in the past several years, Canada may well be enjoying a new surge of interest as a society that has experimented with governments and policies from different ends of the political spectrum and, for the time being, has swung back to more outward-looking and inclusive approaches to international relations. The change of power in Canada in 2015, and in the USA in 2017, has put Canada in the spotlight and, to appropriate the language of economics, this would be a good time to monetize this interest. There are signs that in the Nordic countries, scholars, students, and general audiences are noticing Canada in a new way. The renewed gaze can be kept on Canada, starting with even a modest but determined Canadian investment. The remaining Nordic Canadianists consider the cause very worthwhile and, given the right support, constitute a solid foundation for many years of fruitful Nordic Canadian Studies activities and thus for effective Canadian public diplomacy.

Notes

1. Explored, for example, in the 2005 conference 'Finlande, pays scandinaves, Québec et Canada français: cultures, littératures et langues du Nord?', and in the concept of 'Nordicity' (see e.g. Daniel Chartier's 'Towards a Grammar of the Idea of North: Nordicity, Winterity' (2007)).
2. Jørn Carlsen from Denmark, Bengt Streijffert from Sweden, Per Seyersted from Norway, and Tuomo Laitinen from Finland, who became the association's first president, secretary/treasurer, vice-president, and board member, respectively.
3. Gudrun Gudsteinsdottir joined NACS/ANEC as the first Icelandic member of the board that year.
4. Currently being replaced by a new NACS/ANEC initiative: a Facebook profile.

5. On North American Studies, running at the University of Helsinki since the 1980s.
6. Janne Korkka at University of Turku, Mark Eaton at University of Aarhus, John Erik Fossum at University of Oslo, Úlfar Bragason at University of Iceland, Françoise Sule at University of Stockholm, and Robert C. Thomsen at Aalborg University.

REFERENCES

Chartier, Daniel. 2007. Towards a Grammar of the Idea of North: Nordicity, Winterity. *Nordlit* 22: 35–47.

Cowan, Geoffrey, and Nicholas J. Cull (eds.). 2008. Public Diplomacy in a Changing World. *Annals of the American Academy of Political and Social Science* 616 (1): 6–8.

Dinnie, Keith. 2016. *Nation Branding: Concepts, Issues, Practice*, 2nd ed. London: Routledge.

The Guardian. 2014. Simon Anholt Interview: "There Is Only One Global Superpower: Public Opinion", November 30. www.theguardian.com/politics/2014/nov/30/simon-anholt-good-country-party-global-superpower-public-opinion.

Mikkelsen, Mai Klærke, Robert Christian Thomsen, and Peter Bakker (eds.). 2008. *NACS/ANEC: Chronicle of Activities and Publications, 1997–2007*. Aarhus: University of Aarhus.

Nye, Joseph S. 2004. *Soft Power: The Means to Success in World Politics*. New York, NY: Public Affairs.

Olins, Wally. 2005. Making a National Brand. In *The New Public Diplomacy: Soft Power in International Relations*, ed. Jan Melissen, 169–178. Basingstoke, UK: Palgrave Macmillan.

Pross, A. Paul. 1992. *Group Politics and Public Policy*. Don Mills, ON: Oxford University Press.

CHAPTER 10

Lessons Learned

Stephen Brooks

In recent years between 15 and 17 million persons from outside of France, including about 2 million Americans, roughly the same number of Chinese, and over 2 million British nationals visit Paris annually. London is even more of a draw, attracting between 17 and 19 million international visitors each year. Moreover, the James Bond films, the British monarchy, the Harry Potter franchise, and much more contribute to worldwide awareness of the British brand. Viewers of Euronews, RT (formerly known as Russia Today), the BBC, Al-Jazeera, and other national and international broadcasters, to say nothing of major social media platforms, see, hear and read about what is happening in the United States on a daily basis. Those who do not follow the news typically have ideas and images of America from Hollywood films and other emanations of that country's prodigious cultural industries. And yet despite the fact that each of these countries has a brand that is known throughout the world—not always or in all respects favorably or accurately—their governments all invest significantly in cultural diplomacy and have done so for many decades.

Canada was rather late to this game. The "Unknown Country," as Bruce Hutchison famously described it in his 1942 book, remained largely

S. Brooks (✉)
Department of Political Science, University of Windsor, Windsor, ON, Canada

© The Author(s) 2019   239
S. Brooks (ed.), *Promoting Canadian Studies Abroad*,
Palgrave Macmillan Series in Global Public Diplomacy,
https://doi.org/10.1007/978-3-319-74027-0_10

so for decades after he wrote these words. This situation did not change very much until the Canadian government decided in the 1970s that cultural diplomacy was worth the rather small sums of money that it entailed. The decision to support the study of Canada abroad became an important part of this effort to make Canada better known to the outside world. Returns on this investment were quick to appear, as the previous chapters so clearly demonstrate.

In some countries, the Canadian government's financial support provided an important boost for an already considerable and active community of Canadianists. This was especially true of the United States, Canada's major trading partner, where centers and programs for Canadian studies and even a national association existed before and without anything more than the occasional and rather derisory financial contribution from the Canadian state. In the United Kingdom and France too, although to a much lesser degree, the early architecture of what would become institutionalized Canadian studies communities predated financial support from Ottawa. In other cases—indeed in the majority of the national and regional cases, including those that have not been profiled in this book—Canadian studies depended largely on the efforts of intrepid souls laboring without the benefit of a national association and the other accoutrements of an institutionalized community. For scholars in these countries, the Canadian state's embrace of cultural diplomacy and, in particular, of the idea that there is policy value in encouraging foreign scholars to do research, write, and teach about Canada, was absolutely vital. Without it, it is highly unlikely that the transition from a fledgling to a mature and even institutionalized national community of Canadianists could have been achieved.

As the preceding chapters show, the origins, development, and current state of Canadian studies are different in every national case. Nevertheless, there are some recurrent elements that allow us to generalize about the factors that have shaped Canadian studies abroad. Among them, the following stand out.

Canada's Relationship to the United States

In several of the countries examined in the preceding chapters, and in the majority of those that have not been profiled, Canadian studies began as an extension of American studies. Emerging from the shadow cast by its rather overwhelming neighbor and establishing an identity separate from American studies was often the first challenge that had to be met and in some cases remains so. "The purpose of Canadian studies, as practiced in France and elsewhere," observes Lacroix in his chapter, "is to identify the degree of specificity of Canada in comparison with the United States and to dwell on the distinctions rather than the similarities." Iino observes that, "In the immediate postwar years, the Japanese people as well as the Japanese government were so preoccupied with learning about the United States that Canada received very little attention." Similarly, Klooss writes, "In West Germany [after the War], studies on Canada came under the spell of American Studies which identified North America largely with the U.S." Canada was, for quite some time, seen as simply the "other America," before emerging as a subject whose main interest and reason for study was comparison with the United States.

Even in the case of China, where Canadian studies had its origins in a 1980s Canadian government aid program that was focused largely on university linkages between the two countries, Canadian studies often existed in institutions that had American studies programs. "In this way," says Paltiel, "Canadian studies became an adjunct of American studies." Being associated with American studies, through a common center or program, can have consequences beyond the blurring of Canada's identity. Paltiel notes that "the general salience and critical importance of Sino-American relations usually means that bureaucratic directors of official Canadian Studies programs have their eye more squarely on Sino-American relations both in terms of how they view Canada and in terms of where they wish to move in relation to their professional careers."

In the United States, the country that for many decades has had the largest and, by most measures, the most active Canadian studies community, one might imagine that knowledge of Canada would be more widespread and the need to interpret Canada to opinion leaders, policy-makers and the attentive public less than in other countries. In fact, however, this is far from being the case. University courses on China, Latin America, the Middle East, and Russia are likely to attract several times more students than ones on Canada. In the crowded and highly competitive American academic market and mediascape, Canada must jostle for resources and attention. Notice and knowledge cannot be taken for granted.

THE PHYSICAL AND SOCIAL INFRASTRUCTURE
OF CANADIAN STUDIES

Another lesson that emerges from many of the country chapters in this book, indeed from all of them to varying degrees, is the importance of centers, institutes, programs, administrative hubs, and regular meetings of Canadianists. This is the physical and social infrastructure that typifies an institutionalized Canadian studies community. In the United States, this infrastructure had already developed prior to Canadian government financial support for Canadian studies abroad. To a significant degree, this was due to funding from American corporations and philanthropic institutions. There is no doubt, however, that the dramatic growth that occurred in Canadian studies in the United States in the 1980s and 1990s was due largely to the leveraging effects and incentives provided by Ottawa's rather modest expenditures. The beginnings of this infrastructure existed to lesser degrees in other countries too before the Canadian government began to provide grant money. Typically, however, Canadian studies would be under the same roof as a program or center in American or Commonwealth studies.

Prior to the establishment of university programs, centers, institutes, and even, in the case of the Soviet Union, think tanks engaged in the study of Canada, the opportunities for research collaboration, teaching, and the dissemination of knowledge and interpretations of Canada were fewer and more dependent on the entrepreneurial efforts, vision, and perseverance of particular individuals. Meetings of scholars with interests in Canada might be organized from time to time. Courses might be offered, more often than not with a section on Canada included along with the study of another country or countries. Graduate students were supervised, books, articles, and reports published, and in other ways knowledge and an understanding of Canada would be advanced or at least kept alive. As the preceding chapters show, the creation of a national association and the various activities that are typically associated with this, including regular conferences, a journal, ways of making researchers, teachers and others aware of each other and their work, recognition for outstanding achievements, and other aspects of the social infrastructure of a national or regional community of Canadianists always leads to a more robust community with a sense of professional identity. To these activities, I would add the importance of travel and exchange opportunities for scholars and students to visit Canada and for Canadian scholars, writers, and others to visit other countries and speak to foreign audiences about Canada. None of this happens without money.

In this age of virtual online communities, webinars, and the instantaneous sharing of information, the idea that physical infrastructure might be important to the health and success of Canadian studies may seem rather passé. This is not the case. Physical locations and face-to-face encounters, as occur annually among German Canadianists at Grainau, British Canadianists in London in recent years, or, more typically, at different venues in different years in the case of most Canadian studies associations, provide opportunities for intergenerational renewal, where younger scholars can meet with those already established in the field, present their research, and participate directly in the shaping of Canadian studies. Such meetings are, as all Canadianists know, often attended by Canadian state officials and frequently by Quebec state officials too. They will regularly include one or more prominent Canadian cultural figures or academics as key participants in the program. Webinars are no substitute for these physical encounters and are unlikely to generate the collaboration, invitations, exchanges, and conversations that these meetings produce.

The importance of physical space and meeting places is well known to those familiar with Alliance Française and the Goethe Institute, whose locations may be found on every continent and are immediately recognized as signposts of their respective national cultures. As Lacroix explains, the Canadian Cultural Centre and La Maison des étudiants canadiens perform this role in Paris, hosting activities, providing resources, and serving as meeting points bringing together Canadians and non-Canadians. The tissue of relationships that is vital to keeping Canada relevant in the eyes of others and projecting the country's image abroad is nurtured by such physical spaces and the human interactions that take place at cultural venues like these. China recognizes this and in recent years has been expanding its network of cultural centers across the world.

The Intergenerational Transfer of Interest and Knowledge

The visible and immediate impacts of the Canadian government's 2012 decision to end its financial support for Canadian studies abroad were obvious enough. The secretariats of some national associations were closed; conferences, particularly at the sub-national level, became fewer, if they continued at all; some programs and centers that, in many cases, were already financially precarious and in competition with other areas studies programs or priorities at their universities were eliminated; travel to conferences or to Canada for research declined; and more. Less visible, but no less important, has been the impact on renewal within Canadian studies communities in countries throughout the world. Many of the contributors to this volume make the point that the next generation of Canadianists is likely to be smaller and perhaps even less focused on Canada in their teaching and research than those who came before them.

The reasons for this are easy to understand. Many of those who were attracted to Canadian studies in the 1980s and 1990s benefited from Canadian state funding that supported research visits to Canada, the creation of courses on Canada, and the activities of programs and centers that they directed and in some cases created. Their interest, indeed their enthusiasm for Canadian studies was often passed on to their graduate students whose research and theses they supervised. In the normal course of things some of these students would eventually attend Canadian studies conferences, giving papers, publishing their research, and becoming increasingly engaged in their national Canadian studies community. They would and have assumed leadership roles in these communities.

Today, however, it is more difficult to attract young scholars to Canadian studies. The very modest financial assistance that made possible a research visit to Canada or the creation of a new course with Canadian content is gone. These were financial incentives that, in some cases, kindled a researcher's or teacher's initial interest in Canada or that enabled him or her to build on existing work. It is impossible to know how many potential Canadianists have been lost and will continue to be lost due to the elimination of this financial support. Some idea of the impact, however, is suggested by the 2012 survey of Canadianists in the United States that is discussed in Chapter 2. Respondents expressed significant pessimism about the future prospect for Canadian studies including, in many cases, the likelihood of their continued engagement in research and teaching on Canada. Lacroix, Klooss, and Thomsen and Korkka make this same point about their respective Canadian studies communities. Thomsen and Korkka's observation about the Nordic countries doubtless applies to most Canadian studies communities across the world:

Today...after almost a decade of down-scaling activities, enthusiastic young Canadianists are still present, but they are fewer and farther between than in the past. While some courageously insist on following their scholarly conviction, others whose professional identity involved being Canadian Studies researchers and Nordic Association of Canadian Studies members have been forced to seek greener pastures in such fields as Arctic or American Studies.

Canadian Studies Without the Canadian State

With the exceptions of China and the Nordic countries, all of the other Canadian studies communities examined in this book were characterized by a "pre-institutional" phase during which lone scholars, builders, and academic entrepreneurs had already laid a foundation for the study of Canada. In some cases, these early steps were taken many decades before a national or regional association for Canadian studies was created and well before the Canadian government began to provide financial support. Canadian studies abroad was not a creation of the Canadian government's rather tardy embrace of cultural diplomacy in the 1970s. These activities will not end with the loss of funding by Ottawa, although they are already much diminished.

The Canadian government's decision to end its almost forty years of financial support for Canadian studies abroad did indeed generate considerable criticism at home and abroad. "Fade to black," was how one much-cited article characterized the expected impact on Canada's image abroad (Martin 2012). It is quite possible and even probable, however, that some within the Conservative government that took this decision believed that this spending had no appreciable impact on how the world, outside of the relatively small circle of foreign Canadianists who reaped direct benefits from this spending, viewed Canada. And it may be that some within the Liberal government that replaced them in power in 2015, and which has not reinstituted this program, agree. There is, after all, evidence that Canada's international brand was strong before the 2012 decision and remained strong afterward. Canada's world reputation, as measured by the Reputation Institute's annual survey of national populations, has been either first or second in the world every year between 2010 and 2017. Other international surveys corroborate the high regard in which foreign populations appear to have held Canada for many years. With such a strong international brand, apparently unaffected by the termination of the Understanding Canada Program in 2012, who needs communities of Canadianists throughout the world?

The question is, in fact, based on the false assumption that all that matters when it comes to cultural diplomacy is a country's general reputation in the eyes of foreign populations. For the most part, Canada's reputation has been positive for about as long as the world has paid attention. This does not mean, however, that Canada was not for a very long time what Hutchison called the "unknown country," thought of by many throughout the world as a sort of vast, perhaps friendlier, less violent, and certainly colder America. The facile belief that a country's general reputation correlates positively with and contributes to its success in achieving foreign policy goals and influence in the world is one that lacks serious empirical support.

Moving the needle of global public opinion or opinion in a particular country or region of the world may sometimes be the goal of public diplomacy. The goal of cultural diplomacy, however, is more likely to be to shape the ideas and images that a segment of a foreign population holds, based on the reasonable belief that what policy makers, opinion leaders and the attentive public believe is more important than the beliefs and attitudes of the general public. Moreover, whereas attempts to improve a country's general reputation may rely on grand gestures that are certain to receive extensive media coverage—a speech in front of Brandenburg Gate, a lavish and carefully orchestrated state visit, or the afterglow expected to be generated by hosting the Olympic Games— cultural diplomacy, and certainly that which aims to encourage research and teaching about a country among academics in another country or countries, necessarily involves a long-term commitment of resources that is focused on individuals and institutions that will in turn and over time play an influential role in shaping and sustaining the country's image abroad. It involves the promotion of activities that aim to produce awareness, knowledge, and understandings that are not easily and immediately influenced by a change in government in the studied country, a change in the tone of a bilateral relationship, or some short-term event that suddenly propels the country into the international spotlight.[1]

Most politicians, journalists, and others whose ideas shape the public conversation in the United States, China, France, and other countries do not know much about Canada. But the Canadianists in these countries do. By virtue of being members of their respective societies and able to communicate in its national language or languages, they have a sort of credibility among their fellow citizens that a Canadian public official or someone else from Canada who might be assumed to be less than entirely objective in his or her assessment of their home country, may not have. Moreover, they probably, in most instances, have better access than would many Canadians to their country's decision-makers, media, and the attentive public. This latter group includes their students, some of whom will eventually be the politicians, bureaucrats, journalists, and others whose knowledge of and ideas about Canada may make a difference. These foreign Canadianists are, in a word, informal cultural ambassadors for Canada. And as Jean-Michel Lacroix observes, unlike official Canadian ambassadors, they don't cost much!

NOTE

1. In January of 2017 the Quebec village of Herouxville went from obscurity to worldwide coverage on the BBC, CNN International, The Guardian, and much of the world's media. The cause of this unexpected publicity was a municipal council resolution that was widely perceived to be egregiously Islamophobic. This is not what one would consider to be positive coverage for Canada or for the province of Quebec. At the same time, it did not appear to have any appreciable impact on Canada's generally and strongly positive reputation throughout much of the world.

REFERENCES

Hutchison, Bruce. 2010, first published in 1942. *The Unknown Country: Canada and Her People*. Toronto: Oxford University Press.

Martin, Paul. 2012. Canada's Image Abroad: Fade to Black. *University Affairs*, June 6. https://www.universityaffairs.ca/opinion/in-my-opinion/canadas-image-abroad-fade-to-black/.

INDEX

© The Editor(s) (if applicable) and The Author(s) 2019
S. Brooks (ed.), *Promoting Canadian Studies Abroad*,
Palgrave Macmillan Series in Global Public Diplomacy,
https://doi.org/10.1007/978-3-319-74027-0

Printed by Printforce, the Netherlands